SOUTHERN POLITICS AND THE SECOND RECONSTRUCTION

SOUTHERN POLITICS AND THE SECOND RECONSTRUCTION

NUMAN V. BARTLEY AND HUGH D. GRAHAM

The Johns Hopkins University Press

Baltimore and London

This book has been brought to publication with the
generous assistance of the Andrew W. Mellon Foundation.

Portions of chapter 8 were published by the authors as
"Whatever Happened to the Solid South?" in *New South*
27 (Fall 1972): 28–34.

Manufactured in the United States of America

The Johns Hopkins University Press, Baltimore, Maryland 21218
The Johns Hopkins University Press Ltd., London

Library of Congress Catalog Card Number 74-24377
ISBN 0-8018-1667-X

Library of Congress Cataloging in Publication data
will be found on the last printed page of this book.

For Ann and Morraine

Contents

Illustrations

Tables

Preface

This is essentially an external history of southern political life since the New Deal and World War II, encompassing a crucial epoch, an attempted second Reconstruction of the South. We have focused upon the electoral response to candidates and issues because the need was compelling and the evidence was available; only future historians and political analysts will enjoy the perspective and the access to published, manuscript, and oral data upon which a full account of this turbulent era must be based. We do not pretend that this book is the sequel to V. O. Key's *Southern Politics in State and Nation*, although our debt to Key and his associates is huge and gratefully acknowledged, and we hope that our work is worthy of that high tradition. A definitive political history of this tumultuous period in the South must await the effulgence of time, which alone can produce the necessary evidence and the maturing of the science of policy analysis, in which historical analysis must remain a crucial component.

Our debt to other sources of institutional and personal support is equally enormous. In our research we were generously supported over a period of three years by financial assistance from the National Endowment for the Humanities, the Social Science Research Council, the Institute of Southern History at the Johns Hopkins University, the John Simon Guggenheim Memorial Foundation, the Woodrow Wilson International Center for Scholars, and the Southern Regional Council. We also enjoyed institutional research assistance from the Johns Hopkins University, the Georgia Institute of Technology, the University of Maryland Baltimore County, the University of Georgia, and the Inter-University Consortium for Political Research in Ann Arbor, Michigan, especially by Jerome Clubb and Michael Traugott in the historical archives and Janet Vavra and Karen Sidney of the Survey Research Center.

More personally, we are indebted to Ollie B. Francis, Alan Anderson, Joseph Mercer, and Bernard Wess for assistance in computer programming and data retrieval. For data collection we are indebted to the Inter-University Consortium for Political Research and to the secretaries of state of the eleven southern states (albeit somewhat unevenly); to courthouse bureaucrats in southern cities who for a variety of reasons neglected to throw away old precinct returns and maps; to Richard Scammon and his generous assistant, Alice Vardaman McGillivery; to Chandler Davidson, Gary Orren, and journalists Hugh Baskin Patterson, Guy Friddell, and Ed Yoder; to Joanne Allen of the Johns Hopkins University Press for editorial assistance; to Jim England, who prepared the artwork; and to student assistants Robert Sergott, James Phelps, and Robert Brugger. The errors of omission and comission are our own.

SOUTHERN POLITICS AND THE SECOND RECONSTRUCTION

CHAPTER 1

THE AMERICAN PARTY SYSTEMS
AND THE SOUTH

This first chapter is designed to serve an introductory function, both substantively and methodologically, by locating the study of southern politics within the context of a party-systems mode of analysis. This approach has been developed comparatively recently, less by historians than by political scientists with a keen sensitivity to the importance of the historical dimension in political life. In the pages immediately following, we attempt briefly to describe the construction of the party-systems approach and the empirical discoveries and theoretical assumptions behind it and then to survey the evolution of the five successive American party systems, with special attention to the role of the South within each. This brings us to our point of immediate departure, the structure and functioning of southern politics on the eve of what has been called the Second Reconstruction of the South. It is at this point that we make our major assumptions explicit—or at least own up to them—and briefly describe our research design and methodology, which is explained in greater detail in the Note on Methodology and Data Sources.

Among the central revelations of American political analysis in the post-World War II period has been the discovery, primarily through the relatively new instrument of survey research, of remarkably stable patterns of partisan loyalty. These tenacious party affiliations apparently stemmed far less from specific voter responses to issues and candidates than from basic underlying preferences largely inherited from parents and culture through normal childhood socialization. Upon this stability was predicated the concept of the "normal" vote, the customary partisan distribution of the vote in the absence of unusual external forces. And from this stable distribution there followed the concept of the normal majority, which in the post-New Deal era involved a national partisan distribution fluctuating around just under one-half Democratic, slightly more than one-quarter Republican, and about one-quarter independent or apolitical.[1] This pattern in turn suggested the construction of a threefold typology of partisan elections: maintaining, deviating, and realigning.[2] In *maintaining* elections, such as the election of 1948, the preceding pattern of partisan loyalties constitutes the primary influence governing the vote. In a *deviating* election this basic pattern is not seriously disturbed, but short-term forces, such as the popularity of Eisenhower in 1952 and 1956, bring about the defeat of the majority party (in response to which is a subcategory of the maintaining election, the reinstating election, such as that of 1960, in which the basic partisan loyalties of the "normal" majority are reasserted). The third type of election, relatively rare but of major impact, is the *realigning* election, in which popular excitement associated with politics is sufficiently intense and durable to basically transform the electorate's loyalties and thereby create a new "normal" partisan majority. Both political scientists and historians have recently employed the model of critical realignment to reconstruct our understanding of the entire evolution of American political life, focusing less on ephemeral candidates and issues and even on individual parties than on party systems, of which, by rough consensus, there have been five.[3]

[1]See generally the publications of the Survey Research Center, University of Michigan, particularly Angus Campbell et al., *The American Voter* (New York: John Wiley and Sons, 1960); Campbell, "Voters and Elections: Past and Present," *Journal of Politics* 26 (November 1964): 745–57; and Campbell et al., *Elections and the Political Order* (New York: John Wiley and Sons, 1966).

[2]Campbell et al., *The American Voter*, chap. 16. Gerald Pomper has convincingly argued that a fourth category, the *converting* election, should be added to this trilogy, on the grounds that the realigning category as explicated in *The American Voter* does not distinguish between critical elections which produce a new majority party and those that produce a fundamental rearrangement of the partisan base of a majority party that maintains its hegemony. Hence the following four-cell table:

		Majority Party	
		Victory	Defeat
Electoral	Continuity	Maintaining	Deviating
Cleavage	Change	Converting	Realigning

See Gerald Pomper, "The Classification of Presidential Elections," *Journal of Politics* 29 (August 1967): 535–66.

[3]The next paragraphs are based on generally known secondary studies, including the following: Lee Benson, *The Concept of Jacksonian Democracy: New York as a Test Case* (Princeton: Princeton University Press, 1961); Charles G. Sellers, Jr., "The Equilibrium Cycle in Two-Party Politics," *Public Opinion Quarterly* 29 (Spring 1965): 16–38; Richard P. McCormick, *The Second American Party System* (Chapel Hill: University of North Carolina Press, 1966); William Nesbit Chambers and Walter Dean Burnham, eds., *The American Party Systems* (New York: Oxford University Press, 1967); Michael F. Holt, *Forging a Majority: The Formation of the Republican Party in Pittsburgh, 1848–1860* (New Haven: Yale University Press, 1969); Paul Kleppner, *The Cross of Culture: A Social Analysis of Midwestern Politics, 1850–1900* (New York: Free Press, 1970); and Richard Jensen, *Winning of the Midwest: Social and Political Conflict, 1885–1896* (Chicago: University of Chicago Press, 1971).

The first of these was the Experimental System, lasting from 1789 to roughly 1824. Despite the Founders' theoretical opposition to "divisive faction," and to some extent precisely because of this initial denial of legitimacy to the concept of party, the Federalists and the Republicans clashed bitterly, especially over foreign policy and its domestic implications, and thereby foreshadowed the bimodal partisanship that was to take its modern form after 1824. Following the suicidal demise of the rigidly elitist Federalists after 1800 and the deceptively nonpartisan Era of Good Feelings associated with the administrations of James Monroe, the stage was set for the surprisingly rapid evolution of the first truly modern democratic party system in the world.

The Democratizing System, during the period 1828 to 1854, centered on a democratized presidency and attendant patronage, and both Jacksonian Democrats and Whigs demonstrated extraordinarily creative organizational innovations to mobilize mass participation. This effusive broadening of the franchise focused first on the symbolic figure of Andrew Jackson. Then, as the system matured, the new Whig opposition came to accept the policy and organizational implications of white manhood suffrage, especially after the Jacksonians attempted to dismantle the neomercantilist federal structure they had inherited from the Founders. During this latter period Jackson's previously "Solid South" melted away, and spirited two-party politics became a national tradition, driving voter turnout from an estimated 26.9 percent of the eligible electorate in 1824 to an average of 77.3 percent in the three heated presidential elections of the 1840s. Voters in Alabama, Georgia, Mississippi, and Tennessee turned out at an average rate of 82.1 percent—a performance worth bearing in mind in light of subsequent developments. Indeed, the South has not since been so fully integrated into national politics. Moreover, the division of the two-party vote in presidential elections was consistently close, with the winners' margin during the 1840s averaging a modest 4.1 percent, in contrast to the 15.6 percent average margin for the two elections of the 1830s.

Yet for all its apparent vitality, the volatile second party system rested on localistic, piecemeal coalitions of hostile ethnocultural groups, and the Jacksonian legacy of a weakened federal structure left the national government poorly prepared for the difficult maneuvering necessary in the face of a sectional crisis. Voting alignments outside the South seem to have reflected differences between old-stock Protestants and more recent immigrants and between newly-arrived British and non-British immigrants, as well as settlement patterns and local antagonisms. In the relatively homogeneous white South, partisan voting patterns lacked much of the ethnocultural orientation of northern political divisions but also seemed to reflect differing local perspectives. Some evidence suggests that the more prosperous and growing communities showed a Whig bias while the more isolated and self-contained areas inclined toward the Democrats,[4] although settlement patterns and Protestant denominational concerns may also have influenced partisan preferences. In neither North nor South did Democratic-Whig divisions at the mass level demonstrate significant class-economic conflict.

During the 1850s both local and national events conspired to disrupt these partisan patterns. The growing influx of Catholic immigrants into the northern states, especially in the years following the great potato famine of 1846, sharpened ethnocultural conflict and apparently led evangelical pietist Protestants toward a heightened concern for the morality of American life. In state and local politics, prohibition, Sunday blue laws, and favoritism for public education over parochial schools were issues that attracted support from pietist Protestants, while the emergence of the American, or Know-Nothing, party elevated these provincial concerns into national politics. Ultimately this crusading moralism centered around the slavery question, an issue of sufficient intensity to split the major pietist Protestant denominations into northern and southern wings. The formation of the Liberty and Free Soil parties during the 1840s combined with sharp regional differences in Congress over the expansion of slavery into the West to fuel the slavery controversy in national politics. At the same time, these events forged an alliance between those groups that presumably wanted to escape the moralistic zeal of their countrymen. Catholics, many liturgical Protestants, and white southerners all found refuge in a Democratic party devoted broadly to limited government. As northern Whigs flirted with Free-Soilers, Whiggery became highly suspect in the South, and when the Kansas-Nebraska Act of 1854 overturned the old modalities of compromise that had permitted the antislavery and free-soil controversies to be papered over, the Whigs disintegrated.

The deterioration of party structure during the 1850s foreshadowed the emergence of the Civil War System of 1860–92. The increasingly turbulent national politics drove a traditionalist and entrenched but obsessively fearful southern elite to take desperate measures in response to both real and imaginary threats to the political, economic, and racial status quo. During the Civil War, the new Republican government, suddenly enjoying enormous artificial majorities in Congress, not only delivered the *coup de grace* to slavery but also launched a neo-Whiggish, positive federal program in banking, currency, transportation, tariff, and land-grant policy. This radical transformation had been largely consolidated by the early 1870s. Following the "redemption" of the South by conservative Bourbon state regimes, there ensued, despite the Republican dominance of the White House (textbooks depicting a Republican era are misleading), a

[4]See Thomas B. Alexander et al., "The Basis of Alabama's Two-Party System," *Alabama Review* 19 (October 1966): 243–76.

quarter-century of intense partisan deadlock, in which voting alignments broadly pitting pietist Protestants against a Catholic-liturgical–Protestant-southern white coalition remained generally intact.

In the South during these turbulent years, Redeemer hegemony did not stand unchallenged. The Readjuster insurgency of the 1870s associated with Virginia's William Mahone and the Populist uprising of the 1890s were linked to a Southwide pattern of sporadic effusions of agrarian discontent. Furthermore, voter turnout in presidential elections remained quite high throughout the South, averaging 66 percent in the elections of 1868 through 1892. Indeed, in 1876 the voters of South Carolina, voting early and often in that troubled year, dutifully trooped to the polls in a splendid performance that marshaled 101 percent of the voting-age population. Even the Republicans maintained a modest showing throughout the South during the period of the third party system, generally hovering about the fortieth percentile and periodically threatening to fuse with the agrarian insurgents—a tactic that was particularly successful in North Carolina in 1894, thereby shortly inviting upon the Republicans the same electoral destruction that was to befall their erstwhile agrarian allies.

Hence the third party system grew increasingly unstable as two disadvantaged strata, the cash-crop farmers of the economically colonialized South and West and the ethnically fragmented urban proletariat, grew increasingly restive under the two conservative-dominated major parties. Festering discontents had been heralded prior to previous realignments by the rise of significant third parties—the Anti-Masons in the 1820s and the Free-Soilers and Know-Nothings in the period prior to the Civil War— which had telegraphed the basic clusters of issues that would dominate politics in the next electoral era. Similarly, the Populist party of the 1890s mushroomed in the wake of the "Democratic" Depression of 1893 to attempt the truly formidable task of forging a biracial and multi-ethnic alliance of the rural and urban dispossessed.

The abortive Populist revolt combined with the depression of the 1890s as an important contributing factor to the evolution of the fourth party system, the Industrial System of 1894–1932. Historians continue to debate, with sharp ideological overtones, whether the Populists were rational radicals well in advance of their time or backward-looking provincials with pronounced tendencies toward paranoia and bigotry.[5] Two decades ago, in 1951, in an analysis that was essentially Beardian in its implicit assumptions,[6] the distinguished southern historian C. Vann Woodward penned a

---

[5] Sheldon Hackney, *Populism: The Critical Issues* (Boston: Little, Brown & Co., 1971), contains a balanced assessment of the literature of Populism.

[6] C. Vann Woodward, *Origins of the New South, 1877–1913* (Baton Rouge: Louisiana State University Press, 1951). For a critical assessment of the remarkable impact and durability of Woodward's *Origins*, see Sheldon Hackney, "*Origins of the New South* in Retrospect," *Journal of Southern History* 38 (May 1972): 191–216.

masterful and sympathetic portrait of the Populists' tragic crusade. A grudging admirer of the political acumen if not of the moral compunctions of the outnumbered, neo-Whiggish Redeemers, who ultimately crushed the hapless Populists in the 1890s, Woodward chronicled a tragic epic of chicanery and unrequited hope. The Populists' ill-starred inflationary crusade was probably foredoomed by ancient racial tensions on the farm and by the understandable nervousness of an ethnically variegated urban proletariat too immature and internally fragmented to link arms effectively with Protestant agrarian rebels under the banner of William Jennings Bryan. In any case, the dramatic shift of the Democratic party from the limited government position of Grover Cleveland to the governmental activism and economic reform of Bryan joined with the economic and political turmoil of the 1890s to disrupt the voting coalition that had relied on the Democratic party for protection from moralistic reformers.

Whatever the cause of the Populist insurgents' demise, the movement had a profound impact on southern politics. The agrarian radicals not only challenged the Bourbon strategy of uniting white southerners behind a program of limited government and opposition to outside intervention but, even more crucially, sought to create a mass following based on economic and class divisions, a voting alignment only hinted at by previous agrarian insurgency. This internal conflict between, on the one hand, a white southern quasi-ethnic group defending the region from intrusions into social relations on a program of white supremacy and negative government and, on the other, the masses of exploited blacks and whites of an economically disadvantaged region combining behind the strategy of active governmental reform has in a simplistic but fundamental sense been the underlying division in southern politics during the modern era.

If the recent new-leftist trend in American historiography has been friendly toward the Populists, it concomitantly has invited a concerted assault upon the liberal-reformist credentials of the Progressives, picturing them essentially as nostalgic middle-class conservatives whose crusading rhetoric masked an elitist paternalism.[7] Paralleling and reinforcing this historical critique, political scientist Walter Dean Burnham has severely indicted the politically devastating effects of the Industrial System and the Thermidorian legacy of the Progressive reformers, who, Burnham argues, in the process of reforming the system actually consolidated it as an engine of industrial-elitist domination.[8] The Progressives' electoral reforms bore

---

[7]A perceptive synthesis of and critical commentary upon the recent revisionist literature of the Progressive movement is Otis L. Graham, Jr., *The Great Campaigns* (Englewood Cliffs, N.J.: Prentice-Hall, 1970). See also idem, *From Roosevelt to Roosevelt* (New York: Appleton-Century-Crofts, 1971), chaps. 4–7.

[8]Walter Dean Burnham, "The End of American Party Politics," *TRANS-action* (December 1969): 12–22. See also idem, "The Changing Shape of the American Political Universe," *American Political Science Review* 59 (March 1965): 23. Burnham's most recent and comprehensive statement of this gloomy thesis is *Critical Elections and the Mainsprings of Ameri-*

a host of illiberal consequences. The adoption of the secret ballot deprived political parties of their function of printing and distributing ballots; personal voter registration procedure favored the more politically involved middle-class citizens over those of lower socioeconomic status; the direct primary not only undermined the party leadership's control over the nomination of candidates but also denied the out party its position as the only available alternative; and nonpartisan municipal elections further weakened the party structure. These changes no doubt contributed to greater honesty in the casting and counting of ballots, but at the same time they debased the political parties and decimated voter turnout, especially among lower-status voting groups. By the 1920s on the average only some 52 percent of adult Americans voted in presidential election years, and hardly more than a third made their way to the polls for the off-year congressional contests.

The net result of the fourth party system, Burnham argues, was the virtual destruction of party competition throughout much of the United States. The massive Democratic defections during the 1890s in the greater Northeast created a reliably Republican bastion that effectively controlled a system which served to insulate the dominant industrial elites from the victims of the industrializing process, despite the protesting political movements repeatedly launched from the quasi-colonial West. In the now solidly Democratic South, a shrunken electorate excluded many of the erstwhile agrarians who had sought alliance with the western insurgents, while the consolidation of a legally institutionalized caste system inclined southern politics toward a defense of regional racial and social practices. Nationally the major components of the system included the progressive fragmentation of Congress, corporate domination of the executive branch, and the large but negative role played by the Supreme Court. More broadly, Burnham concludes, the Industrial System of 1896 thrived upon the substantial disappearance of party competition and even the discrediting of party itself as an instrument of government.

Clearly, such a severe interpretation ill comports with our traditional view of the Progressive era as a period in which a broad political reform

---

can Politics (New York: W. W. Norton, 1970), in which he elaborates his argument that the world's most dynamic socioeconomic system has been harnessed since the evolution of the second party system to a moribund political system, one so archaic and shackling that the American government, unlike the polities of modern Europe, lacks the fundamental "sovereignty" necessary to respond effectively to the needs of its exploited people. Jerold G. Rusk has challenged Burnham's use of split-ticket voting as evidence of voter alienation by explaining the phenomenon as primarily a consequence of the adoption of the Australian ballot. See Rusk, "The Effect of the Australian Ballot Reform on Split Ticket Voting," *American Political Science Review* 64 (December 1970): 1220–38. Recent analyses similar to Burnham's are E. E. Schattschneider, *The Semisovereign People* (New York: Holt, Rinehart and Winston, 1960); and Samuel P. Huntington, *Political Order in Changing Societies* (New Haven: Yale University Press, 1968).

movement spread from the cities to the state and federal arenas to cope
with the manifest inequities and dislocations of urban-industrial America.
Yet in recent years several American historians have contributed to a
fundamental reinterpretation of the Progressive era that is more congenial
to the political analysis advanced by Burnham, E. E. Schattschneider, and
Samuel P. Huntington.[9] This new historical interpretation emphasizes a
duality in the ranks of the Progressive reformers which parallels and reflects what Ferdinand Tonnies called the transition of modern society from
Gemeinschaft ("community") to Gesellschaft ("society"). This was "a
transition in which local, personal relations were replaced, through technological change, by a national system of bureaucratic, routinized, relatively impersonal relations in a society where power flowed increasingly
from local elites to be centralized in the hands of a new elite whose claim
to power rested upon expertise rather than reputation."[10] This dualism
goes far toward explaining how men who became reformers in order to
rationalize a chaotic and inefficient society—the "new middle class" of
rising bureaucrats, professionals, and businessmen who endowed Progressivism with its pronounced regulatory character—found themselves rubbing
shoulders with fellow reformers whose goals were quite the opposite: to
defend the threatened, traditional values of the small towns and of the
island communities of the rural hinterland. And it was primarily the latter
who endowed Progressivism with its nostalgic and even reactionary qualities by espousing such reforms as prohibition, immigration restriction,
blue laws, and eugenics. Yet both types of middle-class Progressives
feared the alien values and alleged radical proclivities of the lower social
orders, especially those composed of nonwhite and non-Protestant Americans, and appear to have hedged their faith in democracy by "purifying"
the franchise of its unworthy elements. While the decline in voter turnout,
perhaps especially in the South, seems to have been clearly linked to the
demise of agrarian radicalism and a consequent waning of psychological
involvement in the political process, the Progressive "reforms" served to
consolidate and extend the decimation of voter turnout.

Figure 1.1 diagrams the strikingly positive correlations between the
demise of Populism and the drop in voter participation and the inverse correlation between the rise of Progressivism and the decline in turnout.
Although this marked decline was nationwide, as was the Progressive im-

[9]See Richard Hofstadter, *The Age of Reform* (New York: Alfred A. Knopf, 1955);
Gabriel Kolko, *The Triumph of Conservatism: A Reinterpretation of American History,
1900–1916* (New York: The Free Press, 1963); James Weinstein, *The Corporate Ideal in the
Liberal State: 1900–1918* (Boston: Beacon Press, 1968); Samuel P. Hays, "Political Parties
and the Community-Society Continuum," in *The American Party Systems*, ed. Chambers and
Burnham, pp. 152–81; and Robert H. Wiebe, *The Search for Order, 1877–1920* (New York:
Hill and Wang, 1967). For a critical discussion of this new literature, see Graham, *From
Roosevelt to Roosevelt*, especially pp. 41–124.
[10]Graham, *From Roosevelt to Roosevelt*, p. 114.

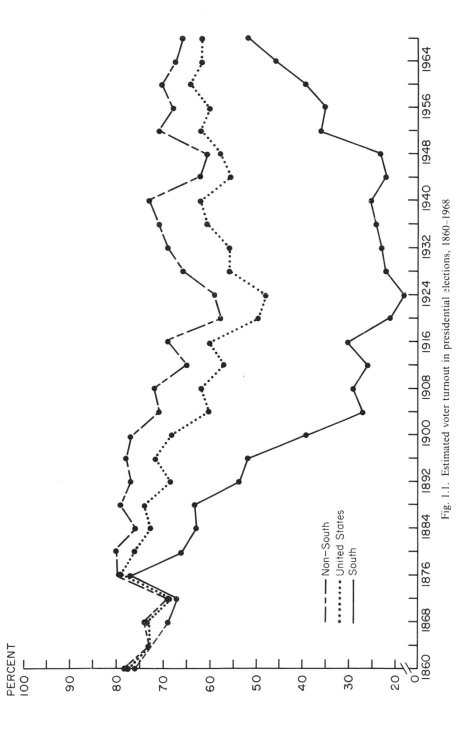

Fig. 1.1. Estimated voter turnout in presidential elections, 1860–1968

pulse itself, nowhere was it more dramatic and devastating than in the South, where by 1924 turnout in presidential elections reached a nadir average of 17.4 percent; in the five Deep South states of South Carolina, Georgia, Alabama, Mississippi, and Louisiana, turnout bottomed at an appalling average of 11.1 percent, with South Carolina once again, as in 1876, claiming supreme honors for descending from the sublime summit of 101.0 percent to a resounding 6.4. In the hands of such a purified electorate, Progressive democracy posed little threat to the established order. Raymond H. Pulley, in a recent study of the Progressive movement in Virginia, concluded that "the reforms undertaken in the Old Dominion during the progressive era returned the state to a political and social system as stable and resistant to innovation as any that had existed prior to the Civil War."[11]

This is not to deny that the Progressive movement was a viable impulse throughout the South, nor that in its range and complexity and even humanitarian concern it mirrored the national movement; indeed, it did so to a remarkable degree for such a distinctive region.[12] But this regional distinctiveness seemed to both magnify and distort as well as to mirror, channeling the regulatory thrust into a more narrow and less controversial business progressivism of more roads, better schools, and cleaner (and minimal) government and accelerating its defense of the South's traditional cultural values down the dark byways of Negrophobia and xenophobia that were to be so thoroughly plumbed by her Tom Watsons and Theodore Bilbos.[13] And in this long and agonizing descent the alleged New South's legacy of massive disfranchisement was enduring, not only for her black native sons, as has been abundantly documented,[14] but for even greater numbers of her less affluent whites as well. The leaders of the South's disfranchising conventions, which clustered about the turn of the century, were often quite candid on this point. Governor William C. Oates of Alabama, a Bourbon whose call for a purified franchise was both typical and hardly distinguishable from the Progressives' stance, openly insisted upon the elimination of "all those who are unfit and unqualified, and if the rule strikes a white man as well as a negro, let him go. There are some white men who have no more right and no more business to vote than a negro and not as much as some of them."[15] The results of this purge of both the

[11]Raymond H. Pulley, *Old Virginia Restored: An Interpretation of the Progressive Impulse, 1870–1930* (Charlottesville: University of Virginia Press, 1968), p. ix.

[12]For a balanced assessment of the democratic tendencies in the Democratic South, see Dewey W. Grantham, Jr., *The Democratic South* (Athens: University of Georgia Press, 1963).

[13]See George B. Tindall, *The Emergence of the New South 1913–1945* (Baton Rouge: Louisiana State University Press, 1967), especially chaps. 7 and 8.

[14]Woodward, *Origins of the New South*, chap. 12; V. O. Key, Jr., *Southern Politics in State and Nation* (New York: Alfred A. Knopf, 1949), pp. 535–39, 597–98, 614–18; and "The Negro Voter in the South," *Journal of Negro Education*, yearbook 26 (Summer 1957).

[15]Quoted in Woodward, *Origins of the New South*, p. 330. Woodward and Key place great emphasis upon the conflict between hill and black-belt whites.

blacks and "the depraved and incompetent men of our own race," in whose alleged interest "the intelligence and wealth of the South" would govern, were both effective and tenacious.[16] Francis Pickens Miller, the frustrated Virginia reformer who twice challenged and twice was crushed by Harry Byrd's formidable machine, recalled with despair the response in 1947 of his white house-painter to his query whether the gentleman was qualified to vote. "Colonel," the man replied, "you know I don't belong to the folks who vote."[17]

As the fourth party system evolved into its mature form in the 1920s, the few folks who voted in the South voted increasingly Democratic. The identification of the Democratic party with the lost cause and white supremacy had been a sacred legacy of the Bourbon redemption that was reinforced by the decimation of the Populist and Republican opposition. The symbolic power of the Democratic party label as representing the Bourbon redemption from black Reconstruction was typified in 1900 by former Governor Murphy J. Foster of Louisiana, who defended his Democratic administration by invoking a higher loyalty: "Because I have sinned don't destroy the Democratic party; strike down the sinner. If I have been recreant in my duty, strike me down, but for God's sake don't destroy

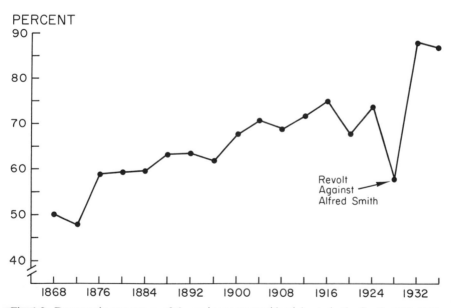

Fig. 1.2. Democratic percentage of the major party presidential vote in the South, 1868–1936

[16]See especially Woodward's discussion of black and white disfranchisement in Louisiana in *Origins of the New South*, pp. 342–49.

[17]Francis Pickens Miller, *The Man from the Valley: Memoirs of a 20th-Century Virginian* (Chapel Hill: University of North Carolina Press, 1971), p. 169.

PERCENT

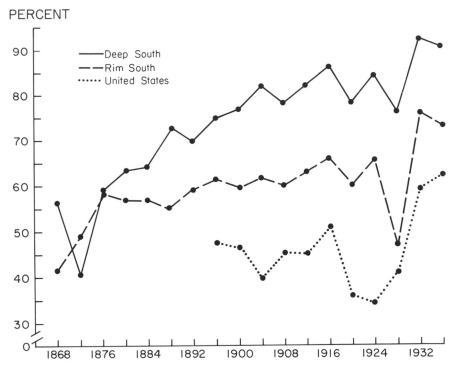

Fig. 1.3. Democratic percentage of the major party presidential vote in the Deep South and in the Rim South, 1868–1936

the Democratic party."[18] In 1924, when South Carolina's Senator Coleman L. Blease noted that Calvin Coolidge had received 1,123 of South Carolina's 50,131 presidential votes, he exclaimed: "I do not know where he got them. I was astonished to know that they were cast and shocked to know that they were counted."[19] Figure 1.2 reflects the incremental ascent of the South's Democratic vote in presidential elections from 1868 to 1936, a pattern of evolving Democratic solidarity marred only by the aberrant revolt against Alfred E. Smith in 1928. That this bolt was largely a defection of the six states of the Rim South—Arkansas, Florida, North Carolina, Tennessee, Texas, and Virginia[20]—is reflected in figure 1.3, which also con-

[18]Quoted in Mark T. Carleton, *Politics and Punishment: The History of the Louisiana State Penal System* (Baton Rouge: Louisiana State University Press, 1971), p. 77.

[19]Quoted in George B. Tindall, *The Disruption of the Solid South* (Athens: University of Georgia Press, 1972), p. 47.

[20]The dichotomy between the five Deep South and the six Rim South states is a useful convention that recognizes the centrality of race in southern political life, but this distinction should be employed with some caution, as it invites an erroneous equation of the relative strengths of the two blocs of states. While the racially sensitive and frequently bizarre political behavior of the Deep South more readily captures our attention and has indubitably endowed

trasts the performance of the Democratic South to that of the normal Republican majority nationally, a majority that abruptly disintegrated following the crash of 1929.

The New Deal System, forged during the critical realignment period of 1928–36, rested upon a dominant coalition formed from such an unlikely amalgam of constituent voting blocs as the Solid South, blacks, organized labor, urban ethnic groups, disgruntled farmers, and liberal intellectuals. That Franklin Roosevelt successfully fused such disparate elements was tribute to his political acumen, as well as to Republican blundering and the purblind opposition of a truculent business community that failed to recognize the vast cooptive possibilities that have always been inherent in the American reform impulse. The critical realignment of 1928–36 produced, through a massive shifting of voting blocs, a new national Democratic majority, but the southern contribution to this realignment flowed less from new electoral pressures than from an acceleration and exaggeration of older electoral forces already inherent in the Industrial System of 1896. Figure 1.4 reflects the degree to which the already Solid South's pronounced Democratic proclivities were further strengthened. This basic pattern of continuity between the fourth and fifth party systems in the South was also reflected in the size of the franchise, which experienced some modest growth during the New Deal years but which nonetheless remained, in striking contrast to the nonsouthern pattern, largely restricted to the region's more affluent white citizens. Never more than a quarter of the South's voting-age population cast ballots. The massive critical realignment that created the New Deal System, of which the Solid Democratic South was a crucial part, ironically witnessed no fundamental modification in southern voting patterns, which were overwhelmingly Democratic and disproportionately low before the realignment and subsequently.

This crucially revealing quality of the southern electorate—its considerable degree of disaggregation relative to the high levels of participation that had characterized so much of the nineteenth-century electorate, North and South—is, again, most readily revealed in the index of turnout, the percentage that major-party voting is of the estimated voting-age population.[21] At the presidential level, the mean turnout of the eleven southern

---

southern politics with its unique regional flavor, it is nevertheless important to bear in mind that in presidential elections since the Civil War the Deep South states have generally contained only two-fifths of the South's voting-age population and have produced only one-quarter of its total major party votes.

[21]Presidential turnout was derived from Walter Dean Burnham, "Sources of Historical Election Data" (mimeographed), which contains estimates of presidential turnout by states from 1824 to 1964. Estimates for 1968 were derived from official estimates of state voting-age populations, which for presidential election years since 1936 are in Bureau of the Census, *Statistical Abstract of the United States: 1969* (Washington, D.C.: U.S. Government Printing Office, 1969), p. 369; voting-age populations of the eleven southern states for 1920 and 1930

PERCENT

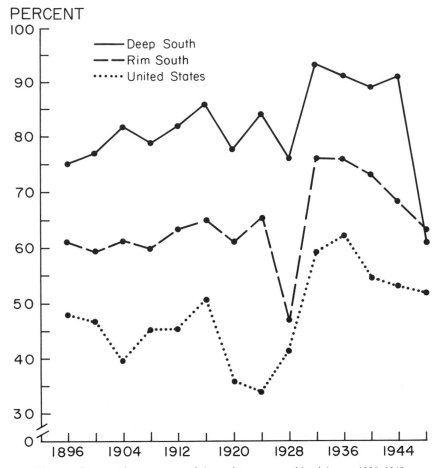

Fig. 1.4. Democratic percentage of the major party presidential vote, 1896–1948

states in 1920 was 20.5 percent, in contrast to a national rate of 56.9; by 1948, the South's participation had increased only to 23.5, and the national figure stood at 53.0, which reflected not only the southern drag but also the decidedly modest popular enthusiasm generated by the 1948 contest. The South's average turnout in the presidential elections between 1868 and 1892 had been 66.0.

This uninspiring portrait of one-party dominance and electoral disaggregation in the South is equally poignant at the gubernatorial level. Illustrative of the steady erosion of southern Republican strength is the

were computed from Bureau of the Census, *Fifteenth Census of the United States: 1930. Population*, vol. 2, and intercensal estimates were calculated from these data to correspond to the dates of the presidential and gubernatorial elections.

G.O.P.'s decline in Tennessee. In 1920 its loyal bloc of Confederate- and Democrat-hating voters in the mountains of east Tennessee, aided by the national Harding sweep, proved sufficient to capture the governor's mansion in Nashville. As figure 1.5 indicates, however, Republican strength slid gradually into impotence thereafter. By 1948 Tennessee Republicans were reduced to nominating hillbilly singer Roy Acuff, star of the Grand Ole Opry, who campaigned against his good friend and the Democratic nominee, Gordon Browning, with entertaining music, warm words of affection, and, ultimately, only a third of the voters. Once again confronted by Browning in the following gubernatorial election, Tennessee's Republicans quietly threw in the towel and nominated no one. Yet during the first half of the twentieth century, the G.O.P. had a better record in Tennessee than in any of the other southern states, where no Republican was elected governor or U.S. senator. During the three decades of decline following 1920, southern Republicans did not bother seriously to contest the Democratic gubernatorial nominees in Georgia, Louisiana, Mississippi, or South Carolina.

Southern voters, then, made their decisions in Democratic primaries, and while the basic continuity of the legacy of 1896—one-party politics and

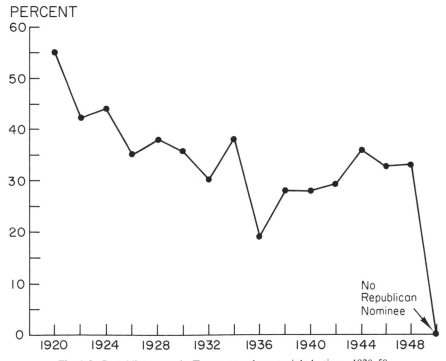

Fig. 1.5. Republican vote in Tennessee gubernatorial elections, 1920-50

electoral disaggregation—remained dominant, the South's minimal transition from the fourth to the fifth party system did produce a small overall improvement in gubernatorial turnout, much as it had in presidential turnout.[22] During the 1920s the South's mean turnout in Democratic gubernatorial primaries was 17.9 percent of her voting-age population; the equivalent figure for the New Deal years 1930–49 was 24.5.[23] This represents a growth in voter participation, but in contrast to the gubernatorial turnout in general elections outside the South, the improvement was minor, and the overall rate of voter participation remained almost pathologically low. A random sample of nonsouthern and nonborder states produced gubernatorial election turnouts (expressed as percentages) as follows: in the presidential year of 1940, Connecticut, 65.9; Illinois, 76.6; Minnesota, 69.6; Montana, 65.8; Nebraska, 71.6. In the off year of 1938, lower turnouts still reached levels vastly beyond the South's performance: New York, 44.0; Oregon, 51.0; Pennsylvania, 60.0.[24]

Expressed in terms of Deep South and Rim South, turnout in gubernatorial primaries was as follows:

[22]The raw data have been compiled by Alexander Heard and Donald Strong in *Southern Primaries and Elections, 1920–1949* (University: University of Alabama Press, 1950).

[23]Gubernatorial turnout was computed for both the Democratic primaries and, where there was significant Republican opposition, the general elections. (When runoff elections were held, they, rather than first primaries, were employed in the calculations.) But the emphasis is upon the primaries because, with the lone exception of Tennessee in 1920, no Republican ever won and because turnout was generally higher in the primaries. The major exceptions to this rule are the three states with significant blocs of mountain Republicans (Virginia, Tennessee, and North Carolina). Mean turnout in Virginia for the 1920–49 period was about the same in Democratic primaries (12.1 percent) and elections (12.8 percent), and both were dismally low. Virginia elected governors to four-year terms in odd years, presumably to insulate her politics from the possible contamination of national presidential elections. (One result of this practice, which has not been unusual in the South, is that elections are constantly being held.) Until 1954 Tennessee elected governors to two-year terms in even years, which practice produced a characteristic pattern, similar to that observed in congressional elections, of a marked drop-off in non-presidential-election years. Consequently, mean turnout for Tennessee's 1920–49 primaries was 16.6 percent, slightly superior to her "drop-off" mean of 15.3 percent for off-year general elections but considerably inferior to her mean turnout of 26.7 percent for general elections in presidential-election years, which raised her election mean turnout to 20.7 percent. A similar pattern of gubernatorial drop-off is found in Arkansas and Texas, which also elected governors to two-year terms in even years, but the Arkansas and Texas Republicans were such a small minority that general election turnout rarely approached that of the crucial primaries. Uniquely among southern states, North Carolina elected governors to four-year terms paralleling presidential terms, which produced a high mean turnout of 41.7 percent for her elections, compared with 19.6 percent for her primaries. Gubernatorial elections elsewhere in the South were largely inconsequential as opposed to the Democratic primaries.

[24]Sources for the state gubernatorial election returns were as follows: *Connecticut State Register and Manual*, 1941, p. 406; *Illinois Blue Book*, 1941–42, p. 703; *Minnesota Blue Book*, 1940, pp. 226–27; Ellis Waldron, *An Atlas of Montana Politics Since 1864* (Bozeman: Montana State University Press, 1958), p. 286; *Nebraska Blue Book*, 1940, p. 411; *New York Legislative Manual*, 1941, p. 1154; *Oregon Blue Book*, 1938, p. 236; and *Pennsylvania Manual*, 1941, p. 147.

	Deep South	Rim South
1920–30	19.6	18.2
1931–49	28.7	22.2

Surprisingly, participation in the Deep South was actually superior. But more revealing is the rank order of mean turnout in gubernatorial primaries in all eleven southern states from 1920 through 1949:

State	Rank	Mean turnout, in percent
Louisiana	1	31.5
Florida	2	28.5
Mississippi	3	26.8
South Carolina	4	26.4
Texas	5	25.9
Arkansas	6	23.3
North Carolina	7	19.6
Alabama	8	18.7 (tie)
Georgia	9	18.7 (tie)
Tennessee	10	16.6
Virginia	11	12.1

South: 22.6

Here the conventional Deep South-Rim South dichotomy makes little sense, and the hoary "Thank God for Mississippi" (for being consistently last) even less, as at least the white voters in the much maligned Magnolia State could legitimately lay claim to a greater measure of participatory democracy than that which obtained in all but one of the Rim South states and in all of Mississippi's fellow Deep South states except Louisiana, where the dynasty founded by Huey P. Long produced unusually intense bifactional competition. In light of this performance, Francis Pickens Miller's white house-painter in Virginia might well have felt more sovereign had he resided anywhere else in the South. But not much.

In 1920, H. L. Mencken pondered the culturally barbarian and politically bankrupt abyss into which the once aristocratic South had allegedly fallen, in a vintage essay entitled "The Sahara of the Bozart."[25] Therein he contemplated this vast regional "vacuity" in characteristic Menckenese ("One thinks of Asia Minor, resigned to Armenians, Greeks and wild swine, of Poland abandoned to the Poles") and concluded that the South's fall from lofty grace, as symbolized by the decay of Virginia, still the South's "best" state but by 1920 in tragic disrepair, came because "the old

[25] In *Prejudices: Second Series* (New York: Alfred A. Knopf, 1920), pp. 136–54.

aristocracy went down the red gullet of war; the poor white trash are now in the saddle."[26] Mencken's genetic theories aside, one may legitimately question whether "the liberated lower orders of whites" were fundamentally responsible for molding and transforming the political structure of a Virginia which sent only 19.4 percent of its voters to the polls in 1920, never attracted to the polls as many as one-quarter of her voting-age population during the following three decades, averaged a mere 12 percent turnout in her gubernatorial primaries and elections during those years, and dispatched Carter Glass and Harry Flood Byrd to the Senate.

In 1949 V. O. Key, Jr., and his research associates published the magisterial *Southern Politics in State and Nation*.[27] With careful attention to parties, candidates, and issues, Key described a political South whose political and social sectionalism was characterized and dominated by four essential and crippling institutions: disfranchisement, malapportionment, the one-party system, and the elaborate structure and pervasive ethos of Jim Crow. Yet, just as Key was writing, the mercurial genie of the race question, that keystone of southern political and cultural life supposedly settled a half-century earlier, was fatefully let out of the bottle by a curious combination of forces. These included the traditional fecundity and massive northern migration of southern blacks; the voting, protests, and demonstrations of blacks and liberal whites; both the liberalism and the expediency of the Democratic party; the demonstrable hypocrisy of the "separate but equal" South, in combination with the hypocrisy of much of the white non-South; the logic of sociological jurisprudence; the decolonization of Africa; the crusading rhetoric of World War II; and the ideological sensitivities of the Cold War.

Key could not know that a veritable Second Reconstruction of the South was in the offing, but, a Texan of liberal persuasions, he was optimistic that a dismantling of the institutional legacy of disfranchisement, malapportionment, the one-party system, and racial segregation would tend to release the South from the constraints of its conservative political establishment. This process, he reasoned, would invite the belated surge of a kind of New Dealish politics which one might plausibly expect from a region of such widespread poverty. "If the blue-collar vote in the South should double, southern conservatives in Congress would probably become less numerous," Key speculated,[28] and he was aware that public opinion polls in the late 1930s had elicited from southerners a higher percentage of self-identifications as "liberals" than from any other region in the United States.[29]

[26]Ibid., p. 139.
[27]Key was assisted by Alexander Heard and Donald Strong.
[28]*Public Opinion and American Democracy* (New York: Alfred A. Knopf, 1961), p. 105.
[29]For a thoughtful assessment of public opinion in the South, see Alfred O. Hero, Jr., *The Southerner and World Affairs* (Baton Rouge: Louisiana State University Press, 1965), especially, on this point, pp. 369–73.

Key introduced *Southern Politics* with the following assertion: "Of books about the South there is no end. Nor will there be so long as the South remains the region with the most distinctive character and tradition."[30] In the more than two decades since the publication of Key's modern classic, two broad developments have occurred that in many ways have been contradictory in their impact. First, the accelerating pace of economic growth and technological change—what C. Vann Woodward has called the Bulldozer Revolution—has tended greatly to reduce the socioeconomic lag which historically had contributed heavily to setting the South apart. A recent comparative study of the South and the non-South, based upon an analysis of urbanization, industrialization, occupational redistribution, income, and education as reflected in census data since 1930, concludes that "in these sectors the South has been changing more rapidly than the rest of the nation for the past forty years and moreover is becoming increasingly indistinguishable from the rest of American society."[31] Second, paralleling this Bulldozer Revolution, especially since World War II, has been an attempt to dismantle those political and sociocultural institutions that were the hallmark of the South's uniqueness. In their alarmed and defensive response to this Second Reconstruction, southern whites reaffirmed, sometimes violently, their allegiance to the old order and their determination once again to defend it against Yankee assault.

Against the background of this paradoxical relationship, in which nationalizing forces exacerbated old regional fears and intensified regional loyalties, a body of literature has been produced by social scientists who have tended to be liberal in persuasion and who hence have seemed at times to function as cheerleaders for the nationalization of the South. These social analysts, and especially the southerners among them, frequently have been somewhat ambivalent, in that their disapproval of the South's elitist caste society has been counterbalanced by an attraction toward a rural folk society and a revulsion against the urban squalor of the industrial North. Nevertheless, an implicit assumption widely shared among social scientists has been that the processes of urbanization and industrialization are fundamentally conducive to the liberalization of political life. In the concluding chapter of his *Political Tendencies in Louisiana*, political sociologist Perry H. Howard observes that the spate of "recent symposiums on change in the South have consisted of papers in which authors wait impatiently for the liberalization of the South and the increasing competitiveness of a two-party politics," and he adds the sobering admonition that "there is nothing inherent in the processes of industrialization and urbanization which foster liberal tendencies."[32]

[30]Key, *Southern Politics*, p. ix.

[31]John C. McKinney and Linda Brookover Bourque, "The Changing South: National Incorporation of a Region," *American Sociological Review* 36 (June 1971): 399–412.

[32]Perry H. Howard, *Political Tendencies in Louisiana*, rev. ed. (Baton Rouge: Louisiana State University Press, 1971), p. 413. See also Charles G. Sellers, Jr., ed., *The Southerner as*

Perhaps some day the homogenizing forces of the Bulldozer Revolution will erase the distinctive patterns of regional diversity in the United States, but at least insofar as the South is concerned, that day has not yet arrived. Samuel Lubell affirmed in 1970 that "the South remains *the* section of the country where business enjoys the widest permissiveness, where labor unions are weakest, where the economic dependence upon military installations is unusually high, where Negroes still struggle for political visibility, where welfare payments are lowest."[33] In a more rigorously empirical study published the same year, political scientist Ira Sharkansky concluded:

> Because the low turnout and single-party character of Southern politics is not explained by the poverty of the region, we must look to centuries of slavery and segregation, together with the corollaries of elitism, the alien reputation of the Republican Party and the reluctance of white politicians to carry their competition outside of the Democratic Party.[34]

The policy impact of this historically inherited, narrow political base, Sharkansky concluded, is reflected throughout the South in the low levels of public service, the regressive nature of state tax systems, and consequently poor public performance generally:

> The region scores below economic expectations on the measures of school completion, exam success, urban and rural road mileage, and benefit payments in all of the major public-assistance programs. Its performance in the program to aid families of dependent children is particularly poor, and reflects AFDC's reputation of being a "Negroes' program." Similarly, the low regional scores on exam success reflect the cultural distance between Southern Negroes and the dominant American society, and the failure of Southern school systems to close the gap since Emancipation.[35]

In short, sociological analysis alone cannot fully explain the observed distinctive phenomena in the absence of historical analysis. C. Vann Wood-

---

American (Chapel Hill: University of North Carolina Press, 1960); Allan P. Sindler, ed., *Change in the Contemporary South* (Durham: Duke University Press, 1963); Avery Leiserson, ed., *The American South in the 1960s* (New York: Praeger, 1964); Robert B. Highsaw, ed., *The Deep South in Transformation* (University: University of Alabama Press, 1964); and John C. McKinney and Edgar T. Thompson, eds., *The South in Continuity and Change* (Durham: Duke University Press, 1965).

[33]Samuel Lubell, *The Hidden Crisis in American Politics* (New York: W. W. Norton, 1970), p. 142.

[34]Ira Sharkansky, *Regionalism in American Politics* (Indianapolis: Bobbs-Merrill, 1970), p. 140. John Shelton Reed, *The Enduring South: Subcultural Persistence in Mass Society* (Lexington, Mass.: D. C. Heath, 1972), provides further support for this theme through an analysis of survey data.

[35]Sharkansky, *Regionalism in American Politics*, pp. 140–41.

ward has posed the rhetorical question: "Is there nothing about the South that is immune from the disintegrating effect of nationalism and the pressure for conformity? Is there not something that has not changed?"[36] To which he replied: "There is only one thing that I can think of, and that is its history . . . the collective experience of the Southern people"—the South's uniquely un-American experience with poverty, failure and defeat, guilt, and the pervasive fear of abstraction.

But if the South persists as a self-conscious entity, the writing of contemporary regional history is doubly perilous. The contemporary historian is largely robbed of the depth of perspective that has been the historian's chief asset. And, to the degree that the essence of social science is comparison, the regional historian risks falling betweeen the two stools of national and state history. Political trends identified as uniquely southern may in fact only mirror national trends.[37] Moreover, there is much truth in the assertion of Donald R. Matthews and James W. Prothro, despite their commitment to regional analysis, that "the most important political and legal fact about the South is its division into 11 states."[38] There is certainly no pretension here that a regional analysis, however comprehensive, can obviate the need for state monographs which reflect the distinctive patterns of state politics within the regional framework.

Our primary assumptions are, first, that despite the nationalizing and homogenizing forces that eroded much of the physical base of the South's distinctiveness during the postwar years, the region's historical legacy perpetuated its distinctive patterns of cultural and political life; second, that regional history remains a legitimate and profitable mode of analysis, despite the real dangers of masking distinctive state and local patterns and of failing to take sufficiently into account the comparative dimension of national politics; third, that the historical narrative, if it is analytical as well as descriptive, is the organizational structure best designed to reveal the evolution of political patterns over time; and finally, we do not assume that liberalism necessarily increases with industrialization and urbanization.

[36]C. Vann Woodward, "The Search for Southern Identity," in *The Burden of Southern History*, rev. ed. (Baton Rouge: Louisiana State University Press, 1968), p. 25.

[37]Assessment of the contrast between regional and national political behavior depends upon the political index employed. In 1962 the Department of Political Science of Duke University sponsored a conference on political change in the postwar South. There Donald Strong focused on the surge of southern Republican voting in presidential elections in the 1950s and concluded that the Republican trend was dramatic. Philip Converse, of the Survey Research Center, University of Michigan, fundamentally disagreed and pointed to the continuity of Democratic party identification in the southern survey sample in support of his contention that the Eisenhower victories were largely a result of short-term "surge" forces rather than fundamental electoral realignment. Their revealing dispute is argued in Sindler, *Change in the Contemporary South*, pp. 174–222.

[38]Donald R. Matthews and James W. Prothro, "Political Factors and Negro Voter Registration in the South," *American Political Science Review* 57 (June 1963): 367.

This fourth assumption may be restated as a hypothesis, namely, that despite the virtual destruction of the South's four inherited institutions of political sectionalism during the years of the Second Reconstruction— disfranchisement, malapportionment, the one-party system, and de jure racial segregation—the new southern politics was not primarily characterized by an unleashing of New Dealish tendencies, as Key had cautiously predicted and clearly hoped. The New Deal model of politics is basically an economic one in which common class interests link together a coalition of the have-nots; and such tendencies did characterize southern politics during the immediate postwar years when Key conducted his analysis, though the effectiveness of this coalition was hampered by low voter turnout and the one-party system. But the South's twentieth-century political legacy was basically Bourbon in character. At the center of this tradition has been a deep racial division that has militated against class coalitions, especially across racial lines, and has permitted government by relatively insulated elites.

To test this hypothesis, we analyzed county and precinct voting returns for primary and general elections from the eleven southern states during the years 1944–72. Since the South contains well over eleven hundred counties, including Louisiana's parishes and Virginia's independent cities, we simplified our analysis by assigning southern counties to three demographic categories (Metropolitan, defined as a county containing a city of more than 50,000 population; Urban, describing a county containing a city of from 20,000 to 50,000; and Rural-small town, denoting any county with no town as large as 20,000) and eight geographic categories: (1) Mountain, containing those counties located in the Appalachian and Ozark mountains; (2) Piedmont, describing the crescent of hill-country counties adjacent to the Appalachians; (3) Black belt, including those counties with a nonwhite population of 40 percent or more; (4) White belt, encompassing those lowland counties with a population more than 60 percent white; and the four peripheral sections of (5) South Florida, (6) Catholic Louisiana, (7) Mexican-American Texas, and (8) West Texas. We further gathered precinct returns from twenty-seven southern cities and classified them by socioeconomic class and race (Black and Lower-class, Lower-middle-class, Upper-middle-class, and Upper-class white). The research design is described in detail in the Note on Methodology and Data Sources at the end of the book, but generally we sought a design that would permit recognition of deviant voting behavior on the part of individual counties and the formulation of generalizations about the voting behavior of rural dwellers and urbanites, of hill country and lowlands, of blacks and whites, and of higher- and lower-status whites.

The identification of trends in voting behavior required examining and discussing a massive number of elections, with the attendant risk of trying the reader's patience with accounts of numerous prosaic campaigns, a risk we resolved to chance in order to minimize impressionistic judgments and overly sweeping generalizations. Among other problems involved in a study of this nature was the extent to which valid inferences might be drawn from aggregate data. We have sought to guard against unwarranted conclusions by being attentive to broad trends in voting patterns and by checking our findings against survey data. There was also the problem of defining multidimensional terms of deplorable ambiguity without which political history is almost impossible to write. For the most part we have relied on the reader's good sense to interpret words within the context of history and southern politics. Although we have used the words "liberal" and "progressive" in a common sense fashion, "liberal" suggests an ideological preference for broadening economic and social opportunities with an orientation toward the have-nots in society, while "progressive" implies a middle-class-oriented business progressivism common to the South's recent past. "Moderate" refers to a relatively tolerant attitude toward race relations. "Conservative" denotes a preference for the economic and social status quo, and "reactionary" represents a general rejection of already accomplished social and economic changes. We offer these general definitions fully conscious of the fact that politicians often cannot be conveniently labeled.

In a very personal sense, Wilbur J. Cash's powerful *Mind of the South* represents the anguished cry of a southern white liberal whose despair over the dominant white South's irrational intransigence, together with unknown personal anxieties, drove him to take his own life on the very threshold of his rise to prominence.[39] Our hypothesis posits a basic continuity of this Bourbon pattern, even in the face of the considerable changes wrought in the South by the Bulldozer Revolution and the Second Reconstruction.

[39]Wilbur J. Cash, *The Mind of the South* (New York: Alfred A. Knopf, 1941).

CHAPTER 2

THE POPULIST-NEW DEAL LEGACY: ONE-PARTY POLITICS IN THE POSTWAR DECADE

Southern politics during the decade following World War II uneasily accommodated two competing and paradoxical historical strains. The Populist legacy of rural liberalism, recently reinforced by the consciousness of class and economic interests that flowed from the Depression and New Deal experiences, conflicted with the tradition of white southern ethnocultural unity that since Reconstruction had shielded the region from outside intervention in social arrangements and in large part had protected entrenched elites from the vicissitudes of mass democracy. The one-party system permitted a Solid South to present a united front to the outside world, while internally a truncated and overwhelmingly white electorate divided over economic and other issues in state and local politics within the Democratic primary elections, which remained the central arena of political conflict through the 1950s. Although the system quadrennially broke apart in presidential elections, the large majority of southerners, even those who voted Dixiecrat or Republican in presidential contests, continued to think of themselves as Democrats, and only occasionally did Republicans make more than token challenges in state and local politics. In Congress the southern delegation not only shielded the region from civil-rights measures but generally opposed national Democratic Fair Deal reform programs, frequently in alliance with Republican legislators.[1]

The Great Depression and the New Deal had emboldened the region's masses of white and black have-nots to press politically for relief, while, at the same time, the South's twentieth-century legacy of racial segregation, malapportionment, and disfranchisement had produced a one-party system that enhanced the dominance of conservative elites. While most

---

[1]W. Wayne Shannon, *Party, Constituency, and Congressional Voting* (Baton Rouge: Louisiana State University Press, 1968), pp. 81–112.

southern voters identified themselves as Democrats, they made their meaningful choices in primary elections, where partisan identification was not a determining influence. The concept of the "normal vote" rested on the assumption that voters would normally express a standing partisan preference at the polls, but in the South, as V. O. Key noted, the one-party system was in reality a non-party system, where factions within the dominant state Democratic parties served often as bewildering substitutes for political parties. While the problem was regional, its political context was dominated by the often arbitrary realities of state jurisdictions, and it is here that a regional analysis must acknowledge the variety of state patterns. At the most cohesive or polarized end of the spectrum was Louisiana, where conflict between the populist Longs and the Bourbon anti-Longs created an intense bifactionalism within the Democratic one-party system that paralleled a two-party model. At the other end were Georgia, where the conservative Talmadge dynasty conquered Georgia's nascent "Little New Deal," and Arkansas, where the chaos of friends-and-neighbors, one-party politics remained supreme.

Generally during the postwar decade the politics of economic class made considerable headway against the inertia of the politics of race and caste. Nevertheless, two broad social and political trends converged on a collision course. On the one hand, New Dealish neopopulism gained impetus with the victories of such men as W. Kerr Scott in North Carolina, Olin D. Johnston in South Carolina, James E. Folsom, John J. Sparkman, and Lister Hill in Alabama, Estes Kefauver and Albert Gore in Tennessee, Lyndon B. Johnson in Texas, and the Longs in Louisiana. On the other hand, the relative ease with which race- and redbaiting destroyed the candidacies of Frank P. Graham in North Carolina and Claude Pepper in Florida suggested a potential that would be realized following the *Brown* decision of 1954. Mass voter behavior in state elections reflected the relatively sharp factional conflicts that took place within state Democratic parties during this transitional period, although the southern franchise experienced only minimal evolution.

Voter participation increased during the period, but registration remained low, especially among black southerners. In 1940 an estimated 250,000 blacks in the eleven former Confederate states, approximately five percent of the black voting-age population, were registered to vote. By 1952 there were slightly more than one million black registrants, or some 20 percent of the voting-age population. The pace then slowed for a decade before spurting upward in the 1960s. An estimated 1.4 million blacks, about 29 percent of the potential, were registered in 1960. Black voter participation varied considerably from state to state, reflecting in part the obstacles placed in the paths of blacks by state constitutional provisions and by the general hostility of state and local authorities to black exercise of the franchise. In Mississippi, where every conceivable impediment blocked black access to the polls, only some 22,000 blacks, about five percent of those eligible, were registered in 1960; in Tennessee, where registration provisions were relatively generous and local hostility to black voting was less common, an estimated 185,000 blacks, almost 60 percent of the voting-age population, were registered. Approximately one of every ten names on the southern registration rolls that year belonged to a black. Of the white voting-age population, roughly 60 percent were registered. White southerners were considerably more likely to cast ballots than black southerners, of course, but nonvoting was also common among whites, especially whites of lower socioeconomic status.[2]

The nature of one-party politics varied substantially from state to state, but some of the underlying inclinations of the voter groups within the southern electorate are suggested by South Carolina election returns. The predominately white population of the Bible Belt uplands traditionally took the conservative side on such social questions as prohibition, while support for the sale of alcohol came from the lowland counties, as figures 2.1–2.4 illustrate. This apparent social toleration of the lowlands terminated at the color line, however. In 1952 the South Carolina legislature, anticipating the U.S. Supreme Court's public-school desegregation decision, submitted to the voters an amendment authorizing the conversion of the public schools into private schools. Lowland voters, the bulk of whom, of course, were whites living in areas heavily peopled with nonvoting blacks, gave the private-school plan overwhelming support. In the Piedmont, where racial issues were less immediately pressing, voters showed less enthusiasm toward the notion of abandoning the public schools in the name of white supremacy.

In Democratic primary elections, the small farmers, millhands, and factory workers of the Piedmont on occasion demonstrated populist inclinations at the polls. Key observed that in the black belt "the overshadowing race question, in which the big farmers have the most immediate stake, blots up a latent radicalism by converting discontent into aggression against the Negro";[3] and the planters, merchants and businessmen of the lowlands often rallied support for conservative candidates. The 1950 senatorial primary campaign pitting Senator Olin D. Johnston against Governor J. Strom Thurmond did not ideally clarify and delineate the issues. Both

[2]Donald R. Matthews and James W. Prothro, *Negroes and the New Southern Politics* (New York: Harcourt, Brace and World, 1966), p. 18; Margaret Price, *The Negro Voter in the South* (Atlanta: Southern Regional Council, 1957); idem, *The Negro and the Ballot in the South* (Atlanta: Southern Regional Council, 1959); U.S. Commission on Civil Rights, *Voting in Mississippi* (Washington, D.C.: U.S. Government Printing Office, 1965), pp. 3–11; Pat Watters and Reese Cleghorn, *Climbing Jacob's Ladder: The Arrival of Negroes in Southern Politics* (New York: Harcourt, Brace and World, 1967), pp. 27–28; and Voter Education Project, *V.E.P. News* 2 (April 1968).

[3]V. O. Key, Jr., *Southern Politics in State and Nation* (New York: Alfred A. Knopf, 1949), p. 44.

Fig. 2.1. South Carolina counties voting 60 percent or more dry in the Prohibition amendment election, 1940

Fig. 2.2. South Carolina counties voting 40 percent or more against the segregationist amendment permitting closure of public schools, 1952

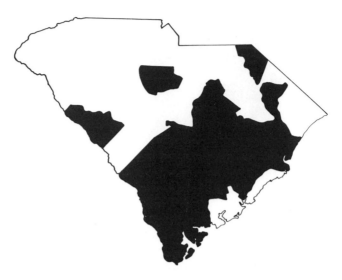

Fig. 2.3. South Carolina counties containing populations 50 percent or more nonwhite in 1950

Fig. 2.4. South Carolina counties voting 50 percent or more for Johnston in the 1950 senatorial primary

candidates spent considerable time espousing their devotion to segregation, and Johnston made extensive use of a picture published in *Life* magazine showing health buff Thurmond standing on his head, as evidence that the governor lacked sufficient maturity to be a U.S. senator. But Johnston was also known to be a friend of New Deal economic policies, and he had received Franklin Roosevelt's endorsement in an earlier senatorial campaign. Thurmond had been the presidental candidate of the Dixiecrats in 1948, and his anti-Fair Deal position was well established.[4] As figures 2.1–2.4 suggest, the hotly contested election resulted in Thurmond capturing the lowlands and Johnston sweeping the uplands and the election with 54 percent of the vote. Johnston won only two downstate counties: Barnwell, which was the home of state Senator Edgar A. Brown, a close Johnston ally, and Beaufort, a coastal county where black voter registration was large.

The absence of two-party organizational structures and the limited size of the southern electorate may well have enhanced the potential influence of local political elites in rural-small town areas. The role played by county leaders in state politics and in Democratic party factional alignments varied enormously over the region. In some cases county officials assiduously avoided involvement in state-level campaigns for fear of offending their own following. Elsewhere, personal and ideological ties bound county leaders into relatively cohesive factional organizations in state Democratic politics. The "banker-farmer-lawyer-doctor-governing class" described by Jasper B. Shannon was most common in the lowland counties, as was a tradition of white solidarity and deference to established authority.[5]

Not infrequently, existing county organizations absorbed the newly—if slowly—emerging black vote. Politicians sometimes talked of "five-dollar counties" and "half-a-pint towns" to describe the cost per vote in black neighborhoods, paid in money or moonshine according to local custom, but local bargains between black leaders and white law-enforcement and other governmental officials were more common. In exchange for black voter support for the slate recommended by the white leadership, black leaders could expect such concessions as protective law enforcement and street repairs and other improvements in the black community, things that perhaps should have been provided by government without local bargaining but which represented an improvement over past practices in any case. As black voters became more numerous, more experienced, and more racially conscious and as voting machines replaced the none-too-secret voting practices common in rural-small town counties, these bargains declined. In the

---

[4]Alberta M. Lachicotte, *Rebel Senator: Strom Thurmond of South Carolina* (New York: Devin-Adair, 1966), pp. 62–76. For the sources of election returns, see the Note on Methodology and Data Sources.

[5]Jasper B. Shannon, *Toward a New Politics in the South* (Knoxville: University of Tennessee Press, 1949), pp. 41–66.

cities, vigorous independence on the part of black voters and black political
organizations was the norm; in the towns and counties, however, black
voting sometimes strengthened the position of the county-seat political
elites.[6]

A judicious use of money, patronage, and pork-barrel projects was
rewarded in the South as often as elsewhere in the nation. Particularly
responsive were the mountain counties of North Carolina and Tennessee,
as exemplified by the two hotly contested North Carolina primary runoff
elections in 1948 and 1950. The 1948 gubernatorial runoff pitted Commissioner of Agriculture W. Kerr Scott, the insurgent candidate who championed increased budgets for roads, schools, rural electrification, and other
services, against State Treasurer Charles M. Johnson, the favorite of most
of the state's political establishment. Johnson did best on the Blue Ridge,
as had other establishment candidates in the past. Scott won the election
and soon afterward appointed Frank P. Graham, the liberal president of
the University of North Carolina, to a vacant U.S. Senate seat. Running
against Graham in the 1950 senatorial campaign was Willis Smith, formerly president of the American Bar Association, who represented somewhat the same conservative viewpoint as Johnson and received support
from many of the same sources that had aided Johnson in 1948, although
Smith conducted a demagogic campaign that made generous use of racism
and redbaiting. Smith won the election, but the mountain counties this time
went to Graham. That the Appalachian counties which had rejected Scott
gave strong support to the liberal university president emeritus was no
doubt related rather closely to the fact that Scott rather than the opposition
now controlled the emoluments of the governor's office.[7]

County organizations provided some structure to one-party politics
while at the same time presenting a formidable barrier to the creation of a
two-party system. County leaders were most cohesive in Virginia, where
they were the foundation for Senator Harry Flood Byrd's statewide organization. They were also important in Georgia, but alliances there were
shifting and uncertain. In Arkansas political informants spoke openly of
"the twenty-one controlled counties." The most "effective" organizations
in the South were no doubt the machine counties in heavily Mexican-
American areas of south Texas, which gained a certain notoriety in 1948

[6]"The Negro Voter in the South," *Journal of Negro Education Yearbook* 26 (Summer
1957); Alfred Clubok, John DeGrove, and Charles Farris, "The Manipulated Negro Vote:
Preconditions and Consequences," *Journal of Politics* 26 (February 1964): 112–29; James R.
Soukup, Clifton McCleskey, and Harry Holloway, *Party and Factional Division in Texas*
(Austin: University of Texas Press, 1964), pp. 108–26; and Watters and Cleghorn, *Climbing
Jacob's Ladder*, pp. 331–58.

[7]Key, *Southern Politics*, pp. 213–15; Samuel Lubell, *The Future of American Politics*,
2d ed., rev. (Garden City: Doubleday, 1956), pp. 108–16; and James R. Spence, *The Making
of a Governor: The Moore-Preyer-Lake Primaries of 1964* (Winston-Salem, N.C.: John F.
Blair, 1968), pp. 7–8.

by continuing well after election day to produce new and revised election returns ultimately sufficient to overcome the opposition's narrow lead and make Lyndon B. Johnson a U.S. senator from Texas. (However, in fairness, Johnson's opponent in the runoff primary, former Governor Coke R. Stevenson, was the favored candidate in a number of east Texas court-houses, a fact that netted Stevenson some highly questionable returns of his own and led a Texas historian to observe that "Johnson men had not *defrauded* Stevenson, but successfully *outfrauded* him.")[8] But the influence of county organizations, while providing the most persuasive explanation for deviant voting behavior otherwise difficult to explain, could easily be exaggerated.

Within this system, South Carolina might again serve as a microcosm of the fundamentally paradoxical situation wherein the tensions between Piedmont and Tidewater, black and white, rural and urban, Populist and Bourbon worked themselves out along a spectrum of state responses. In the South Carolina elections mentioned previously, the cities differed relatively little from the adjacent countryside in the percentage of votes they cast for or against prohibition, private schools, and Olin Johnston or Strom Thurmond. But within the cities the balloting etched divergent tendencies on the part of affluent whites, lower-status whites, and blacks. New Dealish Johnston, the uplands candidate, ran considerably better in Columbia, located in the center of the state at the edge of the Piedmont, than he did in the lowland city of Charleston. But in either case Johnston prospered politically in black precincts and did well in the white working-class districts. Dixiecrat Thurmond won the upper-income precincts, and his majorities in the prestigious residential area along the Battery in Charleston were truly impressive. The urban coalition that helped to elect Johnston often disintegrated in other types of elections, as indicated by the voting patterns in Columbia on constitutional amendments pertaining to segregation and the sale of liquor. Like the hill-country counties, the lower-status white wards supported the dry position; upper-income whites, this time joined by blacks, favored liberalizing the laws governing the sale of alcohol. But on the 1952 private-school segregation amendment, skin color rather than class dominated voter behavior: whites generally, in both Columbia and Charleston, banded together in support of segregation; blacks understandably were reluctant to endorse closing the public schools in preference to desegregating them.[9] The election results presented in tables 2.1*a*, 2.1*b*, and 2.1*c* suggest some of the differing political inclina-

[8]T. R. Fehrenbach, *Lone Star: A History of Texas and the Texans* (New York: Macmillan, 1968), p. 659.

[9]This white-versus-black voting alignment on the private-school referendum differed from the voting patterns on similar questions in the cities of most other southern states. The class division among whites on the liquor question, however, was consistent in numerous elections checked in cities throughout the region.

Table 2.1*a*

Percentage of the Vote for Johnston and Thurmond
in the 1950 Senatorial Runoff in Columbia and Charleston,
by Socioeconomic Class and Race

Vote category	Columbia			Charleston		
	Percentage of vote received by Johnston	Percentage of vote received by Thurmond	(N)[a]	Percentage of vote received by Johnston	Percentage of vote received by Thurmond	(N)[a]
Black	94.5	5.5	(1,321)	66.7	33.3	(616)
Lower-class white	62.3	37.7	(1,899)	42.8	57.2	(1,927)
Lower-middle-class white	58.8	41.2	(2,468)	37.8	62.2	(760)
Upper-middle-class white	51.4	48.6	(2,096)	25.8	74.2	(2,154)
Upper-class white	49.1	50.9	(1,694)	13.9	86.1	(908)
County vote[b]	62.5	37.5	(24,855)	43.6	56.4	(27,036)

Note: For the source of election data and the methodology used in classification of precinct votes, see the Note on Methodology and Data Sources.

[a](N) denotes the number of votes upon which the percentages are based. Thus Johnston received 94.5 percent of the 1,321 votes cast in the predominately black precincts used in this analysis. The difficulties involved in selecting relatively homogeneous precincts account for variations in the size of N.

[b]County-vote percentages are based on the total number of votes cast in the county, in this case Richland County (Columbia) and Charleston County. Thus, in Richland County, Johnston won 62.5 percent of the total number of 24,855 votes actually cast in Richland County, and Thurmond won 37.5 percent.

Table 2.1*b*

Results of the 1952 Vote in Columbia
on the Private-School-Segregation Amendment,
by Socioeconomic Class and Race

Vote category	Percentage for	Percentage against	(N)[a]
Black	17.9	82.1	(1,189)
Lower-class white	81.6	18.4	(1,141)
Lower-middle-class white	82.9	17.1	(1,808)
Upper-middle-class white	72.2	27.8	(2,065)
Upper-class white	80.1	19.9	(2,121)
County vote[b]	74.5	25.5	(18,315)

[a](N) denotes the number of votes upon which the percentages are based.

[b]County-vote percentages are based on the total number of votes cast in the county.

Table 2.1c
Results of the 1966 Referendum in Charleston
on Liberalization of State Liquor Laws,
by Socioeconomic Class and Race

Vote category	Percentage of vote for liberalization	Percentage of vote against liberalization	(N)[a]
Black	63.4	36.6	(737)
Lower-class white	42.1	57.9	(1,813)
Lower-middle-class white	48.0	52.0	(3,123)
Upper-middle-class white	60.6	39.4	(2,001)
Upper-class white	65.8	34.2	(3,759)
County vote[b]	56.5	43.5	(27,265)

[a](N) denotes the number of votes upon which the percentages are based.

[b]County-vote percentages are based on the total number of votes cast in the county.

tions of the affluent and the nonaffluent and of blacks and whites in the cities.

Senator Johnston had rallied the farmers and mill workers of the hills and the lower-class whites of the cities, and similar neopopulist voting alignments appeared in other southern states. This Populist-New Deal coalition of have-nots, allied across color lines in opposition to the haves, generated the votes that swept into office a number of economically liberal candidates who frequently differed on specifics but who broadly oriented their campaigns toward higher expenditures for schools, roads, public health, old-age pensions, and other state services. Such relatively loyal New Dealers as Governors Earl K. Long, James E. Folsom, and W. Kerr Scott and Senators John J. Sparkman, Estes Kefauver, and Albert Gore relied generally upon Populist economic programs and common-man campaign styles rather than race-baiting. The resultant voting patterns during the postwar decade could often be interpreted as relatively realistic expressions of economic self-interest.

These patterns were most consistent and most effectively factionalized in Louisiana. After the death of Huey P. Long, his followers within the state Democratic party fell upon hard times. Rocked by scandals shocking even by Louisiana standards, the Long faction was driven from power by conservative "reform" forces in 1940. But the bifactionalism bequeathed by Long remained. Voters favored with some consistency either the Long or the anti-Long factions, and candidates customarily campaigned for state and local offices as members of a factional ticket. First-primary campaigns for major state offices were frequently free-for-all contests involving numerous contestants; the runoff primaries, however, were normally clear-cut struggles between the two factions.

In 1948 the Longs returned to power. Russell Long, Huey's son, won a seat in the U.S. Senate; Earl Long, Huey's brother, was victorious in the gubernatorial election; and the Long slate captured a majority in the state legislature. The incoming governor issued an open invitation to his inauguration, held in the Louisiana State University football stadium, and a sufficient number of people attended to consume some 200,000 hot dogs and 240,000 soft drinks. Following these formalities, the new administration set about fulfilling its campaign promises. The state budget promptly doubled from what it had been four years earlier at the beginning of the previous anti-Long administration; taxes went up; public health, schools, and welfare services benefitted; and such things as civil-service standards, governmental administration, and industrial development programs suffered. Buccaneering liberalism was back in Baton Rouge.[10]

Unable constitutionally to succeed himself as governor, Earl Long in 1952 supported District Judge Carlos Spaht of Baton Rouge, while the reform faction united in the runoff election behind Appellate Judge Robert F. Kennon of Minden. Spaht ran best in areas that traditionally supported Long contenders, but he proved to be a relatively weak candidate, and Kennon and the anti-Long faction won a substantial victory. Four years later, however, Earl Long again headed the Long ticket and swept past four opponents for a first-primary victory. Before leaving office, the anti-Long administration did head off another hot dog extravaganza by limiting the funds available for the inauguration ceremony, and, more important, successfully sponsored a constitutional amendment requiring a two-thirds vote in the legislature to levy new or increased taxes, all of which created difficulties for the new administration. Long forced a tax increase through the legislature in 1958, and his legislative followers repealed the right-to-work law for nonagricultural workers, thereby making Louisiana the only state in the South without one. But the Long administration of the late 1950s accomplished less in terms of new and expanded programs than had the previous one.[11]

The candidates of the Long faction consistently appealed most strongly to rural-small town dwellers, as figure 2.5 indicates. The Protestant hill country in the northern and central parts of the state included a disproportionate number of the faction's most consistently loyal parishes, as well as the Longs' home parish of Winn, and several of the Mississippi River Valley black-belt parishes demonstrated a fairly consistent

[10]Allan P. Sindler, *Huey Long's Louisiana: State Politics, 1920–1952* (Baltimore: Johns Hopkins Press, 1956), pp. 207–9, 262; Stan Opotowsky, *The Longs of Louisiana* (New York: E. P. Dutton, 1960), pp. 148–51; and Perry H. Howard, *Political Tendencies in Louisiana*, rev. ed. (Baton Rouge: Louisiana State University Press, 1971), pp. 278–80.

[11]*New Orleans Times-Picayune*, June 17, November 7, 1956; and William C. Havard, Rudolf Heberle, and Perry H. Howard, *The Louisiana Elections of 1960* (Baton Rouge: Louisiana State University Press, 1963), pp. 35–36.

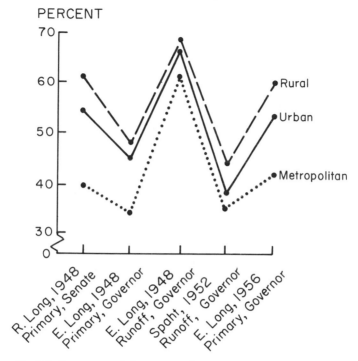

Fig. 2.5. Percentage of the vote received by Long faction candidates
in rural, urban, and metropolitan parishes in Louisiana, 1948–56

anti-Long bias in voting patterns. But generally the Long ticket, at least
when headed by a Long, could expect to fare well across the Louisiana
countryside. The Long faction championed programs designed to benefit
rural areas, and the style of its candidates, especially that of "Uncle Earl,"
was oriented toward the hinterlands. In 1956, Long eschewed the use of
television in his campaign, stating that "it makes me look like a monkey on
a stick,"[12] and carried his campaign to the backwoods. He attacked his
leading opponent, New Orleans Mayor deLesseps S. Morrison, whom
Long referred to as Del-a-soops, for wearing a "toopee," spraying perfume
under his arms, and dressing in four-hundred-dollar suits, all of which
may not have been particularly relevant to the issues at hand but which
made Uncle Earl an attraction in rural areas.

As figure 2.5 suggests, Longism did not flourish in metropolitan areas.
Virtually all of the major city newspapers were anti-Long, although the
New Orleans Times-Picayune may have been to the Longs, as A. J. Lieb-
ling observed, "what the Austrian armies were to Napoleon"—they made

[12]As quoted in Thomas Martin, Dynasty: The Longs of Louisiana (New York: G. T.
Putnam's Sons, 1960), p. 198.

his "reputation by being easy to lick."[13] The united opposition of the press and most of the state's business and industrial leadership helped to make the cities strongholds of the anti-Long opposition. In the 1948 runoff primary, Earl Long ran well virtually everywhere, winning majorities in sixty-two of Louisiana's sixty-four parishes and crushing former Governor Sam Jones. But normally the anti-Long, good government, "reform" forces enjoyed sufficient support from upper- and middle-income whites to dominate the urban returns. While voting patterns were by no means identical from city to city and from election to election, the Longs with some consistency did well in black and lower-status white neighborhoods. Figures 2.6 and 2.7 identify the sources of Long faction support in Shreveport, Baton Rouge, and New Orleans in a series of gubernatorial primary elections. In the 1948 primary, Earl Long received the bulk of the votes cast by blacks in Shreveport and won a plurality in low-income white neighborhoods. But as income, education, and house values increased, the Long vote declined, until he received a scanty 6.5 percent in the most prestigious white neighborhoods, compared with the 92.8 percent shared by the two leading anti-Long contenders, Jones and Judge Kennon. These general patterns remained evident in other gubernatorial primaries. In the 1948 runoff election against Jones, Long ran more poorly in Baton Rouge than

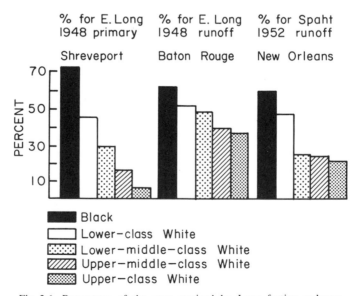

Fig. 2.6. Percentage of the vote received by Long faction gubernatorial candidates in Shreveport, Baton Rouge, and New Orleans, by socioeconomic class and race

[13]A. J. Liebling, *The Earl of Louisiana* (New York: Simon and Schuster, 1961), p. 152.

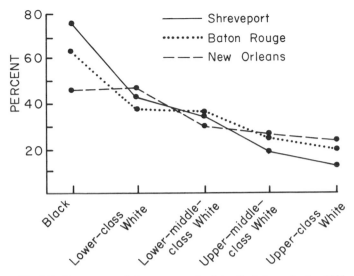

Fig. 2.7. Percentage of the vote received by Earl Long in the 1956 primary

in other Louisiana cities, but, in light of the customarily anemic Long support in the cities, he did quite well, and he held together the New Deal coalition of black and white have-nots. Judge Spaht fared badly in New Orleans and elsewhere against Kennon in the 1952 runoff primary; but Uncle Earl was irresistible in 1956, when he won a first-primary majority. Long ran best in black neighborhoods in Shreveport and Baton Rouge in the 1956 race; but in New Orleans Mayor Morrison cut heavily into his black support. Generally, however, the class and racial bias of Long's appeal in the cities remained broadly consistent.

The relatively disciplined and organized factionalism in Louisiana contrasted with the more fluid Democratic infighting in most other southern states. In Alabama shifting political alliances encouraged friends-and-neighbors parochialism at the voting booths and generally was less successful in channeling the populist impulses that fueled the Long organization in Louisiana into a consistent and cohesive force. The election successes of Governor James Folsom and Senators Lister Hill and John Sparkman evidenced the continuing vitality of what Key called Alabama's "inclination to defend liberty and to bait the interests."[14] But while Folsom, Hill, and Sparkman emerged victorious from a half-dozen relatively clear-cut election clashes between liberals and conservatives during the postwar period, each conducted his own campaign, and each drew support from overlapping but independently distinguishable voter bases.

[14]Key, *Southern Politics*, p. 36.

Governor Folsom betrayed a continuing concern for the disheveled state of Alabama liberalism and struggled sporadically to replace every-man-for-himself practices with a more cohesive factionalism. He attempted to introduce a Louisiana-type ticket system by energetically supporting his own choices for state and local offices. These efforts, however, were rarely successful. Folsom won gubernatorial primary elections by smashing margins in 1946 and in 1954, but he was unable to transfer this voter following to other candidates.

A gargantuan man who stood six feet, eight inches, weighed 260 pounds, and wore size 16 shoes, he also had gargantuan appetites. Midway through his first term as governor, he suffered a severe loss of prestige when he became the object of a highly publicized paternity suit.[15] During his second term his heavy consumption of alcohol became an increasing problem, particularly when he invited Harlem Congressman Adam Clayton Powell to the governor's mansion for a drink. Drinking was bad enough in Alabama, but when it was with an uppity black who entered the governor's mansion through the front door, it became too much for many whites to accept.[16]

Folsom made no secret of his distaste for civil service and competitive bidding on state contracts, and he was accused of maladministration, conflict of interest, and nepotism, charges to which he often responded with such disarmingly frank replies as: "I don't know why others should get the gravy. I'm governor."[17] But he also fought for higher expenditures for schools and teachers' salaries, farm-to-market roads, old-age pensions, and other state services and for progressive tax measures, reapportionment of the legislature, and repeal of the poll tax. And he demonstrated a magnetic appeal to voters residing in the backwoods. With a hillbilly band, a folksy style, and a splendid ability to bait the metropolitan newspapers, millionaires, Big Mules, and monopolies, Big Jim, "the little man's big friend," rolled up impressive majorities in the hills and mountains of north Alabama and the wire-grass region in the south. In 1954 Folsom won a first-primary majority over six opponents by taking almost 60 percent of the votes cast in rural-small town areas (while losing almost 60 percent of the votes in metropolitan counties). But Folsom developed little in the way of a cohesive campaign organization. County political elites were usually suspicious if not downright hostile toward Folsom—more often than not he delivered campaign speeches without benefit of introductions from local leaders—and his attempts to build his own factional following failed. Folsom did create an administration faction in the state legislature, but,

[15]William Bradford Huie, "Draughts of Old Bourbon: Pregnancy and Politics in Alabama," *American Mercury* 72 (June 1951): 748–66.

[16]*Montgomery Advertiser*, June 8, 1958.

[17]As quoted in Robert Sherrill, *Gothic Politics in the Deep South: Stars of the New Confederacy* (New York: Grossman, 1968), p. 274.

except for the early years of his second term, he had difficulty commanding a majority on controversial legislation.[18]

In 1946 Folsom supported Sparkman, then a north Alabama congressman, in a special election to fill an unexpired Senate term. Sparkman won the election, but by 1948 Folsom and Sparkman were at odds, and in the Senate primary of that year the governor unsuccessfully attempted to unseat the senator by supporting the candidacy of Philip J. Hamm.

Sparkman was generally regarded as a friend of New Deal policies, and Senator Lister Hill even more so. "[Hill] must be classed," according to the editors of the *New Republic*, "among the half-dozen or so most effective progressives in the upper house."[19] Formerly a congressman from Montgomery, Hill in his early Senate races ran best in the lowland counties around his home. With the emergence of the civil-rights issue and the Fair Deal, Hill's base of support shifted toward the northern hills and mountains and the southeastern wire grass.

Folsom, Sparkman, and Hill attracted vaguely similar followings, but the differences were also substantial and were exaggerated by the friends-and-neighbors appeal of various opponents. Folsom's victory over Lieutenant Governor Handy Ellis in the 1946 gubernatorial runoff and his sweep of the 1954 gubernatorial primary, Hill's defense of his Senate seat against Lawrence McNeil in 1950 and against retired Rear Adm. John G. Crommelin in 1956, and Sparkman's victories over Congressman Frank W. Boykin and Birmingham lawyer James A. Simpson in 1946 and over State Representative Laurie C. Battle and Crommelin in 1954 all involved relatively well-defined liberal-conservative conflicts.[20] In these elections, a number of rural counties in the northern part of the state, as well as Coffee County in the wire-grass area, consistently appeared in the top third of the counties offering the strongest support to Folsom, Hill, and Sparkman. The Mobile area and a number of black-belt counties consistently ranked high in opposition, while Jefferson County (Birmingham) more often than not was in the top third of the opposition counties.

In a typical postwar primary election, Alabama's metropolitan counties cast up to a third of the state's total vote, and city election returns

[18]Murray C. Havens, *City Versus Farm?: Urban-Rural Conflict in the Alabama Legislature* (Tuscaloosa: University of Alabama Press, 1957), pp. 9–19. On Folsom, see William D. Barnard, *Dixiecrats and Democrats: Alabama Politics 1942–1950* (University: University of Alabama Press, 1974); Neil O. Davis, "The Mystery of Big Jim," *Nation* 163 (August 31, 1946): 240–42; Douglas Cater, "Governor Folsom: Big Man in a Tight Spot," *Reporter* 14 (April 19, 1956): 30–32; and W. Bradley Twitty, *Y'All Come* (Nashville: Hermitage, 1962).

[19]Potomacus, "Hill of Alabama," *New Republic* 110 (May 1, 1944): 602; "People in the Limelight: Lister Hill," *New Republic* 112 (March 26, 1945): 407; "Sparkman's 'Liberalism,'" *Nation* 175 (August 9, 1952): 101; "John Sparkman and the Civil Rights Issue," *New Republic* 127 (August 18, 1952): 5–6; and William S. White, "Medicine Man from Alabama," *Harper's* 219 (November 1959): 90–94.

[20]Sparkman's 1948 race against Philip Hamm and one other candidate is excluded here, since both major candidates were progressives.

often reflected the same voter divisions along socioeconomic class lines that appeared in Louisiana, although substantially fewer blacks voted in Alabama. During the mid-1950s only an estimated 55,000 Alabama blacks were registered, with Birmingham and Mobile, the state's largest cities, each having little more than 5,000 black registrants.[21] Table 2.2 suggests the basic continuity underpinning Alabama politics, as well as the inconsistencies of individualistic and unstructured political competition. In 1946 Folsom and Sparkman attracted a similar voter following in Birmingham, despite the huge drop-off in voter turnout between the gubernatorial runoff primary and the special election some two months later. Both Folsom and Sparkman carried Jefferson County by piling up sufficient majorities in lower-status white and in black precincts to overcome heavy upper-class opposition. In 1954 Folsom's candidacy again elicited sharp class cleavages in both the lowland city of Montgomery and in the upland city of Gadsden. But on the same ballot Sparkman drew a significantly different vote. Now a veteran senator, Sparkman was opposed by two major candidates, both resident in the southern half of the state, and sectional divisions outweighed class conflicts in the balloting. Although Sparkman did best in black and lower-income white precincts in both cities, he fared well generally in the northern city of Gadsden and not so well generally in the southern city of Montgomery. Hill, who had been in the Senate since 1938, projected little in the way of class appeal. Despite the mishmash of class and sectional conflict, the basic reformist thrust came from the lower socioeconomic neighborhoods, and conservatism was resident in the high-rent districts. The black belt and the suburbs stood broadly for the status quo, or perhaps the status quo ante, while the hills and the wire grass and the working-class districts in the cities demonstrated a distinct liberal bias.

In Texas sharp ideological conflict transformed the relatively placid politics of the early war years into an increasingly acute factional struggle during the postwar period. Heralding the emerging dissension was the race in 1946 between Homer P. Rainey, former president of the University of Texas and an outspoken proponent of the New Deal, and Railroad Commissioner Beauford Jester, who lambasted with equal vehemence communists, labor unions, taxes, and Rainey. Jester won the governorship by a wide margin in a runoff primary. Then two years later, Lyndon Johnson and Coke Stevenson became embroiled in a bitter senatorial primary runoff contest. The moderately New Dealish Johnson earned the nickname "Landslide Lyndon" by beating the conservative former governor by a total of eighty-seven votes in an election in which almost a million votes were cast. Beauford Jester died in 1949, shortly after winning reelection as governor. Lieutenant Governor Allan Shivers inherited the office, and he

[21]Donald S. Strong, *Registration of Voters in Alabama* (University: University of Alabama Press, 1956), pp. 57–58, 75.

Table 2.2

Percentage of the Vote for Folsom and Sparkman
in Selected Alabama Cities in 1946 and 1954,
by Socioeconomic Class and Race

Birmingham, 1946

Vote category	Folsom (runoff)		Sparkman (special)	
	Percentage of vote received	(N)[a]	Percentage of vote received	(N)[a]
Black	85.1	(509)	83.7	(282)
Lower-class white	67.5	(2,986)	65.8	(1,578)
Lower-middle-class white	59.9	(2,013)	58.3	(1,036)
Upper-middle-class white	47.6	(2,070)	51.1	(1,079)
Upper-class white	19.6	(3,007)	29.1	(2,200)
Jefferson County[b]	53.0	(49,784)	53.9	(28,899)

Montgomery, 1954 primary

Vote category	Folsom		Sparkman	
	Percentage of vote received	(N)[a]	Percentage of vote received	(N)[a]
Black	61.3	(2,128)	56.6	(1,960)
Lower-class white	57.7	(3,206)	49.2	(2,886)
Lower-middle-class white	45.4	(2,937)	45.2	(2,665)
Upper-middle-class white	38.7	(2,739)	44.0	(2,545)
Upper-class white	24.0	(5,217)	39.7	(5,029)
Montgomery County[b]	43.2	(20,300)	45.2	(18,676)

Gadsden, 1954 primary

Vote category	Folsom		Sparkman	
	Percentage of vote received	(N)[a]	Percentage of vote received	(N)[a]
Black	76.1	(820)	80.9	(643)
Lower-class white	66.7	(3,307)	76.7	(2,905)
Lower-middle-class white	55.3	(3,385)	75.6	(3,181)
Upper-middle-class white	32.0	(3,266)	69.9	(3,044)
Upper-class white	21.1	(2,683)	57.1	(2,543)
Etowah County[b]	52.7	(24,734)	71.9	(22,784)

[a](N) denotes the number of votes upon which the percentages are based.

[b]County-vote percentages are based on the total number of votes cast in the county.

retained it against weak opposition in 1950; in 1952 he was challenged by Ralph W. Yarborough, an Austin attorney. At the same time, Congressman Lindley Beckworth of Gladewater and state Attorney General Price Daniel announced for the Senate seat being vacated by Tom T. Connally. Both Yarborough and Beckworth campaigned as Fair Deal Democrats. Shivers and Daniel banded together in opposition to Trumanism and the Fair Deal and in support of state rights and state control of offshore oil lands.

All of these campaigns presented similar conflicts, but they elicited little consistency on the part of the voters. There was virtually no relationship between support for Rainey in the 1946 runoff and support for Johnson in the 1948 runoff. Similarly, Johnson in 1948 and Yarborough and Beckworth in their losing efforts in 1952 tapped no common voter following. Relatively typical were the election returns from the east-central Texas city of Waco in McLennan County. Johnson carried the county with 54 percent of the vote, and he received roughly equal support from voters, regardless of socioeconomic class. Beckworth lost the county heavily, and he too projected little in the way of class appeal. Yarborough, on the other hand, did attract strong black and relatively substantial lower-class white backing, although Shivers won the county.

But the acrimonious clash along New Deal-Fair Deal lines in the 1952 primaries marked the emergence of more cohesive factional divisions. No other modern governor, one student of Texas politics observed, "matched Shivers in his frankly ideological appeal and in his capacity to mobilize and lead the right-of-center camp."[22] While Shivers warred against "the socialistic philosophy that has crept into our national party" by supporting Eisenhower in the 1952 presidential election, the liberal-loyalist forces created the Democratic Organizing Committee (successively superseded by the Democratic Advisory Council and the Do-It-Yourself Democrats) to mobilize support for the national Democrats and for Fair Deal progressives in state politics.[23] The hero of the liberal-labor-loyalist organization was Ralph Yarborough, who, like Shivers, projected a frank ideological and class appeal. In a series of bitterly fought primaries during the mid-1950s, Yarborough lost to Shivers, after forcing him into a runoff in 1954; barely lost to Price Daniel, who resigned from the U.S. Senate to run for governor, in the 1956 runoff primary; and finally emerged victorious from a special election in 1957 to fill the Senate seat vacated by Daniel. Yarborough achieved success by winning a plurality in a field of twenty-two candidates, since runoff contests were not required in special elections.

---

[22]Clifton McCleskey, *The Government and Politics of Texas*, 2d ed. (Boston: Little, Brown, 1966), p. 107.
[23]O. Douglas Weeks, *Texas Presidential Politics in 1952* (Austin: University of Texas Press, 1953), p. 39. On Texas factional politics during the 1950's, see also Soukup, McCleskey, and Holloway, *Party and Factional Division in Texas*, pp. 67–139; O. Douglas Weeks, *Texas One-Party Politics in 1956* (Austin: University of Texas Press, 1957); and idem, *Texas in the 1960 Presidential Election* (Austin: University of Texas Press, 1961).

Table 2.3

Percentage of the Vote for Yarborough in Waco and Fort Worth
in the 1954 and 1956 Runoffs and the 1957 Special Election,
by Socioeconomic Class and Race

	Waco		Fort Worth	
Vote category	Percentage of vote received	(N)[a]	Percentage of vote received	(N)[a]
1954 runoff				
Black	86.7	(1,079)	93.9	(1,302)
Lower-class white	60.5	(2,514)	60.1	(4,414)
Lower-middle-class white	48.7	(2,346)	52.1	(5,130)
Upper-middle-class white	34.4	(2,246)	29.4	(5,647)
Upper-class white	30.8	(2,144)	18.8	(3,490)
County vote[b]	53.5	(25,271)	45.8	(63,963)
1956 runoff				
Black	85.0	(818)	96.5	(1,630)
Lower-class white	59.9	(3,856)	59.7	(4,472)
Lower-middle-class white	48.9	(3,357)	55.0	(5,945)
Upper-middle-class white	41.1	(3,754)	27.8	(5,322)
Upper-class white	29.1	(2,274)	19.9	(4,816)
County vote[b]	52.7	(24,413)	47.7	(71,793)
1957 special				
Black	75.6	(418)	86.3	(1,038)
Lower-class white	61.8	(2,135)	47.8	(3,395)
Lower-middle-class white	50.3	(1,886)	44.4	(4,177)
Upper-middle-class white	42.0	(2,265)	21.3	(4,654)
Upper-class white	31.6	(1,597)	15.7	(4,185)
County vote[b]	49.1	(15,656)	34.7	(51,716)

[a](N) denotes the number of votes upon which the percentages are based.

[b]County-vote percentages are based on the total number of votes cast in the county.

[c]Yarborough had only one opponent in the runoff elections in 1954 and 1956; in the 1957 special election, he had twenty-one opponents, two of them major candidates. He won a plurality in McLennan County (Waco) and finished second behind a conservative Democrat in Tarrant County (Fort Worth).

Through all of these electoral clashes, voters responded in a broadly consistent fashion. With only one exception—the wild 1956 first gubernatorial primary scramble, in which six candidates battled for runoff positions—Yarborough ran best in the hills and piney woods of east Texas; he fared worst in the heavily Chicano machine counties of south Texas; and he lost west Texas, though usually by relatively narrow margins. He ran better in rural areas than in the cities, but in the metropolitan counties, which during this period normally cast approximately 50 percent of the total state vote, Yarborough appealed strongly to the familiar New Deal alliance of blacks and lower-status whites.

Yarborough commanded a relatively consistent following, but when Henry B. Gonzalez carried the liberal banner in the 1958 gubernatorial primary, the earlier voting patterns disintegrated. A Mexican-American, Gonzalez ran well in the Chicano counties and poorly elsewhere. In the cities Gonzalez won strong black support, but he lost the white precincts by lopsided margins, regardless of the prestige of the neighborhoods in which they were located. Given the nature of Texas politics in the 1950s, it is not at all surprising that a Chicano candidate would fare badly among Anglo voters, but this does suggest the immaturity of Texas factionalism.

Class and sectional conflicts were less persistent in the upper southern states of Tennessee and North Carolina. Insurgent Democrats in Tennessee overthrew the Crump organization's long domination of state politics, but they did not create a cohesive progressive faction. Edward H. Crump, once reform mayor of Memphis, had accomplished a genuine rarity in the South, an effective biracial urban machine, and from this base in Tennessee's largest city Crump had extended his influence over the state, creating a loosely structured, status quo-oriented statewide organization that had not failed at the polls since 1932. But in 1948 the organization was vulnerable. Its candidate for governor, incumbent James Nance McCord, had made enemies, especially by sponsoring a state sales tax. Also up for reelection was Senator Thomas Stewart, a lackluster campaigner generally regarded as a weak link in the organization. As the primary election approached, Crump chose to abandon Stewart and shifted his support to Judge John S. Mitchell. Stewart sought reelection without Crump's endorsement, thus splitting the organization forces.

Estes Kefauver, a congressman from the Chattanooga area, and Gordon Browning, who had made a strong showing in the gubernatorial primary two years previously, led the anti-Crump effort. Although Kefauver and Browning were political friends and were popularly identified as the leading anti-Crump candidates, they conducted their campaigns independently and created separate statewide organizations. Kefauver relied heavily upon his ability to inspire a devoted band of amateur workers, who even mounted a major challenge to Crump on his home grounds in Memphis. When Crump compared him to a pet coon, Kefauver scored a major campaign success by donning the coonskin cap that became his trademark and announcing that, unlike his major opponents, he was not Crump's pet coon. Kefauver won the Senate nomination by a plurality and went on to build a national reputation for liberalism. His following, however, remained more of a movement than a faction. Browning, who won the gubernatorial nomination with a comfortable 56 percent of the vote, in office turned out to be as safely conservative as the Crump-supported governor he replaced. Two years later Browning defended his seat by beating back a primary-election challenge from Clifford Allen, a liberal state legislator from Nashville. In 1952 Congressman Albert Gore com-

pleted the rout of the Crump organization by unseating Senator Kenneth
D. McKellar, a six-term veteran. Gore made a political issue of the incumbent senator's advanced age (McKellar was eighty-three at the time of the
election), but the campaign also delineated a relatively clear clash between
the liberal positions expounded by Gore and the conservative record defended by McKellar. A similar ideological division occurred when Kefauver
sought renomination to the Senate in 1954. His chief opponent, Congressman Pat Sutton, denounced Kefauver as a left-winger and generally conducted a racist and redbaiting campaign. Kefauver concentrated on sub-
stantive national issues and swept to a substantial victory.[24]

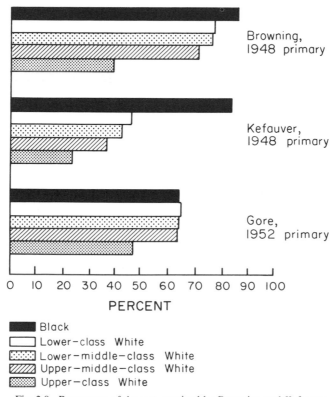

Fig. 2.8. Percentage of the vote received by Browning and Kefauver
in 1948 and by Gore in 1952 in Nashville, by socioeconomic class
and race

[24]Crump enjoyed one last triumph when he supported the candidate who defeated
Browning for the gubernatorial nomination in 1952, but well before Crump's death in 1954
his organization had lost its influence in state politics. This discussion of Tennessee politics is
based on Key, *Southern Politics*, pp. 58–81; William Goodman, *Inherited Domain: Political
Parties in Tennessee* (Knoxville: University of Tennessee Bureau of Public Administration,

In these primary contests the anti-Crump reform candidates ran best in Nashville among black and lower-income white voters and drew only grudging support from upper-income whites. As figure 2.8 suggests, Browning and Kefauver, as the anti-Crump candidates in 1948, and Gore, in his 1952 race against McKellar, drew their basic support from black and from lower- and middle-income white residential areas, although class cleavages normally were less acute in Tennessee than in cities in a number of other southern states. But county returns clearly demonstrate the disheveled state of Tennessee liberalism. The primary victories by Browning and Kefauver in 1948, Gore in 1952, and Kefauver again in 1954 suggest friends-and-neighbors voting patterns, the influence of county leaders, and a generally low level of political maturity among the state's voters. Although Browning and Kefauver were the anti-Crump candidates in 1948, their voter appeal lay in different parts of the state. Browning ran best in middle Tennessee, though he did well almost everywhere, except in the Memphis area. Kefauver's strength was concentrated in the eastern mountains, especially in his old congressional district, and his poorest showing was in the central part of the state. In the 1950 primary between Allen and Browning, all three of Tennessee's grand divisions voted similarly, although Allen fared considerably better in rural counties than in urban. In 1952 Gore, while running best in middle Tennessee, carried the eastern and western sections as well. In 1954 Kefauver still did slightly better in the mountains, but he also appealed generally to Tennessee's voters. In both 1948 and 1954, Kefauver reaped his highest percentages in counties containing cities and larger towns; other progressive candidates ran better in rural areas.

In North Carolina, two major factions existed within the Democratic party, and the North Carolina press often reported political developments in terms of factional relations. The conservative, urban-oriented, establishment wing of the Democratic party leadership and the progressive, farm bloc followers of Kerr Scott clashed sharply in a series of heated primary contests during the early 1950s. But the influence of both factions rested primarily upon their ability to command campaign chests and to negotiate alliances with county leaders rather than upon a mass base of support.[25] Neither precinct nor county returns pointed toward consistent identifiable voter divisions. The Democratic leadership was factionalized, but North Carolina voters were considerably less so.

One-party factional competition in Louisiana channeled populist voting tendencies into a relatively consistent and cohesive force; in states like

1954), pp. 37–65; Hugh Davis Graham, *Crisis in Print: Desegregation and the Press in Tennessee* (Nashville: Vanderbilt University Press, 1967), pp. 62–66; and Joseph Bruce Gorman, *Kefauver: A Political Biography* (New York: Oxford University Press, 1971), pp. 7–191.
[25]Spence, *The Making of a Governor*, pp. 1–20.

Alabama and Texas, intraparty divisions expressed similar patterns in cruder form; and in such states as Tennessee and North Carolina, Democratic factionalism was generally less successful in providing an orderly and continuing structure for a populist-New Deal politics. The ecological correlation analysis in tables 2.4–2.6 suggests the wide state-to-state diversity of voter response to progressive candidates. In Louisiana the Long candidates appealed to a similar voter base in election after election; in Alabama voter support for progressive candidates was less consistent; and in Tennessee it showed little continuity at all. To be sure, coefficients of correlation based on broad ecological units of analysis are methodologically crude, but the evidence suggests that they provide an essentially accurate portrayal of the wide variations in the effectiveness of factional politics in building reliable sources of support for candidates of similar ideological orientation.

The alliance of lower-status whites and blacks in the cities and rural dwellers, especially those residing in predominately white counties, generated a viable impetus in southern politics during the postwar period, but even after recognizing the inadequacies of factional politics, care should still be taken not to make voter behavior more consistent and rational than it really was. In Georgia, for example, entirely different voting alignments prevailed. The staunchly conservative Talmadge faction, led by Eugene Talmadge until his death and then by his son Herman, so dominated Georgia politics that the moderately progressive anti-Talmadge forces won not a single major election during the postwar period—although, with the death of "Ole Gene," following his election to the statehouse in 1946, the governorship passed to the incoming anti-Talmadge lieutenant governor, Melvin E. Thompson. Herman E. Talmdge beat Thompson in the gubernatorial primaries of 1948 and 1950, Lieutenant Governor S. Marvin Griffin won the governorship in 1954, and Talmadge was elected to the U.S. Senate in 1956. Despite shifting alliances and counteralliances between state factional leaders and county-seat elites, the Talmadge faction maintained a relatively consistent voter following. Talmadge candidates ran well in rural areas and fared poorly in the cities; they did better in the lowland counties in the southern half of the state than in the hills and mountains to the north; and in the cities they ran well in lower-income white neighborhoods and badly in black and upper-income white areas.

The ability of the conservative faction consistently to woo rural and lower-income whites set Georgia apart from most other southern states. In part this situation testified to the importance of image or style in politics and to the influence of Negrophobia. Such candidates as Eugene and Herman Talmadge and Marvin Griffin projected a hell-of-a-fellow, common-white-man image. They were "good ole boy" segregationists who effectively manipulated the race issue, in that time-honored manner, as an instrument for dividing the have-nots along color lines. Georgia's peculiar

Table 2.4

Consistency in Voter Support for Long Candidates in Louisiana
in 1948, 1952, and 1956

	R. Long, 1948	E. Long, 1948	E. Long, 1948	Spaht, 1952	Spaht, 1952	McKeithen, 1952	E. Long, 1956	Frazar, 1956
R. Long, 1948	–	.99	.91	.78	.78	.78	.91	.94
E. Long, 1948	.99	–	.94	.78	.80	.75	.91	.93
E. Long, 1948	.91	.94	–	.82	.75	.75	.84	.84
Spaht, 1952	.78	.78	.82	–	.89	.93	.85	.75
Spaht, 1952	.78	.80	.75	.89	–	.92	.92	.85
McKeithen, 1952	.78	.75	.75	.93	.92	–	.91	.83
E. Long, 1956	.91	.91	.84	.85	.92	.91	–	.98
Frazar, 1956	.94	.93	.84	.75	.85	.83	.98	–

Notes: The elections included are: Russell Long, 1948 Senate primary; Earl Long, 1948 gubernatorial primary and 1948 gubernatorial runoff; Carlos Spaht, 1952 gubernatorial primary and 1952 gubernatorial runoff; John J. McKeithen, 1952 runoff for lieutenant governorship; Earl Long, 1956 gubernatorial primary; and Lether E. Frazar, 1956 primary for lieutenant governorship.

The units of analysis employed were: north (Protestant) Louisiana metropolitan, urban, and rural; south (Catholic) Louisiana metropolitan, urban, and rural; and Black belt (seven cases). See the Note on Methodology and Data Sources for precise definitions.

Table 2.5
Consistency in Voter Support for Progressive Candidates in Alabama
in 1946, 1950, 1954, and 1956

	Folsom, 1946	Sparkman, 1946	Hill, 1950	Sparkman, 1954	Folsom, 1954	Hill, 1956
Folsom, 1946	–	.61	.34	.69	.67	.71
Sparkman, 1946	.61	–	.59	.80	.15	.91
Hill, 1950	.34	.59	–	.76	.12	.74
Sparkman, 1954	.69	.80	.76	–	.19	.85
Folsom, 1954	.67	.15	.12	.19	–	.40
Hill, 1956	.71	.91	.74	.85	.40	–

Notes: The elections included are: James Folsom, 1946 gubernatorial runoff; John Sparkman, 1946 senatorial special election; Lister Hill, 1950 Senate primary; Sparkman, 1954 Senate primary; Folsom, 1954 gubernatorial primary; and Hill, 1956 Senate primary.

The units of analysis employed were: south Alabama metropolitan, urban, and rural; Black-belt metropolitan, urban, and rural; Piedmont metropolitan, urban, and rural; and mountains (ten cases).

county-unit system, an arrangement whereby each county was assigned two, four, or six unit votes and primary elections were determined by the number of unit votes won by each candidate, grossly magnified the ballots cast in the small, rural counties and tended to draw blacks and affluent whites in the cities together in opposition to rural domination and in support of urban progress.[26]

Table 2.6
Consistency in Voter Support for Progressive Candidates in Tennessee
in 1948, 1950, 1952, 1954, and 1958

	Browning, 1948	Kefauver, 1948	Allen, 1950	Gore, 1952	Kefauver, 1954	Gore, 1958
Browning, 1948	–	.11	-.05	.51	.23	.16
Kefauver, 1948	.11	–	.08	-.57	.37	-.36
Allen, 1950	-.05	.08	–	-.29	.42	.17
Gore, 1952	.51	-.57	-.29	–	-.10	.21
Kefauver, 1954	.23	.37	.42	-.10	–	.62
Gore, 1958	.16	-.36	.17	.21	.62	–

Notes: The elections included are: Gordon Browning, 1948 gubernatorial primary; Estes Kefauver, 1948 Senate primary; Clifford Allen, 1950 gubernatorial primary; Albert Gore, 1952 Senate primary; Kefauver, 1954 Senate primary; and Gore, 1958 Senate primary.

The units of analysis employed were: west Tennessee metropolitan, urban, and rural; Black belt; middle Tennessee metropolitan, urban, and rural; and east Tennessee metropolitan, urban, and rural (ten cases).

[26]See generally Joseph L. Bernd, *Grass Roots Politics in Georgia . . . 1942-1954* (Atlanta: Emory University Research Committee, 1960); Louis T. Rigdon II, *Georgia's County Unit System* (Decatur, Ga.: Selective Books, 1961); and Numan V. Bartley, *From Thurmond*

In Arkansas the "pure one-party politics" described by Key flourished unperturbed by the sharpened class cleavages in neighboring states. Although Arkansas produced its share of Fair Deal loyalists, they created little in the way of a factional or even a class following. Sidney McMath, who initiated his political career as leader of a G.I. revolt against corruption in Hot Springs, gave Arkansas four years of relatively vigorous governmental leadership from the statehouse and was the recognized leader of the reform forces in state politics. He won the governorship by beating a segregationist opponent in the 1948 runoff election, and in 1950 he defended the office against a field of candidates that included the conservative former governor and former Dixiecrat leader Ben Laney. In 1952 he lost the governorship in a runoff campaign to Francis Cherry, a relatively unknown opponent, and in 1954 he failed in his effort to unseat Senator John L. McClellan. Through all of this, Arkansas voters betrayed few indications that there were any differing interests between lowlands and mountains, countryside and city, affluent and nonaffluent. In Little Rock black voters showed somewhat more loyalty to McMath than did white citizens, but the returns are free of the class conflict common in neighboring states. County returns told a similar story. Whether counties were located in the black belt or mountains or whether they were metropolitan or rural made little consistent difference. In 1950 McMath was a winner, and he won almost everywhere; by 1952 his star had set, and he lost almost everywhere.[27]

V. O. Key ably described southern politics at mid-century, and during the early 1950s there were few basic changes in the patterns he described. While wide variations flourished from state to state, the region as a whole demonstrated New Dealish inclinations, and the have-nots often banded together across color lines to support a politics of reform. It did not seem at all far-fetched to conclude, as Key hopefully predicted, that if more blacks and lower-income whites voted within the more structured framework of a two-party politics, the notion of a conservative South would become a thing of the past. But the late 1950s generated a different dynamics and a new thrust in southern politics that were to call some of these assumptions sharply into question.

to Wallace: Political Tendencies in Georgia, 1948-1968 (Baltimore: Johns Hopkins Press, 1970).

[27]The best study of Arkansas politics during this period is Boyce A. Drummond, Jr., "Arkansas Politics: A Study of a One-Party System" (Ph.D. diss., University of Chicago, 1957).

CHAPTER 3

ONE-PARTY STATE POLITICS AND THE
IMPACT OF DESEGREGATION

One-party factionalism was acutely vulnerable on the issue of race, the primeval fault that had divided the have-nots at crucial junctures in the southern past. In many nonsouthern states, New Deal voting alignments were more or less entrenched behind party identification, the political orientation of ethnic and religious minorities, and the organizational structures of labor unions and urban machines. In southern state politics, New Dealish politicians relied upon personal followings, factional loyalties, alliances with county leaders, a common-man style, and the individual voter's ability to recognize and support his own economic self-interest. The *Brown* v. *Board of Education* decision of 1954 struck directly at the Jim Crow system, and large numbers of southern whites reacted with the same defensiveness and hostility toward outside intervention with which they had responded to previous assaults on peculiar southern social institutions. The focus of southern politics began to shift from economic issues to matters of race.

To be sure, racial demagoguery was by no means a stranger to political conflict prior to the *Brown* decision. The Dixiecrats sprang to the defense of white supremacy in 1948, and Herman Talmadge won the Georgia governorship in a campaign that played upon white racial fears. In 1950 what was later to be christened the Social Issue[1] was particularly salient. That year saw Congress deadlocked in a bitter debate over enactment of a permanent Fair Employment Practices Commission; Senator Joseph R. McCarthy of Wisconsin become a household word as he pursued communists in and out of government; Richard M. Nixon win a U.S. Senate seat with a redbaiting campaign in California; and Senator McCarthy claim credit for what Franklin Roosevelt had failed to do, namely, unseating Senator Millard E. Tydings of Maryland. In the South, former Secretary

---

[1]The term was popularized by Richard M. Scammon and Ben J. Wattenberg, *The Real Majority* (New York: Coward-McAnn, 1970).

of State James F. Byrnes won election to the statehouse in South Carolina, which he used as a forum to vent his hostility toward Harry Truman, the Fair Deal, and desegregation; Herman Talmadge was reelected governor of Georgia; and incumbent Senators Claude Pepper of Florida and Frank P. Graham of North Carolina went down in defeats that Samuel Lubell described as "the most crushing setbacks Southern liberalism has suffered since the coming of Franklin Roosevelt."[2]

The campaigns that upset Pepper and Graham were remarkably similar. Florida Congressman George A. Smathers, characterized by one student of Florida politics as an attractive candidate with "political ambition and surprising flexibility in his political position,"[3] and Willis Smith, the favorite of the establishment forces in North Carolina, both sought to capitalize on the incumbent senators' identification with socially and economically liberal causes. The challengers vigorously attempted to link their opponents to an overlapping trinity of communism, Trumanism, and racial integration, and in Florida, for good measure Smathers added labor bossism. Their campaigns achieved the desired results. It was not surprising that most of Florida's major newspapers opposed Pepper, nor that he ran poorly in upper-status white precincts. But Pepper also lost in rural areas, and his majorities in lower-status white neighborhoods, when they materialized, were by no means overwhelming. Pepper ran strongly in Jewish and black districts, but a substantial majority of Protestant white voters supported Smathers.[4] In North Carolina Graham enjoyed support from Governor Kerr Scott and almost won a first-primary victory. In the runoff, however, the Smith camp launched a "White-People-Wake-Up" campaign that was labeled "a display of race bitterness such as this state had not witnessed for fifty years."[5] Graham suffered heavy defections in the eastern lowlands, where his vote dropped by almost five percent. But despite the impact of these elections, they were relatively isolated. They pointed to the soft underbelly of southern liberalism; however, Pepper, who had cast Senate votes in favor of civil rights, and Graham, who was a member of President Truman's Commission on Civil Rights, occupied particularly exposed positions.

Not until the late 1950s did a politics of race become a regional phenomenon. The reaction to the *Brown* decision demonstrated the depth of southern white opposition to basic changes in racial practices. Black-belt whites organized the Citizens' Council movement to defend white suprem-

[2]Samuel Lubell, *The Future of American Politics*, 2d ed., rev. (Garden City: Doubleday, 1956), p. 107.

[3]Hugh D. Price, *The Negro and Southern Politics: A Chapter of Florida History* (New York: New York University Press, 1957), p. 119.

[4]On the election, see ibid., pp. 60–63; *New York Times*, April 7, May 3, 1950; and Lubell, *The Future of American Politics*, pp. 106–15.

[5]*New York Times*, June 26, 1950. On the election, see *New York Times*, May 28, June 25, 26, 1950; and Lubell, *The Future of American Politics*, pp. 108–13.

acy and to spread the resistance to public-school desegregation. Spurred on by the Councils, important southern political leaders vowed resistance, and southern state legislators enacted more than 450 laws and resolutions designed to prevent, delay, or limit public-school desegregation and to suppress or handicap the National Association for the Advancement of Colored People and other civil-rights groups. The Councils often behaved as local vigilante committees self-commissioned to enforce racial orthodoxy; governmental investigating committees searched for communists and found integrationists; and state governments laid plans to abolish the public schools rather than desegregate them. "Massive resistance" to the *Brown* decision became the dominant theme of southern state politics.[6]

The defense of white supremacy and southern traditions shifted the thrust of southern politics. The rural and lower-status whites who had provided much of the impetus for the populist-New Deal politics of the early 1950s were also the people most likely to feel threatened by black advancement and to express confidence in southern customs. The urban-suburban bourgeoisie, past mainstays of southern conservatism, were apt to be somewhat more tolerant on racial matters or at least sufficiently devoted to business and industrial progress that they were soon to become frightened that the excesses of massive resistance, especially the threat of school closures, would be detrimental to economic progress. Blacks were the most liberal of all southerners, at least concerning issues of economics and race.[7] During the post-World War II decade, blacks often allied with the economically liberal but socially conservative lower-status whites; as the segregation issue became increasingly pressing, blacks frequently found themselves in a coalition with affluent white "moderates" in opposition to white-supremacy extremism. These shifting issues and changing voter patterns disrupted and modified Democratic party factional alignments throughout the region.

The dynamics of the politics of massive resistance are well illustrated by voting tendencies in Arkansas. Orval E. Faubus won the governorship in 1954 by upsetting the vaguely conservative, largely nondescript incum-

[6]See generally Numan V. Bartley, *The Rise of Massive Resistance: Race and Politics in the South during the 1950s* (Baton Rouge: Louisiana State University Press, 1969); and Neil R. McMillen, *The Citizens' Councils: Organized Resistance to the Second Reconstruction, 1954–64* (Urbana: University of Illinois Press, 1971).

[7]See Donald R. Matthews and James W. Prothro, *Negroes and the New Southern Politics* (New York: Harcourt, Brace and World, 1966), especially pp. 398–400, 472–79; Alfred O. Hero, Jr., *The Southerner and World Affairs* (Baton Rouge: Louisiana State University Press, 1965), especially pp. 389–93; Melvin M. Tumin et al., *Desegregation: Resistance and Readiness* (Princeton: Princeton University Press, 1958), especially pp. 80–81, 144; and John Shelton Reed, *The Enduring South: Subcultural Persistence in Mass Society* (Lexington, Mass.: D. C. Heath, 1972), especially pp. 39–42. See also James W. Vander Zanden, *Race Relations in Transition: The Segregation Crisis in the South* (New York: Random House, 1965), pp. 100–117; Charles H. Stember, *Education and Attitude Change: The Effect of Schooling on Prejudice against Minority Groups* (New York: Institute of Human Relations, 1961); and William H. Form and Joan Huber, "Income, Race, and the Ideology of Political Efficacy," *Journal of Politics* 33 (August 1971): 659–88.

bent, Francis Cherry, who had defeated Sidney S. McMath two years previously. In Arkansas, a governor was virtually assured a second term, although not in a half-century had an incumbent been permitted a third term in office. Faubus was to overturn both traditions. Raised in an Ozark mountain county so isolated that the first paved thoroughfare was not constructed until the early 1950s, Faubus worked variously as a migrant fruit picker, a logger, and a schoolteacher, ultimately purchasing a small weekly newspaper in his home county of Madison. Faubus also dabbled in politics. He once ran for a state legislative seat and solved the problem of living in a Republican county in a Democratic state by calling himself a "Lincoln-style Democrat." McMath introduced Faubus to state politics, appointing him to an administrative position. (McMath was later to say: "I brought Orval down out of the hills and every night I ask forgiveness.")[8]

With McMath's support, Faubus sought the governor's office in 1954. He ran sufficiently well in the mountains and in rural areas to force Cherry into a second primary. In the runoff Faubus won hardly more than a third of the votes cast in metropolitan counties, and he lost the larger towns, although by a narrower margin. But in a rural state with a substantial mountaineer population, Faubus was the rural and mountain candidate, and he won approximately 55 percent of the votes cast in the countryside, and the election. In Little Rock, the state's largest city, Faubus fared poorly everywhere, but he did worse in prestige districts than in black and lower-status white neighborhoods. In upper-class Little Rock precincts, the "hillbilly" candidate failed to win as much as 10 percent of the votes in either the first or the second primary.

As governor, Faubus proved to be a capable politician, carefully balancing competing interests and strengthening his ties with county leaders. He catered to rural areas with increased state support for public education and higher old-age pensions, which he paid for by raising both income taxes and sales taxes. He propitiated business by granting various favors, including controversial rate increases for the Arkansas-Louisiana Gas Company, and by strengthening the Arkansas Industrial Development Commission, appointing Winthrop Rockefeller as its director and supporting its industry-hunting activities (until Rockefeller later became identified with the anti-Faubus forces, at which time the governor slashed the Commission's budget). Faubus's administration drastically reduced the number of welfare (Aid to Families with Dependent Children) recipients, which action hit poor blacks hardest, and supported segregation legislation

[8]As quoted in Robert Sherrill, *Gothic Politics in the Deep South: Stars of the New Confederacy* (New York: Grossman, 1968), p. 76. See also *New York Times*, September 4, 1957; Boyce A. Drummond, Jr., "Arkansas Politics: A Study of a One-Party System" (Ph.D. diss., University of Chicago, 1957), pp. 223–26; and Thomas F. Pettigrew and Ernest Q. Campbell, "Faubus and Segregation: An Analysis of Arkansas Voting," *Public Opinion Quarterly* 24 (Fall 1960): 436–47.

designed to forestall public-school desegregation; at the same time the University of Arkansas began accepting black undergraduates, and a half-dozen blacks were added to the state Democratic Central Committee.[9]

By the time of the 1956 primary elections, Faubus had covered all flanks. His chief opponent in the gubernatorial contest was James D. Johnson, past president of the Arkansas Citizens' Councils and an avid segregationist. Despite Johnson's racist appeal, the rural counties and the mountains stayed with Faubus; and the governor, now the moderate candidate, also won majorities in the cities, running best in black and higher-income white neighborhoods. The precincts that had given more than 90 percent of their votes to the opposition in 1954 now gave almost 60 percent to Faubus. In 1954 rather vaguely the economically progressive candidate, Faubus fared best in the mountains and in rural areas, and he did relatively better among blacks and lower-class whites than among middle- and upper-status whites in the cities. In 1956, when the racial issue was paramount, Faubus was, still as vaguely as he could manage, the moderate candidate; while again running best in mountain and rural areas, his appeal was more general, and in the cities it was to a coalition of blacks and affluent whites.

Then came the Little Rock desegregation crisis of 1957, from which Faubus emerged as a hero among segregationists. After Little Rock Faubus was unstoppable. He breezed past the opposition to win first-primary victories in the next four gubernatorial primaries. In 1958 two moderate candidates sought to capitalize on a temperate reaction to the racial hysteria in Little Rock, and aiding the anti-Faubus effort were such diverse political powers as former Governors Ben Laney, Sidney McMath, and Francis Cherry, all of whom professed distaste for Faubus's actions in Little Rock and feared, no doubt, that the governor was becoming too politically dominant in Arkansas. Faubus largely ignored his opponents and campaigned instead against the federal government, outside agitators, the *Arkansas Gazette*, the NAACP, and a variety of other people, ideologies, and organizations that had no particular relevance to the gubernatorial primary election in Arkansas. Displaying a genuine knack for demagoguery, Faubus promised to call out the National Guard in Little Rock again "if they push me."[10] The silent vote for moderation failed to materialize, and Faubus won overwhelmingly.

In 1960 Attorney General Bruce Bennett was the best known of the four candidates challenging Faubus. During the late 1950s, Bennett had kept his name before the public by warring on the NAACP, communists, and integrationists and had waited for Faubus to step down. That failing, Bennett ran anyway, promising to restore segregation throughout the

[9]*Arkansas Gazette*, June 16, 1955; March 16, 1957; July 1, 1958; April 7, September 17, 1959.

[10]As quoted in *Memphis Commercial Appeal*, July 5, 1958; and *Arkansas Gazette*, July 1, 5, 8, 26, 30, 1958.

Table 3.1
Triptile ranking of counties in support for Faubus, 1954–62

Counties	Top 1/3	Mid 1/3	Low 1/3	Top 1/3	Mid 1/3	Low 1/3
	1954 Primary			1958 Primary		
Rural mountain	22	7	5	7	14	13
Rural lowland	2	14	16	17	9	6
Urban[a]	1	4	4	2	1	6
	1954 Runoff			1960 Primary		
Rural mountain	23	9	2	9	11	14
Rural lowland	1	13	18	15	13	4
Urban	1	3	5	1	1	7
	1956 Primary			1962 Primary		
Rural mountain	19	11	4	10	12	12
Rural lowland	3	12	17	14	10	8
Urban	3	2	4	1	3	5

[a]The nine counties in Arkansas containing a city of more than 20,000 population (1960).

state. Again demonstrating the admirable flexibility of a latter-day Vicar of Bray, Faubus appealed to "all the people" and spoke of the accomplishments gained "by working together, not by fighting, not by yielding to the agitators of whatever race or creed."[11] Faubus won easily. In 1962 the governor faced threats from both right and left. Sidney McMath returned to the political fray to oppose his former protégé, and, on the right, Dale Alford, an extreme segregationist and former congressman, sought to keep alive his political cause. Together with three minor candidates, McMath and Alford held Faubus to his smallest majority since 1954, but the governor still won the first primary by a comfortable margin. By 1964 no major candidates were willing to oppose Faubus for the nomination.

The governor's post-Little Rock opposition varied, but his voter support remained relatively consistent during the 1958–64 period. In both 1958 and 1960 Faubus won more than three-quarters of the ballots cast in lower- and lower-middle-class white precincts in Little Rock. This vote dropped off slightly in 1962, though Faubus still won majorities in both classes. The upper-status white neighborhoods, which had opposed him in 1954 and joined him in 1956, now staunchly rejoined the opposition. The sharp class cleavages provoked by Faubus's candidacy were unusual in Little Rock and testified to the divisive impact of the race issue. The poor whites followed Faubus, and the affluent whites, concerned about adverse publicity and the closure of the public high schools in Little Rock during the 1958–59 school

[11]As quoted by Patrick J. Owens, in *Arkansas Gazette*, May 23, 1960. See *Arkansas Gazette*, October 3, December 4, 9, 1958; January 17, 1959; February 25, 1960.

year, opposed him. Blacks, not surprisingly, joined the affluent whites in an anti-Faubus coalition.[12] In the countryside, the mountain counties that had originally formed the governor's voter base continued to support him, but, after the Little Rock crisis, they were figuratively elbowed aside by the stampede of lowland counties into the Faubus camp. Arkansas's most racially conscious whites, those of the plantation lowlands and the working-class districts of the cities, contributed heavily to Faubus's extended tenure in the governor's mansion.

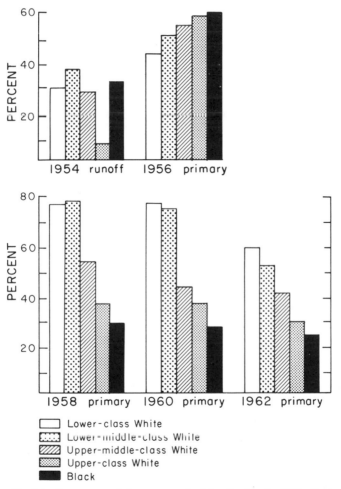

Fig. 3.1. Percentage of the vote received by Faubus in Little Rock, 1954–62, by socioeconomic class and race

[12]See Corinne Silverman, *The Little Rock Story*, rev. ed. (University: University of Alabama Press, 1959), especially pp. 36–38; and Bartley, *The Rise of Massive Resistance*, especially pp. 251–69, 327–32.

In Louisiana the political dynamics generated by the race issue disrupted customary factional alignments. The Long faction's concentration on economic issues had overridden the social and cultural differences between Catholics and Protestants and blacks and whites, but the reemergence of a politics of race not only divided blacks from whites but also accentuated the differences between the French-Catholic culture of south Louisiana, where the practices of white supremacy found less support,[13] and the southern traditionalism of north Louisiana. This sectional fissure had long existed within the anti-Long, reform faction. One wing of the anti-Long forces was Bourbon-oriented, socially conservative, and strong in north Louisiana, especially in the larger towns and Protestant plantation counties. The other wing, oriented toward good government and a good business atmosphere, was socially moderate and attracted some black support; it fared best in south Louisiana, especially in the suburban communities in the New Orleans area. This division was clear in the 1952 first-primary election, when Congressman Hale Boggs was the candidate of the progressive side of anti-Longism, and James McLemore and, perhaps to a lesser degree, Judge Robert Kennon led the Bourbon forces. In 1956 Mayor deLesseps Morrison was the progressive, good government, south Louisiana candidate; and Fred Preaus, who had Governor Kennon's endorsement, was the north Louisiana anti-Long contender. Both groups, however, shared a mutual distaste for buccaneering liberalism, and the necessity of uniting against the Longs held their intrafactional differences in abeyance.

But as social matters replaced economic concerns as the center of political contention, the Long forces found their north Louisiana following defecting on the race issue and their south Louisiana support disintegrating over the religious issue, and these same impulses sharpened divisions within the anti-Long faction. Seizing leadership of Louisiana's massive resistance movement was William E. Rainach, a little-known state senator from north Louisiana. Rainach became chairman of the Joint Legislative Committee to Maintain Segregation, which plotted segregationist strategy, concocted and drafted all manner of anti-integration legislation, carried out white-supremacy propaganda campaigns, investigated integrationists and communists, and encouraged purges of blacks from the voter registration rolls. Rainach was also president of the Citizens' Councils, and it was the Councils that utilized a provision in the Louisiana state constitution permitting citizens to challenge "illegally" registered voters on a variety of technical grounds to purge some 31,000 blacks from the registration lists.[14] So long as Rainach and his associates were writing

[13]See John H. Fenton, *The Catholic Vote* (New Orleans: Hauser, 1960), pp. 43–44, 109–12.

[14]Perry H. Howard, *Political Tendencies in Louisiana*, rev. ed. (Baton Rouge: Louisiana State University Press, 1971), pp. 335–36; Kenneth N. Vines, "A Louisiana Parish: Wholesale

segregationist statutes and searching for communists, Governor Earl Long avoided a direct confrontation. But disfranchising voters who normally supported the Longs was another matter. "If those colored people helped build this country, if they could fight in its Army, then I'm for giving them the vote," Long stated, and he added, "a candidate should go after every vote he can get."[15] Such statements were anathema to Rainach, who insisted that the voter purges were making Louisiana "a shining example to the nation on how to thwart the National Association for the Advancement of Colored People."[16] "I'm sick and tired of you yellin' nigger, nigger, nigger," Long snapped at Rainach. "People aren't with you; they're just scared of you."[17] When the Louisiana legislature met in 1959, Rainach and his Committee to Maintain Segregation introduced legislation to facilitate voter purges, and Governor Long countered with legislation to protect registered voters. But the governor was under great strain, and in May 1959 he had his much-publicized breakdown.[18]

Against this background Louisiana voter alignments shifted massively in the 1959–60 gubernatorial elections. Three anti-Long candidates led the first-primary balloting, and the two contenders from the Long camp trailed behind in the fourth and fifth positions. Mayor Morrison, himself a Catholic, ran strongly in the Catholic parishes of south Louisiana to lead in the first primary; Rainach, making his first statewide race, fared well in the north Louisiana black-belt parishes and in the Shreveport area and came in third. Finishing second and thus gaining a runoff spot with Morrison was former Governor Jimmie H. Davis, who wrote and sang country music and promised to "govern sincerely, honestly, impartially and with feeling."[19] Davis claimed to be a "one-thousand percent" segregationist in the first primary; in the second primary he concluded an alliance with the Rainach forces and made defense of segregation the central theme of the campaign.[20] Earl Long, who after recovering from his breakdown had run unsuccessfully for lieutenant governor, endorsed Davis, presumably concerned that Morrison might win control of the patronage in both New Orleans and the state government. Morrison campaigned as a segregationist, but, given his relatively enlightened record as New Orleans mayor and the racist onslaught from the Davis forces, there could be no doubt that he was the racial moderate in the runoff campaign.

Purge," *The Negro and the Ballot in the South* by Margaret Price (Atlanta: Southern Regional Council, 1959), pp. 34–46.

[15]As quoted by Robert Wagner, in *New Orleans Times-Picayune*, September 21, 1958.

[16]As quoted in *The State* (Columbia, S.C.), December 17, 1956.

[17]As quoted by Harnett T. Kane, in *New York Times Magazine*, January 1, 1961.

[18]This episode is related with wit and feeling in A. J. Liebling, *The Earl of Louisiana* (New York: Simon and Schuster, 1961).

[19]As quoted by Robert Wagner, in *New Orleans Times-Picayune*, September 7, 1959.

[20]William C. Havard, Rudolf Heberle, and Perry H. Howard, *The Louisiana Elections of 1960* (Baton Rouge: Louisiana State University Press, 1963), pp. 34–54.

For the first time in a generation, a Long candidate failed to appear in a gubernatorial runoff primary, and the election returns, as Perry H. Howard has observed, portrayed "a cleavage which pitted North against South, Protestant against Catholic, and rendered race the primary issue in the place of economic realities."[21] Morrison carried French-Catholic south Louisiana substantially, but Davis won every other parish in the state, most by whopping majorities. The sectional appeal of Davis in 1960 differed fundamentally from the statewide following attracted by Earl Long in the 1956 primary. Urban returns reflected the north-south split: Caddo Parish (Shreveport) in the far north gave Davis better than 70 percent of its votes, East Baton Rouge on the edge of the Catholic parishes granted him almost 55 percent, and Orleans Parish went for Morrison by almost 60 percent. Within the cities, the Long alliance of blacks and non-affluent whites collapsed. Morrison was clearly the candidate of a coalition of blacks and upper-income whites, while lower-income whites followed Davis.

A similar sectional split appeared in Florida. North Florida differed not basically from north Louisiana: it too was Protestant, old-stock southern, and its politics reflected a similar devotion to social and racial conservatism. And rural-small town citizens were particularly numerous in north Florida. South Florida, of course, had little in common with French-Catho-

Table 3.2

Percentage of the Vote for Long in the 1956 Primary
and for Davis in the 1959 Runoff, by Rural, Urban, and
Metropolitan Counties

Counties	Long, 1956 Primary			Davis, 1959 Runoff		
	65+ percent	50+ percent	−50 percent	65+ percent	50+ percent	−50 percent
Statewide						
Rural	31	13	7	28	6	17
Urban	1	5	1	2	2	3
Metropolitan	–	1	5	2	2	2
North						
Rural	21	6	5	27	5	–
Urban	1	2	–	2	1	–
Metropolitan	–	–	3	2	1	–
South						
Rural	10	7	2	1[a]	1	17
Urban	–	3	1	–	1	3
Metropolitan	–	1	2	–	1	2

[a]Plaquemines Parish, bossed by Leander Perez, a Davis ally.

[21]Howard, *Political Tendencies in Louisiana*, p. 355.

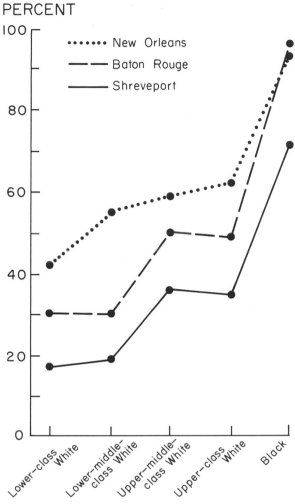

Fig. 3.2. Percentage of the vote received by Morrison in the 1960 runoff in New Orleans, Baton Rouge, and Shreveport, by socioeconomic class and race

lic south Louisiana, except that neither seemed overtly devoted to lost-cause mythology or to white supremacy. Heavily metropolitan, south Florida contained substantial Jewish and Latin as well as black minorities, and economically it was particularly dependent on the good will of non-southern tourists and immigrants.[22] While south Florida was not noted for political liberalism, its citizenry possessed a social toleration that was

[22]Charlton W. Tebeau, *A History of Florida* (Coral Gables: University of Miami Press, 1971), pp. 433–35.

foreign to the northern part of the state, and the racial issue contributed along with other factors to a growing divorce between rural-oriented, socially conservative north Florida and predominately metropolitan, socially heterogeneous south Florida.[23]

Florida voters had rejected Claude Pepper, the state's preeminent New Dealer, in 1950, and they did so again in 1958, when Pepper challenged Senator Spessard Holland for his U.S. Senate seat. In neither election was there a major split between the northern and southern portions of the state. Pepper ran best in the cities by swamping the opposition in Jewish and black precincts and by winning significant if uneven support in lower-income Protestant neighborhoods. But he ran poorly in upper-income Protestant areas, and in a rapidly growing state with an ever proliferating suburbia, this inability to appeal to the affluent was fatal, at least for a candidate who was vulnerable in rural areas to charges of being soft on communism and integration, themes which both Smathers and Holland played upon freely. In his 1958 comeback effort, Pepper sought to win the voters who had entered the electorate since 1950, but when the ballots were in, Pepper had lost by a larger margin than before.[24]

In the 1952 gubernatorial campaign, Dan McCarty was more successful, combining a winning coalition behind a program of progressive moderation, a program sufficiently progressive to win minority support, sufficiently "safe" to attract affluent voters, and generally urban-oriented in a state where the metropolitan counties cast a majority of the ballots in a gubernatorial primary. McCarty promised efficiency and economy in government, encouragement of business and industrial growth, and expanded financial aid to education, highway construction, and public services. McCarty's runoff opponent, Brailey Odham, ran a relatively nondescript campaign centering around such noncontroversial homilies as "I'll clean up your government or close it up—and get the dirty hands of the racketeers off your kids' government."[25] McCarty died just after assuming office, and since the Florida constitution at that time provided for no lieutenant governor, the statehouse passed to the president of the state senate, who in Florida's grossly malapportioned legislature was "Pork Chop Gang" favorite Charley E. Johns. A former railroad conductor representing a tiny north Florida district, Johns, as Hugh Douglas Price noted, "had distinguished himself in the senate by voting for the 1947 white primary bill and for legalized slot machines, but against expanded school construction and against unmasking the Ku Klux Klan."[26] Johns

---

[23]Neal R. Peirce, *The Megastates of America: People, Politics and Power in the Ten Great States* (New York: W. W. Norton, 1972), pp. 450–94.

[24]See Frank Trippett, in *St. Petersburg Times*, August 5, 1958.

[25]As quoted in *Miami Herald*, May 27, 1952.

[26]Price, *The Negro and Southern Politics*, p. 98. Also helpful on Florida politics are William C. Havard and Loren P. Beth, *The Politics of Mis-Representation: Rural-Urban Conflict in the Florida Legislature* (Baton Rouge: Louisiana State University Press, 1962); and

promptly fired many of McCarty's appointees and steered the government toward policies favored by rural conservatives.

In a special gubernatorial election two years later, LeRoy Collins, McCarty's senate floor leader and friend, sought revenge. Collins promised to return to McCarty's program and generally conducted an urban-oriented "media" campaign, by-passing county political elites to appeal directly to the voters. Johns relied heavily on winning the support of local leaders, and it is highly probable that Johns's organizational superiority rather than the issues accounted for his curious majorities in the black precincts in Jacksonville.[27] Although Johns led in the first-primary balloting, Collins won the runoff and the election. Collins again sought the gubernatorial nomination in 1956, and this time his leading opponent was Sumter L. Lowry, a retired army general and a rabid segregationist. So aggressively did Lowry promote the racial issue that the moderate Collins shifted rightward to protect his exposed flank, notably after *Look* magazine insulted traditionalist white Floridians by picturing Florida in gray as a wavering state rather than in black as a state totally resistant to desegregation. Collins quickly convened a high-level strategy conference, after which a spokesman assured reporters: "I think what we've done here today will definitely put us in the black."[28] Collins won a first-primary victory and, after the election, resumed his socially moderate policies.

Collins was constitutionally unable to succeed himself in 1960, and voters chose Doyle E. Carleton, Jr., and C. Farris Bryant as the runoff candidates from a large field of first-primary contenders. Governor Collins dismissed Bryant as an apostle of "reaction, retreat, and regret" and endorsed Carleton.[29] A legislative supporter of the Collins administration, Carleton promised a continuation of "the same progressive service we have had the last six years."[30] Bryant campaigned on a staunchly conservative program, promising governmental economy, avowing himself "a firm believer in segregation," and attacking the moderate Carleton as the candidate who "stands for moderate integration."[31] Bryant won, and four years later Haydon Burns, mayor of Jacksonville, running on a platform very similar to that of Bryant, also emerged victorious. Burns's runoff opponent, whom he denounced as the "candidate of the NAACP,"[32] was Robert King

---

Tebeau, *A History of Florida*, pp. 437ff. V. M. Newton, Jr., *Crusade for Democracy* (Ames: Iowa State University Press, 1961), chap. 10, includes a devastating critique of the "Pork Chop Gang."

[27]See Steven Trumbell, in *Miami Herald*, May 26, 1954; and Havard and Beth, *The Politics of Mis-Representation*, pp. 27–29 *passim*.

[28]As quoted by John L. Boyles, in *Miami Herald*, March 25, 1956.

[29]As quoted in *St. Petersburg Times*, May 24, 1960.

[30]As quoted in ibid., May 23, 1960.

[31]As quoted in ibid., May 10, 1960.

[32]As quoted in Reed Sarratt, *The Ordeal of Desegregation: The First Decade* (New York: Harper and Row, 1966), p. 24.

High, mayor of Miami. High was more openly "liberal" on both social and economic issues than Collins or Carleton had been, but generally the 1964 runoff primary was a replay of the 1960 one.

These gubernatorial elections exhibited a certain continuity in the sense that Collins identified himself with McCarty, Carleton identified with Collins, and High was obviously in their tradition. All were moderate on racial matters, and all espoused generally progressive policies. Their opponents were for the most part conservative on economic issues and vigorously racist in social matters. The voter response in these elections revealed not only a general trend toward conservatism but a deepening split between the northern and southern halves of the state, with north Florida becoming increasingly solidified in opposition to the more progressive candidates. In the 1952 runoff McCarty won almost 55 percent of the ballots cast in north Florida, running somewhat better there than in the

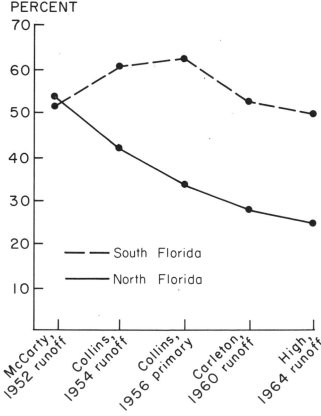

Fig. 3.3. Percentage of the vote received by progressive candidates in north and south Florida, 1952–64

southern portion of the state. Two years later, Collins, in his runoff against Johns, won only 42 percent in the north and carried the election by harvesting 61.5 percent of the south Florida vote. Collins dropped to just over a third of the north country's votes in his 1956 first-primary victory, again winning more than 60 percent in the south. Carleton won less than 30 percent in the north in his 1960 runoff effort against Bryant, while his south Florida vote was only 53 percent, insufficient to swing the election. High fared even worse, winning 25 percent in the north and just barely over 50 percent in the south. Thus the north Florida tally for progressive gubernatorial candidates fell steadily from 1952, when McCarty won better than one out of every two votes, to 1964, when High received one of every four.

There was in these campaigns something of a rural-urban as well as a sectional cleavage. A Collins or Carleton ran better in metropolitan counties than in rural-small town areas. But the basic cleavage was sectional. Progressive candidates ran better in south Florida metropolitan counties than in south Florida rural counties, but they also fared better in south Florida rural areas than in north Florida metropolitan counties. Although Collins was a resident of Leon County on the Georgia border, south Florida adopted him as its own, and his two campaigns in the mid-1950s marked a high tide of progressivism in the south.

Insofar as Jacksonville is illustrative of voting trends in urban north Florida,[33] the progressive decline resulted from a general collapse of support in the white community. In 1952 McCarty had been the coalition candidate in Jacksonville, winning overwhelmingly in black precincts, solidly in upper-status white neighborhoods, and trailing off to just above 40 percent in lower- and lower-middle-income white areas. Against Johns, Collins had done even better in white areas, sweeping affluent white districts with more than 60 percent and semi-affluent precincts by above 55 percent. He lost the lower-status whites, with about 45 percent of the vote, and black voters rejected him by a more substantial margin. But in 1956 blacks massively flocked to Collins, giving him 93 percent of their votes, while white support slipped sharply. Collins lost in every category of white voters, winning above 40 percent only among the affluent. Lower- and lower-middle-class whites allowed Collins less than 20 percent. Carleton did worse in the 1960 runoff, falling below a quarter of the vote in every white category. Like Collins, Carleton won huge majorities in black communities. This growing black-white polarization became almost complete in 1964, when High won just under 95 percent of black votes and lost more than 85 percent of the white votes.

---

[33]Since the consolidated vote in Escambia County (Pensacola, the only other metropolitan center in the north) and the counties containing larger towns followed the same general patterns from election to election as Duval County (Jacksonville), it is probable that somewhat similar patterns prevailed in urban north Florida generally.

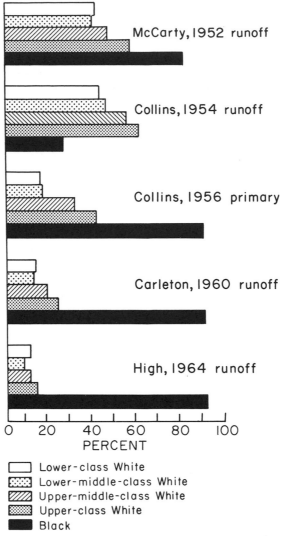

Fig. 3.4. Percentage of the vote received by progressive candidates in Jacksonville, 1952–64, by socioeconomic class and race

Light-years from the voting patterns in Jacksonville were those in Dade County and Miami,[34] where voters of all races, creeds, and colors tended to support the progressive candidate. McCarty in 1952 and Collins in 1954 and 1956 fared best in upper-status, predominately Protestant

[34]Dade County (Miami) could not be considered a typical south Florida metropolis, since such cities as Orlando, St. Petersburg, Tampa, and Miami are distinctively different. See Peirce, *The Megastates of America*, pp. 450–94.

precincts. As social issues became increasingly salient, Jewish and black voters cast ever mounting majorities for the progressive candidates. But in not a single instance did Collins in the 1954 runoff or the 1956 primary, Carleton in the 1960 runoff, or High in the 1964 runoff manage to lose more than 40 percent of the votes in any voter category. Not that Miami voters were by any means homogeneous; there was a considerable gap between the 60 percent majority that Carleton received in lower-status white neighborhoods and the 91 percent he collected in black precincts. An aggressive economic liberal, such as Claude Pepper in his 1950 and 1958 Senate races, sparked strong opposition from affluent whites; an aggressive racial liberal, such as state Representative John B. Orr, Jr., drew an unfriendly reception in lower-status white precincts.[35] For relatively "safe" progressive candidates, however, Dade County regularly delivered impressive majorities.

The vigorous if sometimes chaotic rural liberalism so prevalent in Alabama during the 1940s and early 1950s also fell victim to the race issue. In the 1958 primaries, all major gubernatorial candidates disavowed association with "Folsomism," a nebulous term that included maladministration and laxity in state government but especially a generous attitude toward race. Voters might forgive Governor Folsom for having a drink or two, but not with Adam Clayton Powell. Attorney General John Patterson and Circuit Judge George C. Wallace, a former Folsom protégé, emerged from the first primary as the runoff contenders. The central question in the runoff was the same as in the first primary: Which candidate could convince the voters that he was more avidly segregationist than his opponent? Patterson won hands down, leaving Wallace to ruminate, significantly as it turned out, "they out-niggered me that time, but they'll never do it again."[36] In the runoff Wallace carried urban black precincts handily; but neither candidate projected a consistent class appeal.

The gubernatorial primaries four years later gave Alabama voters wider choices. The leading contenders were Wallace, state Senator Ryan DeGraffenried, and James Folsom. This time Wallace easily outdistanced competitors for the position on the extreme right of the racial issue, but on economic matters he talked in a populist vein. DeGraffenried campaigned as an economic conservative and was comparatively moderate on racial issues. Folsom was the liberal candidate, socially and economically. In his last term as governor, Folsom had battled the Citizens' Councils and encouraged black voter registration. In 1962 he called for "Peace in the

---

[35]Norman I. Lustig, "The Relationships between Demographic Characteristics and Pro-Integration Vote of White Precincts in a Metropolitan Southern County," *Social Forces* 40 (March 1962): 205–8.

[36]As quoted in Sherrill, *Gothic Politics in the Deep South*, p. 267. On the campaign see the reports by Fred Taylor, in Atlanta *Journal and Constitution*, March 16, 23, 1958, and in *Birmingham News*, April 27, May 18, June 4, 1958. See also Marshall Frady, *Wallace* (New York: World, 1968).

Valley" and a termination of racial strife. Folsom might well have made the runoff had it not been for a disastrous statewide election-eve television appearance, in which Big Jim appeared to be fall-down drunk, attempting to introduce his family but forgetting some of their names. "How many votes that TV show cost Folsom," observed a veteran Alabama journalist, "is beyond calculation."[37] At the polls Wallace cut heavily into Folsom's rural and lower-class white following. Folsom led in the mountain counties, and he won heavily in urban black precincts, but Wallace's racial appeal served him well in lower-status white districts and in rural areas, especially in the black belt. DeGraffenried ran well enough in metropolitan counties, where he was the favorite in affluent white neighborhoods, to nose past Folsom and make the runoff with Wallace.

In the second primary Wallace swept the lowland counties and ran well in the countryside generally. (Wallace, like Folsom before him, was the rural candidate, but the sources of their support, if overlapping, also differed. Wallace appealed most strongly to voters in the black belt, the area that had shown a decidedly limited enthusiasm for Folsom.) In the cities Wallace was the white common man's candidate. DeGraffenried won the support of blacks and upper-status whites. This now familiar coalition carried metropolitan Alabama for DeGraffenried but not by large enough margins to overcome Wallace's majorities in the hinterlands.

The same voting patterns—in which rural, lowland, lower-status whites were pitted against metropolitan, upland, blacks and higher-status whites—were customary in Georgia during the entire postwar period. The Talmadges and Griffins prospered in rural areas, ran best in rural counties in the southern half of the state, thrived in lower-status white precincts in the cities, lost the more affluent white precincts, and might as well have not been on the ballot at urban black polling places.[38]

Georgia voters divided along similar lines over such issues as expanding and constitutionally formalizing the county-unit system and authorizing the substitution of a private-school system for the public schools in order to avoid desegregation. In 1950 and again in 1952 the Talmadge forces in the legislature submitted county-unit amendments to the electorate, and both times the voters turned them down. After the 1950 defeat, Talmadge and his associates went all out in support of the 1952 amendment, insisting that it was insurance against: "1. Mixed Schools and Colleges; 2. Boss Rule; 3. Organized Crime; 4. County Consolidation."[39] But to no avail. A major-

---

[37]Bob Ingram, in *Montgomery Advertiser*, May 6, 1962.

[38]For a more detailed treatment of Georgia voting patterns, see Numan V. Bartley, *From Thurmond to Wallace: Political Tendencies in Georgia, 1948-1968* (Baltimore: Johns Hopkins Press, 1970).

[39]From a pamphlet bearing Talmadge's name supporting passage of the amendment, cited in Louis T. Rigdon II, *Georgia's County Unit System* (Decatur, Ga.: Selective Books, 1961), pp. 38–39.

ity of Georgia's voters saw through such nonsense; and ratification of a constitutional amendment required a majority of the ballots, not a majority of the county-unit votes. The Talmadge camp was more successful in 1954, when voters ratified the private-school amendment. Voter response in these elections was generally consistent, as evidenced by the coefficients of correlation between the vote for Herman Talmadge in 1948 and 1950, for the county-unit amendments in 1950 and 1952, and for the segregation amendment in 1954 (see table 3.3).

The presence of nine candidates, three of them from the Talmadge camp, disrupted voting patterns somewhat in the 1954 gubernatorial primary, although the combined vote for the two leading Talmadge candidates, Lieutenant Governor Marvin Griffin and Commissioner of Agriculture Tom Linder, compare closely to past voting patterns. During the late 1950s political conflict subsided. Talmadge went to Washington as a U.S. senator, and Lieutenant Governor S. Ernest Vandiver, a close political friend of Senator Talmadge, won the 1958 gubernatorial primary overwhelmingly against weak opposition.

But the old cleavages reappeared in the 1962 gubernatorial campaign, when former Governor Marvin Griffin opposed state Senator Carl Sanders of Augusta. That same year the U.S. Supreme Court upheld a lower federal court decision declaring the county-unit system unconstitutional,[40] and for the first time in the modern period, popular ballots decided the election—a factor no doubt important in accounting for the greatly increased turnout in metropolitan counties. Griffin had served as lieutenant governor under Talmadge in the early 1950s and had enjoyed Talmadge's support in his successful gubernatorial effort in 1954. But Griffin proved something of an embarrassment to the Talmadge-oriented leadership in the state because of his heavy-handed administration, alleged corruption and malpractices on the part of his appointees, and generally what Atlanta journalist Charles Pou called "the 'if-you-ain't-for-stealing-you-ain't-for-segregation' modus operandi of Griffin's administration."[41] Griffin and Vandiver became particularly acrimonious political enemies; indeed, when Griffin asked his former lieutenant governor what support he could expect in his 1962 campaign, Vandiver thundered "none whatsoever."[42] Griffin ran in 1962, as he had in previous races, as a "good ole boy" segregationist, but without support from the state's top political leadership. Sanders conducted an urban-oriented campaign, avowing his belief in segregation but promising moderation and fairness. Sanders won overwhelmingly, sweeping the cities with whopping majorities in affluent white and in black districts and even winning a slight plurality in the countryside. Griffin ran best

[40]*Sanders* v. *Gray*, 203 F. Supp. 158; *Gray* v. *Sanders*, 372 U.S. 368.
[41]As cited in Sherrill, *Gothic Politics in the Deep South*, pp. 90.
[42]As quoted in *Atlanta Journal*, February 16, 1960.

Table 3.3

Consistency in Voter Support for the Conservative Position in Georgia, 1946–62

	Talmadge, 1946	Talmadge, 1948	Talmadge, 1950	County-unit amendment, 1950	County-unit amendment, 1952	Private-schools amendment, 1954	Griffin, 1962
Talmadge, 1946	–	.96	.85	.96	.87	.78	.85
Talmadge, 1948	.96	–	.82	.90	.83	.85	.86
Talmadge, 1950	.85	.82	–	.75	.55	.48	.55
County-unit amendment, 1950	.96	.90	.75	–	.95	.80	.86
County-unit amendment, 1952	.87	.83	.55	.95	–	.86	.93
Private-schools amendment, 1954	.78	.85	.48	.80	.86	–	.84
Griffin, 1962	.85	.86	.55	.86	.93	.84	–

Notes: The elections included are: Eugene Talmadge, 1946 gubernatorial primary; Herman Talmadge, 1948 special gubernatorial election and 1950 gubernatorial primary; for county-unit amendment, 1950 special election and 1952 general election; for private-schools amendment, 1954 general election; and Marvin Griffin, 1962 gubernatorial primary.

The units of analysis employed were south Georgia metropolitan, urban, and rural; Black-belt metropolitan and rural; Piedmont metropolitan, urban, and rural; and Mountain urban and rural (ten cases).

in the traditionally Talmadge strongholds. In the cities Griffin appealed to the lower- and lower-middle-status white voters, the same voter groups that had given relatively strong support to Herman Talmadge, the county-unit and segregation amendments, and Griffin himself in previous races.

The black-affluent white coalition that helped to give Sanders more than two-thirds of the votes in metropolitan counties reappeared in a variety of elections in Georgia and elsewhere. In Atlanta the affluent whites and the blacks opposed the private-school scheme and supported liberalizing local ordinances governing the sale of alcohol. Their votes kept Mayor Ivan Allen, Jr., in office and replaced the Fifth District's antediluvian congressman, James C. Davis, by making Charles L. Weltner, a moderate Atlanta lawyer, the Democratic nominee for U.S. representative.

The racial issue provoked similar alignments in other southern cities. In Little Rock, blacks and upper-status whites ultimately elected a moderate school board that helped to resolve the desegreation crisis in that city. In Birmingham, blacks and higher-income whites retired Eugene "Bull" Connor from his position as police commissioner, first by outvoting the lower- and lower-middle-status whites to approve a new form of government that abolished Connor's office and then by again outvoting the same groups to prevent Connor from becoming mayor. (Having been driven from office in Birmingham, Connor was now a martyr, and he promptly won the important office of president of the Alabama Public Service Commission in a statewide election in 1964.)

Voting patterns varied from state to state of course, but a central theme was the breakdown of the New Deal alliance, as the Faubuses, Davises, Wallaces, Bryants, Burnses, and Griffins siphoned off rural and lower-income white voters. Blacks reacted by supporting the moderation of upper-status suburbanites. In some states, such as Arkansas or Mississippi, this division took on the basic character of a rural-urban cleavage; in others, as in the case of Louisiana or Florida, it accentuated sectional differences. In most instances, voting patterns reflected all of these factors—race, class, sectional, and rural-urban division—which were so clearly etched in the election returns of Alabama or Georgia. In Mississippi and South Carolina, the pervading influence of the race issue transcended the sporadic primary-election conflict between black belt and hills.

Mississippi, Key speculated in *Southern Politics*, "only manifests in accentuated form the darker political strains that run throughout the South,"[43] and surely Ross R. Barnett was the ultimate caricature of the racist demagogues of the massive resistance period. But before Barnett, the conflict between the Mississippi River Valley black-belt counties and the predominately white northeastern hills and southeastern coastal areas

[43]V. O. Key, Jr., *Southern Politics in State and Nation* (New York: Alfred A. Knopf, 1949), p. 229.

mapped the contours of state politics. During the postwar period the black-belt whites and their allies in the high-rent districts of Jackson, the state's only metropolis, supported an uncompromising conservatism that could have been matched by few other areas of the nation.

In 1947 the Delta gubernatorial candidate was Fielding L. Wright, who defeated the vaguely New Dealish Paul B. Johnson, Jr., and went on to become the Dixiecrat vice-presidential nominee. Wright was replaced in the statehouse by Hugh White, another black-belt favorite, who defeated Johnson by a relatively narrow margin. In 1954 James O. Eastland defended his Senate seat against the moderately progressive Carroll Gartin. Himself a Delta planter, Eastland won an impressive 71 percent in the black-belt counties, which was the same margin by which he carried the silk-stocking neighborhoods in Jackson. In 1960 Mississippi voters ratified a constitutional amendment placing right-to-work provisions in the state constitution, thus reinforcing the right-to-work law already in the Mississippi statute books. Only four of eighty-two counties voted against the amendment, but the majorities delivered by some of the Delta counties were truly impressive, though most could not live up to the 94.3 percent provided by Jackson's upper-income precincts. In a 1952 prohibition

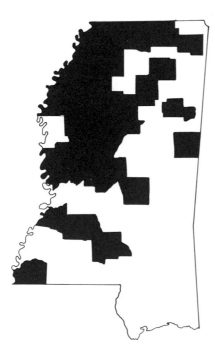

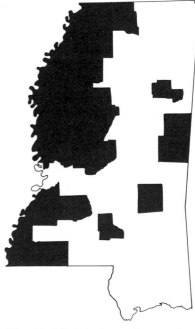

Fig. 3.5. Mississippi counties voting 80 percent or more for the right-to-work amendment in 1960

Fig. 3.6. Mississippi counties containing 50 percent or more nonwhite population in 1960

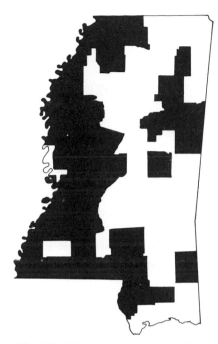

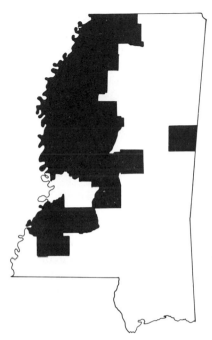

Fig. 3.7. Mississippi counties voting
50 percent or more for White in the 1951
runoff

Fig. 3.8. Mississippi counties voting
70 percent or more for Eastland in the
1954 primary

referendum, the black belt turned in a relatively sizable minority for the
wet position, but on few other matters could the area's voting residents lay
claim to the liberal side of an issue. James Eastland insisted that "segregation lives in the minds and hearts of southerners. It is integral to southern
culture."[44] Walter Sillers, perennial speaker of the Mississippi house of
representatives and a leading Delta spokesman, opposed progressive taxation for the support of public education on the grounds that, "after all, the
people who have the children should pay the tax, and you know the favored
few don't have many children."[45] What Key called "the delta mind" was
aptly expressed in a 1960 resolution passed by the Mississippi legislature
commending "the determined stand of the government of the Union of
South Africa in maintaining its firm segregation policy."[46]

Against this background the 1955 gubernatorial election marked something of a break with tradition. In the first primary Fielding Wright won a
plurality in the black-belt counties and a majority in the affluent and semi-
affluent precincts in Jackson, while Ross R. Barnett exhibited some appeal

[44]As quoted in U.S. Congress, *Congressional Record*, 81st Cong., 2d sess., 1950, 9043.
[45]As quoted in *Jackson Daily News*, March 16, 1958.
[46]As cited in *Southern School News*, May 1960.

to lower-status white voters. But neither made the runoff, which was fought out between Johnson and James P. Coleman. The black belt and, indeed, most of the northern and central portions of the state adopted Coleman in preference to the liberal-tinged Johnson, and the upper-income Jackson neighborhoods gave him two-thirds of their votes. But Coleman was by no means a typical Delta candidate; he brought to the governorship a refreshing concern for dignity, rationalized governmental procedure, and such things as honest elections and a higher budget for Mississippi's starved public schools.[47] Whatever impetus Coleman might have provided toward a more responsible conservatism, however, was soon absorbed by racial hysteria.

Ross Barnett made his third assault on the statehouse in 1959. In the first primary he ran well enough in rural areas and, insofar as Jackson returns are representative, in lower-status white precincts to lead the balloting and enter the runoff. His runoff opponent, Carroll Gartin, was the coalition candidate, winning majorities in black and high-income white neighborhoods. But too few blacks voted, and Gartin's majorities in Jackson's prestige areas were too narrow to overcome the massive support Barnett received from the lower socioeconomic levels of whites. Barnett carried Jackson and the election. Despite his success in Jackson, however, Barnett was distinctly the candidate of the countryside; of Mississippi's seventy-one rural-small town counties, Barnett won majorities in sixty-one. Gartin's strength lay in the larger towns. Of the eleven counties containing a city of 20,000 or more, Gartin carried nine, losing only Hinds (Jackson) and Adams (Natchez) Counties.

Barnett promised little in his campaign other than absolute devotion to the policies of white supremacy and, reputedly, an unusually large number of patronage positions for his supporters. So preoccupied did Barnett become with finding jobs for worthy allies that when a reporter asked him about Quemoy and Matsu he allegedly answered: "They're good men, and I'm sure I can find a place for them in Fish and Game [Commission]."[48] Barnett was never able to get the grasp of the governorship and always seemed a bit incredulous when things went wrong. After a prison trusty assigned to the governor escaped, Barnett philosophized memorably: "If you can't trust a trusty, who can you trust?"[49] The first session of the Mississippi legislature to meet under Barnett's guidance distinguished itself primarily by lowering the income tax and raising legislative salaries; commending South Africa's racial policies, enacting a series of anti-sit-in and anti-civil-rights laws, and opening the state treasury to the Citizens' Councils; and submitting to the electorate constitutional amendments

[47]Coleman's tenure is perceptively reviewed by Kenneth Toler, in *Atlanta Journal and Constitution*, January 3, 1960.

[48]As quoted in Sherrill, *Gothic Politics in the Deep South*, p. 184.

[49]Ibid., p. 3.

guaranteeing right-to-work and erecting yet further barriers to voter registration.[50] As time passed, the Barnett administration came under increasing criticism for inefficiency and corruption. But Barnett "stood in the school house door" in defense of segregation at the University of Mississippi, and so did his lieutenant governor, Paul Johnson, Jr.

Consequently, Johnson made continuation of the struggle against the federal government and its racial policies his principle campaign issue in his 1963 quest for the governorship. Once known as something of an economic liberal, Johnson followed the drift of Mississippi, and indeed southern, politics from economics to race. His leading opponent, as in 1955, was James P. Coleman, and the two once again met as runoff opponents. By this time the mood of the electorate had changed, however, and Johnson won a substantial victory. Coleman swept Jackson's black and upper- and upper-middle-class white precincts, but Johnson won in lower-status white neighborhoods and carried most of the state's rural counties. Johnson won more than 55 percent in only three of the eleven urban counties, but he did better than 55 percent in three-fourths of the rural-small town counties.

The darker political strains exemplified in Mississippi were a formidable force in Democratic factional politics in the upper-South states, splitting even the venerable Byrd organization in Virginia. Senator Harry Flood Byrd had coined the term "massive resistance," and the Byrd organization was instrumental in formulating a strategy of southern opposition to public-school desegregation. But when the defense of segregation became a matter of closing affected schools, Governor J. Lindsay Almond, Jr., chose to abandon massive resistance and to reopen on a desegregated basis the nine schools he had ordered closed during the fall of 1958. Senator Byrd and many of the organization stalwarts considered the governor's strategic retreat a sellout. "I stand now as I stood when I first urged massive resistance," the senator stated,[51] and the division between the organization's hard-core segregationists, who stood with Byrd, and its more moderate members, who followed Almond, widened during the governor's final years in office.

Each faction entered candidates for the gubernatorial nomination in 1961. The organization regulars selected Attorney General Albertis S. Harrison to oppose Lieutenant Governor A. E. S. Stephens, who was closely associated with Almond's policies. Virginia voters for the first time since the 1940s were treated to the unseemly spectacle of a hotly contested Democratic primary election. The Byrd organization weathered the rebellion. Harrison won substantial majorities in nonmetropolitan areas,

[50]*Jackson Daily News*, May 6, 1960; *Southern School News*, May, June 1960.

[51]As quoted by Laurence Stern, in *Washington Post*, August 30, 1959. See Benjamin Muse, *Virginia's Massive Resistance* (Bloomington: Indiana University Press, 1961); and J. Harvie Wilkinson III, *Harry Byrd and the Changing Face of Virginia Politics, 1945-1966* (Charlottesville: University of Virginia Press, 1968), pp. 113-54, 237-40.

especially in the southern and central parts of the state, to finish with 56.7 percent of the vote. Stephens carried the mountain counties and almost broke even in the metropolitan areas. In Richmond and Norfolk, Stephens massively carried the black precincts and lost the white ones, though he made a creditable showing in lower-status areas. Harrison held together the Byrd organization's basic following—the Southside whites, the urban upper class, and the rural-small town voters generally. Nevertheless the public bloodletting damaged the prestige of the organization's aging leadership.

In North Carolina the racial issue catapulted I. Beverly Lake, a Columbia Ph.D. and former Wake Forest law professor, into a major force in state politics. Making his first statewide campaign in the 1960 gubernatorial primary, Lake relied heavily on the volunteer efforts of former students and on an aggressive defense of segregation. Lake ran sufficiently well in the lowland counties and in blue-collar districts in the cities to enter the runoff against Terry Sanford, former campaign manager for Kerr Scott. Horrified by Lake's virulent racism, Governor Luther H. Hodges and the establishment forces, who had divided their efforts between two contenders in the first primary, threw their support to Sanford. Opposed by virtually all the Democratic party regulars, Lake went under in the runoff with 44 percent of the vote. He carried the black belt and made a creditable showing everywhere except in the mountain counties. In the cities he projected a sharp class appeal, running well among lower-status whites. Sanford, who campaigned on a progressive platform, won almost unanimous support in black precincts and carried higher-income white precincts by handsome majorities.

Four years later Lake again sought the governor's office. This time, however, the establishment faction united behind Judge Dan K. Moore, while the more liberal Sanford forces supported Judge L. Richardson Preyer. Lake finished third, again demonstrating a strong appeal to voters in the eastern lowland counties and in lower-status white neighborhoods. Eliminated from the runoff campaign, Lake supported Moore, who apparently attracted the bulk of Lake's voter following. In the runoff, as in the primary, Preyer won massive majorities in black neighborhoods and lost generally in white neighborhoods. In North Carolina the race issue alone was not adequate for victory, but the impact of Lake on the state's politics testified to its disruptive potential.[52]

Similarly, in Tennessee hardly a campaign passed without some candidate accusing the opposition of integrationist leanings. Both Gore and Kefauver won renomination over segregationist opposition. In 1958 former Governor Prentice Cooper based his campaign to dislodge Gore on a

---

[52]James R. Spence, *The Making of a Governor: The Moore-Preyer-Lake Primaries of 1964* (Winston-Salem, N.C.: John F. Blair, 1968), pp. 8–105.

Table 3.4

Percentage of the Vote for Lake in the 1960 Gubernatorial
Runoff Primary in Charlotte, Greensboro, and Raleigh,
by Socioeconomic Class and Race

Vote category	Charlotte		Greensboro		Raleigh	
	Percentage of vote received	$(N)^a$	Percentage of vote received	$(N)^a$	Percentage of vote received	$(N)^a$
Lower-class white	44.8	(1,843)	53.9	(321)	51.9	(503)
Lower-middle-class white	29.6	(769)	54.6	(960)	47.0	(1,135)
Upper-middle-class white	23.9	(1,314)	39.8	(1,958)	41.0	(1,263)
Upper-class white	27.9	(3,105)	32.9	(3,096)	35.8	(3,943)
Black	.9	(1,704)	.3	(2,234)	1.7	(2,491)
County vote[b]	34.2	(10,098)	40.8	(11,897)	41.7	(28,616)

[a](N) denotes the number of votes upon which the percentages are based.

[b]County-vote percentages are based on the total number of votes cast in the county.

stringent defense of social conservatism; two years later Judge Andrew T. Taylor conducted a similar though more folksy, more effective campaign in his effort to unseat Kefauver.[53] In neither case did the tactics prove effective. Both Cooper and Taylor won majorities in the rural-small town counties of the western Tennessee lowlands, but the incumbents swept the central and eastern parts of the state to claim impressive victories. In Nashville Gore and Kefauver carried precincts of all socioeconomic categories, running best in black and lower- and middle-income white areas. Beginning their Senate careers with substantially different voting bases, Kefauver and Gore were repeatedly challenged in the Democratic primaries by demonstrably more conservative, segregationist candidates. The sharp escalation in their ecological correlations clearly suggests the convergence of their voter constituencies and the polarization of politics in the era of desegregation:

Kefauver in 1948 and Gore in 1952	–.57
Gore in 1952 and Kefauver in 1954	–.10
Kefauver in 1954 and Gore in 1958	.62
Gore in 1958 and Kefauver in 1960	.85
Kefauver in 1960 and Gore in 1964	.87

Racial and ideological division was less obvious in Tennessee's gubernatorial politics. Liberal candidates in Tennessee gubernatorial primaries

[53]Hugh Davis Graham, *Crisis in Print: Desegregation and the Press in Tennessee* (Nashville: Vanderbilt University Press, 1967), pp. 278–87.

consistently went under, but so too did the extreme segregationists. In 1952 Frank G. Clement defeated Governor Gordon Browning and two years later overwhelmed Browning's comeback effort. As governor, Clement increased educational expenditures and state services, promoted industrial expansion, and followed a moderate policy on racial matters. Unable to succeed himself in 1958, Clement supported the successful campaign of Buford Ellington, his commissioner of agriculture and former campaign manager, who in turn supported Clement's return to the governor's office in 1962. The administration machine failed in 1964, when Clement sought to move from the governor's office to the Senate seat vacated by Kefauver. Ross Bass, a progressive congressman who had voted for the 1964 civil-rights bill, ran extremely well in the middle part of the state and combined black and lower-status white support to carry the cities and the election. Clement got revenge two years later, beating Bass in a rematch by a narrow margin. The administration forces continued in power, moreover, as Ellington returned to the governorship, defeating liberal John J. Hooker.

The Clement-Ellington administration forces fielded candidates in election after election and thus provided some structure for Tennessee politics, but they did not create a consistent identifiable voter following, and the ecological correlations suggest a surprisingly minimal relationship between their voter bases: Clement in 1954 and Ellington in 1958, .14; Ellington in 1958 and Clement in 1962, .11; Clement in 1962 and Ellington in 1966, .26. Like the Crump organization that it replaced, the administration faction relied on loose alliances with county leaders and the patronage and favors dispensed by the governor. In the cities white upper-income areas provided the basic support. In Nashville and in Memphis, both consistently did best in high-prestige neighborhoods.

New Deal voting alignments continued more or less to hold together in Texas. In 1958 Ralph Yarborough successfully defended the Senate seat he had won in the 1957 special election by defeating William A. Blakley of Dallas. An insurance man, banker, rancher, and lawyer, Blakley was regarded as wealthy even by Texas standards, and his ideological views corresponded to popular stereotypes of the outlook of the very rich in the Lone Star State. So reactionary were Blakley's positions on the issues that moderate leaders, such as U.S. Speaker of the House of Representatives Sam Rayburn, and numerous right-of-center voters supported Yarborough, who won convincingly. As in previous races, Yarborough ran best in black and lower-status white precincts, and he carried eastern Texas by a hefty margin. But unlike in his previous elections, Yarborough made a creditable showing in higher-income neighborhoods and was the favorite of the south Texas machine counties.

Yarborough's 1958 victory was a relatively isolated event, however. Texas liberalism had no other leader with a statewide following. In the 1960 gubernatorial primary, the only contenders were two conservatives,

Governor Price Daniel and challenger Jack Cox. When Lyndon B. Johnson resigned his Senate seat to become vice-president, the 1961 special election to fill the seat was a true free-for-all, with seventy-one candidates on the ballot and one write-in contestant, but the two major liberal candidates, Henry B. Gonzalez and Maury Maverick, Jr., together won only 20 percent of the votes, as William Blakley and Republican John Tower captured runoff slots.

Then, in 1962, both the conservatives and the liberals found new leadership. Don Yarborough, a Houston lawyer and no relation to Senator Yarborough, entered the gubernatorial primary as a New Frontier liberal. Yarborough had made only one previous campaign, a strong though unsuccessful effort for lieutenant governor in 1960, but he was an attractive candidate and a persuasive advocate of social and economic reform. Price Daniel was expected to be the strongest conservative contender but as the campaign got underway, that role passed to John B. Connally. In both the first and second primaries Connally's campaigns were among the best financed and most effective in Texas history. His five-minute "Coffee with Connally" television spots between seven and eight o'clock each morning proved popular, and his "John Connally Victory Special" whistle-stop speaking tour was reminiscent of Harry Truman's 1948 presidential campaign.[54] Although making his first race, Connally was a veteran aide to Lyndon Johnson and during 1961 served as secretary of the navy. The hotly contested runoff between Connally and Yarborough resulted in a narrow Connally victory. Don Yarborough, like Ralph before him, carried east Texas and ran up heavy majorities in lower-status white precincts. Connally won in west Texas, and his financial and organizational resources appeared in the returns from the Mexican-American counties, which he took handily, and probably in the returns from black precincts, where he reaped a sizable share of the vote. Connally won a third of the black votes in Yarborough's hometown of Houston, almost 45 percent in his own hometown of Fort Worth, and a majority in the black precincts of intermediate Waco. But Connally's basic constituency was the upper-income whites; in Yarborough's Houston, Connally won more than 80 percent of the ballots cast in affluent white districts, and he did almost as well in Fort Worth and Waco.[55]

The 1962 race had been close; in a clear-cut contest pitting liberal versus conservative, the liberal had reaped almost half the votes cast, despite defections from minority voters. Then came the assassination of President John F. Kennedy in Dallas in 1963. Connally, who was riding

[54] Fred Gantt, Jr., *The Chief Executive in Texas: A Study in Gubernatorial Leadership* (Austin: University of Texas Press, 1964), pp. 293–97.

[55] For a more detailed discussion of voting patterns in Houston, see Chandler Davidson, *Biracial Politics: Conflict and Coalition in the Metropolitan South* (Baton Rouge: Louisiana State University Press, 1972), pp. 52–105.

with Kennedy and who suffered wounds from the assassin's bullets, immediately became a living martyr. When Don Yarborough again challenged Connally in 1964, the Houston liberal polled less than a third of the ballots, as Connally, his arm still bandaged from his wounds, swept to a massive victory. In this instance the frontier tradition of violence, rather than the southern tradition of racism, undermined the liberal cause in Texas. Nonetheless, the New Deal voting alliance remained potentially intact, as Ralph Yarborough demonstrated in his reelection to the Senate in 1964. Yarborough faced relatively weak primary opposition, thanks in some measure to arm-twisting on the part of President Lyndon Johnson, who wanted to prevent factional bloodletting in his home state.[56] As he had against Blakley, Yarborough rolled up massive majorities in black and lower-income white precincts to cruise to a first-primary victory.

But over much of the region the racial issue slashed through the fabric of one-party politics. Voting patterns varied, of course, but in state after state the populist-New Deal alignments of the early postwar years broke apart, as rural and low-income whites shifted from support of economic reform to defense of social conservatism. Black voters increasingly joined with the economically conservative upper-income whites in opposition to racial extremism. These shifting voting alignments disrupted the factional competition that had served as an inadequate substitute for a two-party system. By this time, however, the days of the Solid Democratic South had passed. A surging southern Republicanism represented a new force in southern politics.

[56]O. Douglas Weeks, *Texas in 1964: A One-Party State Again?* (Austin: University of Texas Press, 1965), pp. 10–19.

CHAPTER 4

THE EMERGENCE OF TWO-PARTY POLITICS: REPUBLICANISM IN THE NEW SOUTH

Southern voters expressed their preferences in the Democratic primaries, and the victorious candidates had little to fear in the ritualistic November general elections. By the end of World War II, the twentieth-century decline of two-party competition had evolved into a pattern of self-perpetuating stagnation. Republicans could realistically expect to win no electoral votes, no governor's chairs, and no U.S. Senate seats in the South. In the South's 105-seat House delegation in the 79th and 80th Congresses (1946–1950), the only Republicans were Representatives B. Carroll Reece and John Jennings, both from east Tennessee's mountain redoubt. The resultant moribund, patronage politics of southern Republicanism has been ably analyzed by Key and Heard.[1] Grass-roots Republicanism, according to Heard, was so paralyzed and defeatist that presidential Republicanism seemed to offer the sole available avenue of growth.

The weakness of the G.O.P.'s southern constituency is reflected in its performance in the presidential election of 1944 (illustrated in table 4.1). That fallow year Thomas E. Dewey won only a quarter of the South's popular votes, and he failed even to carry the mountains. His showing in south Florida gave early promise of future Republican gains from in-migration in that booming retirement haven, although regionally his performance in the metropolitan counties did not differ significantly from his strength in the towns and the countryside. Similarly, the Republican showing at the state level in 1944 plainly suggested that G.O.P. support in the South rested upon its mountain base in Tennessee, Virginia, North Carolina, and Arkansas and upon the in-migration attracted to south Florida.[2]

---

[1]V. O. Key, Jr., *Southern Politics in State and Nation* (New York: Alfred A. Knopf, 1949), especially chap. 13; and Alexander Heard, *A Two-Party South?* (Chapel Hill: University of North Carolina Press, 1952).

[2]The Republican percentage in the mountain counties of these states was: 38.2 in Arkansas, 46.0 in North Carolina, 55.6 in Tennessee, and 46.8 in Virginia; the South Florida percentage was 34.5.

Table 4.1
Percentage of the Vote for Dewey in 1944,
by Geographic and Demographic Category

	Number of counties	Total presidential votes	Percentage of total vote	Percentage voting Republican
Geographic category				
Mountain	182	829,366	17.5	46.7
South Florida	30	318,457	6.7	34.5
South Texas	36	90,007	2.0	26.8
Piedmont	163	817,896	17.3	24.9
West Texas	146	631,220	13.3	19.0
White belt	316	1,433,150	30.2	18.1
Catholic Louisiana	19	191,140	4.1	16.9
Black belt	242	419,434	8.9	12.3
Demographic category				
Rural	946	2,464,935	52.1	26.4
Metropolitan	82	1,672,058	35.4	24.5
Urban	106	593,677	12.5	21.7
Region	1,134	4,730,670	100.0	25.1

The Democratic hammerlock on the prestigious gubernatorial and congressional offices, in addition to the gerrymandered legislatures and, outside the mountains, the courthouse machines, was so demoralizing during the postwar decade and a half that genuine contests in the general elections were almost nonexistent. This was least true at the congressional level, although east Tennessee's two Republican congressmen remained in lonely isolation until in 1952 four new colleagues were brought in on Eisenhower's coattails. During the next ten years, however, the South's G.O.P. House ratio never exceeded 7 to 99.

In the five Deep South states, Republican gubernatorial and senatorial candidates rarely carried as much as one-fifth of the vote until the early 1960s. In Georgia, Mississippi, and South Carolina there were no Republican nominees for governor until 1966; there was no serious nominee for senator in Mississippi until 1966 and in Georgia none at all until 1968. The only minor exceptions to this rule of Republican invisibility in the Deep South were in Alabama and Louisiana.

In Alabama the Republicans at least offered a sacrificial entry in most state contests, often attempting to capitalize upon the divisive Democratic primaries so characteristic of Alabama's turbulent Democratic factionalism. In 1954 Republican gubernatorial candidate Tom Abernethy drew a protest vote of 26.6 percent against the controversial Jim Folsom, and in 1960 Julian Elgin attracted a surprising 30 percent of the senatorial vote against John Sparkman. The ebullient, populistic Folsom and the veteran New Dealer Sparkman were both beholden to the Democrats' traditional rural-small town constituency, and Republican inroads against them were most marked in the spreading suburbs surrounding Birmingham and Mobile. Similarly, in Louisiana Republicans stood to profit from the constant feuding of the Long and the anti-Long factions in the Democratic primaries and from metropolitan suspicion of the Longs' roots in rural populism. In 1948, when Russell Long first ran for the Senate, Republican Clem Clarke captured 25 percent of the votes; Clarke ran especially well in the New Orleans suburbs. Even so, in no case was a Democratic victory seriously in doubt, and the fact remained that, during the postwar decade and a half, no general election in the Deep South was remotely close.

Even in the six states of the Rim South, where elections were more often serious contests, there were no Republican gubernatorial or senatorial victories until the 1960s. In Texas in 1948, Republican Jack Porter drew almost one-third of the Senate vote against Lyndon Johnson, whose eighty-seven-vote margin in the Democratic runoff primary had doubtless made him appear vulnerable. Otherwise, the advantages of seniority and an electorate that overwhelmingly identified with the Democratic party shielded the South's Democratic senators from real partisan threats. In Texas the three-term gubernatorial regimes of Allan Shivers and Price Daniel were sufficiently conservative to effectively blunt Republican challenges.

The pattern in Texas illustrates the shrewd ability of conservative Democratic governors to rally to their standards in the hard-fought primaries sufficient upper-income voters to edge the liberal coalition of blacks and lower-income whites. Then in the general elections the Democratic voters remained in the fold, and the G.O.P. suffered biannual humiliation. Little wonder that the morale of both liberal Democrats and loyal Republicans remained chronically low in Texas.

In Florida and in the four mountain states of the peripheral South, prior to the 1960s, Republican gubernatorial challenges could range as high as one-fourth to one-third of the vote. In only one instance did the Republicans offer a serious contest, and although they lost it, it was close and revealing. In Virginia, as in Texas, the dominance of conservative Democrats in the statehouse—in Virginia's case the entrenched Byrd machine— had also long plagued liberal Democrats and loyal Republicans. In 1949 Francis Pickens Miller led a crusade of moderate and liberal Democrats against Byrd's gubernatorial nominee, John S. Battle, in a primary that bore striking similarities to the intraparty class warfare waged in Texas. In Roanoke, Miller captured 96 percent of the black vote and 67.2 percent of the lower-income white vote, while Battle countered with 88.5 percent of the upper-class and 68.4 percent of the upper-middle-class whites. (Roanoke was Miller territory, but the same general pattern is reflected in precinct returns in Norfolk.) The Byrd organization's strength in the rural areas, and especially the conservative Southside, gave Battle a plurality of 42.8 percent, as against Miller's 35.3 percent (Virginia had no primary run-off provision then).[3] Battle then easily defeated his Republican opponent in the general election with over 70 percent of the vote.

In 1953 the Byrd organization nominated a loyal if colorless conservative, Thomas B. Stanley, to succeed Battle as governor. The Republican nominee was state Senator Theodore Roosevelt Dalton, an aggressive, attractive, young candidate whose campaign was a Republican version of Miller's attack on the Byrd machine, which was heavily reliant upon Virginia's withered electorate.[4] Dalton called for repealing the poll tax, lowering the voting age to eighteen, and increased expenditures for education, mental health, and highways, as against Stanley's standard Byrd litany of "sound fiscal policies." Precinct returns suggest that traditional class and racial divisions were considerably blurred in this contest, which pitted a conservative Democrat against a progressive Republican and very likely confused much of the electorate. Clear patterns do emerge from the county returns, however. Dalton drew well in the mountain and metropolitan counties (51 percent and 48.6 percent, respectively) but fell off in the Piedmont (33.4 percent); and Stanley's margin of 72.3 percent in the black belt held Dalton's total vote to 44.3 percent. It was by far the best showing of any southern Republican in a statewide race between 1945 and 1960, and it presaged the victory of moderate Republican Linwood Holton in Virginia in 1969. But Dalton's second attempt, against J. Lindsay Almond in 1957, drew only 36.4 percent of the vote. By then the politics of massive resistance was in full flower, and Democrats were simply better at it. They had been shielding the white South from intrusion into its social folkways for decades, and their credentials as resisters against federal interference were more believable.

Outnumbered and outflanked on the racial question in state politics, southern Republicans found an opening in presidential politics when the national Democrats nominated Harry S. Truman and wrote into the party platform unprecedented proposals for reform in civil rights. There had been premonitory symptoms of revolt in 1944, when disgruntled States' Rights Democrats defected from the Roosevelt ticket in Texas (11.8 percent for the Texas Regulars), South Carolina (7.5 percent), and Mississippi

[3]See Francis Pickens Miller's *The Man from the Valley: Memoir of a 20th Century Virginian* (Chapel Hill: University of North Carolina Press, 1971), chaps. 14 and 15. In 1952, Miller challenged Senator Harry Flood Byrd directly, losing by a vote of 128,869 to 216,438. County and precinct returns show that Miller's campaign of 1952 was largely identical to that of 1949: his liberal coalition of blacks and lower-income whites in the cities was not strong enough to overcome Byrd's upper-income and rural coalition of conservatives.

[4]The Dalton-Stanley contest is discussed in J. Harvie Wilkinson III, *Harry Byrd and the Changing Face of Virginia Politics, 1945–1966* (Charlottesville: University of Virginia Press, 1968).

(5.8 percent). The story of the Dixiecrat revolt of 1948 is a familiar one,[5] although most analyses concentrate on the individual states, wherein the Thurmond-Wright ticket carried the thirty-eight electoral votes of Alabama (where it was impossible to vote for Truman), Louisiana, Mississippi, and South Carolina, plus one from Tennessee, and the South's remaining eighty-eight electoral votes went to Truman.[6] Interestingly, politically volatile Catholic Louisiana was most receptive to Democratic defection, and heavily Catholic Mexican Texas was least receptive. The Southwide Democratic fall-off in the popular vote was 20.9 percent, and while the bulk of it was lost to the Dixiecrats, the Republicans made small gains in most categories. The most notable exception was the black belt, where the small number of presidential Republicans could more effectively punish the national Democratic party by voting for Thurmond and Wright. The Southwide Republican gain in 1948 was only 1.5 percent, but the geographic distribution of these gains is revealing: there was a significant 6.1 percent increase in the metropolitan counties and only a 1.0 percent increase in the town counties, while in the rural counties there was a decline of 1.8 percent.

Despite the apparent magnitude of the Dixicrat revolt, its impact was localized in the black belt, and there was a surprisingly high degree of partisan continuity from the election of 1944 to the election of 1948. The Southwide coefficients of correlation by county for the Republicans and Democrats in the two elections are in fact identical: .83 for the Democrats and .83 for the Republicans.[7] In North Carolina, a state unusually well endowed with the four basic geographic categories of counties (24 white belt, 27 black belt, 20 Piedmont, and 29 mountain), Pearson's r for the Democrats, 1944 and 1948, is .91; for the Republicans it is .97. In North Carolina the ecological correlations of the two major parties in 1944 against the Dixiecrats in 1948 are mirror images of insignificance: Democrats, .10; Republicans, .10.

In many cities of the Deep South the States' Rights presence grossly distorted the two-party mold, such as in Birmingham, where Truman was a nonperson, or in Charleston, where Strom Thurmond humiliated both Truman and Dewey. But in the metropolitan counties of the peripheral

[5] An able summary is Heard, *A Two-Party South?* chap. 2; and Key has demonstrated the discontinuity between Hoovercrats and Dixiecrats in *Southern Politics*, chap. 15. But see also Numan V. Bartley, *The Rise of Massive Resistance: Race and Politics in the South during the 1950s* (Baton Rouge: Louisiana State University Press, 1969), chap. 2.

[6] The electoral votes for the States' Rights Democratic Party were: Alabama, 11; Louisiana, 10; Mississippi, 9; South Carolina, 8; and Tennessee, 1. The popular votes in the four states carried by the Dixiecrats were: Alabama, 79.7 percent; Louisiana, 49.1 percent; Mississippi, 87.2 percent; and South Carolina, 72.0 percent.

[7] Because the regional regression analysis by county was employed to assess continuity for the two major parties, Alabama was excluded because in 1948 no votes could be cast for Truman, and Mississippi and South Carolina were excluded because the proliferation of state parties prevented the application of a two-party model.

South, which cast 77.9 percent of the total southern metropolitan vote in 1948, the class-based New Deal coalition held up fairly well, as the precinct returns in table 4.2 suggest. Not only was the performance of Thurmond poor, in the Rim South cities he fared worse among working-class whites than among the more affluent, and his very modest showing in precincts classified as black doubtless reflects a sprinkling of whites within them. Dewey was poorly endowed by partisan or regional affiliation and personal appeal to warm the hearts of southerners, but the Republican base of support among the more affluent whites promised to bloom with the burgeoning of suburbia.

The watershed election for presidential Republicanism was the contest of 1952, which clearly established the G.O.P. as the respectable party of the urban and suburban affluent whites in the South's large and small cities and a visible threat in presidential elections in the South.[8] While campaigning in Columbia, South Carolina, in 1952, Dwight Eisenhower heard the band strike up "Dixie" and arose to exclaim: "I always stand up when they play that song." During that campaign Eisenhower visited nine southern states, while Adlai Stevenson campaigned in only four, and the results were dramatic. Eisenhower carried the fifty-seven electoral votes of Florida, Tennessee, Texas, and Virginia and made substantial gains in every

Table 4.2

Percentage of the Vote for Truman in 1948
in Nashville, Richmond, and Miami,
by Socioeconomic Class and Race

	Nashville		Richmond		Miami	
Vote category	Percentage of vote received	$(N)^a$	Percentage of vote received	$(N)^a$	Percentage of vote received	$(N)^a$
Black	67.8	(2,346)	76.9	(1,625)	64.9	(12,479)
Lower-class white	85.4	(2,813)	71.1	(2,181)	60.5	(11,128)
Lower-middle-class white	61.9	(214)	61.0	(6,163)	58.6	(10,071)
Upper-middle-class white	57.9	(797)	42.4	(3,839)	48.6	(5,748)
Upper-class white	13.4	(808)	31.5	(615)	34.9	(2,541)
County vote[b]	55.5	(37,643)	47.2	(34,907)	53.5	(111,512)

[a](N) denotes the number of votes upon which the percentages are based.

[b]County-vote percentages are based on the total number of votes cast in the county.

[8]For an analysis of the 1952 election by states, see Donald S. Strong, *The 1952 Presidential Election in the South* (University: Bureau of Public Information, University of Alabama, 1955).

Table 4.3
Percentage of the Vote for Thurmond and Dewey in 1948
in Nashville, Richmond, and Miami,
by Socioeconomic Class and Race

Vote category	Nashville		Richmond		Miami	
	Thurmond	Dewey	Thurmond	Dewey	Thurmond	Dewey
Black	3.8	26.0	1.5	21.6	5.9	29.2
Lower-class white	7.1	7.4	3.5	25.4	6.1	33.4
Lower-middle-class white	19.6	18.1	9.2	29.8	6.3	35.1
Upper-middle-class white	20.6	21.5	11.2	46.4	6.8	44.7
Upper-class white	42.2	43.4	12.0	56.5	9.4	56.4
County vote[a]	21.5	22.2	11.1	41.7	6.4	37.0

[a]County-vote percentages are based on the total number of votes cast in the county.

geographic and demographic category of counties, as figure 4.1 demonstrates. Eisenhower's striking appeal to upper-income white voters is evident from table 4.4.

The contest between Eisenhower and Stevenson in 1956 was a rerun. The Republicans added Deep South Louisiana to the four Rim South states they had carried in 1952, and the Southwide county correlations between the two elections were uniformly high: Democrats, .84; Republicans, .83.[9] There were also significant differences. The intervening years had witnessed the school desegregation decision of *Brown* v. *Board of Education*, a decision which President Eisenhower repeatedly refused to endorse but which was announced by Chief Justice Earl Warren, a Republican whom Eisenhower had appointed, and this in turn had accelerated the massive resistance movement led by southern Democrats. In response, a pronounced shift of black voters toward the G.O.P. is reflected in the precinct returns. In Richmond, the birthplace of massive resistance, the Republican vote in the selected black precincts rocketed from 25.1 percent in 1952 to 74.9 percent in 1956; and in Norfolk, from 16.2 percent to 77.7 percent. In Atlanta, Eisenhower's share in the selected black precincts soared from 25.7 percent to 85.3 percent. The Republican surge among black voters elsewhere in the South was generally somewhat less spectacular, but everywhere it was substantial, and while local variations were occasionally wide, it would appear reasonable to estimate that black southerners in the cities chose Eisenhower over Stevenson in 1956. Correspondingly, support for Eisenhower fell off among black-belt whites. The only geographic category

[9]South Carolina was excluded from the 1952–56 correlation because the proliferation of state parties made the two-party model inapplicable.

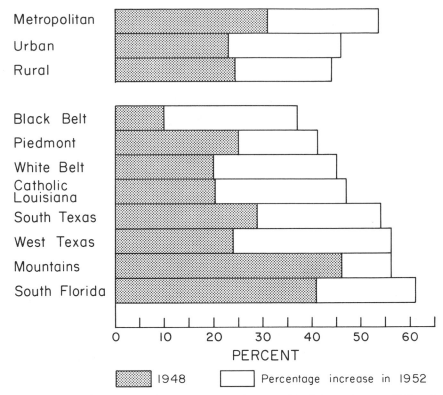

Fig. 4.1. Increase in the Republican percentage of the presidential vote between 1948 and 1952, by demographic and geographic categories of counties

of counties in which Eisenhower did not gain in 1956 was the black belt, where the Republican vote fell from 36.5 percent in 1952 to 30.7 percent in 1956.

Southern white disenchantment with the two major parties resurfaced in 1956 in the form of third-party, States' Rights tickets, which drew 29.5 percent of the vote in South Carolina, 17.3 percent in Mississippi, 7.2 percent in Louisiana, and 6.2 percent in Virginia. In South Carolina 46.2 percent of the black belt's vote went to the States' Rights party, while only 30.8 percent went to the Democrats, and 23 percent went to the Republicans; but it was to no avail, as the Democrats carried South Carolina, with a plurality of 45.4 percent, and Mississippi as well. They lost Virginia and Louisiana to the Republicans, but the small States' Rights vote in these two states could have made no difference in the outcome had it been allocated to either major party. The third-party effort clearly could not work unless it could attract a large enough following to threaten the balance of power between the two major parties, and it could not do this under the

Table 4.4

Percentage of the Vote for Eisenhower in 1952
in Norfolk, Birmingham, Waco, and Gadsden,
by Socioeconomic Class and Race

Vote category	Norfolk		Birmingham		Waco		Gadsden	
	Percentage of vote received	(N)[a]	Percentage of vote received	(N)[a]	Percentage of vote received	(N)[a]	Percentage of vote received	(N)[a]
Black	16.2	(653)	19.0	(633)	17.9	(1,322)	17.1	(368)
Lower-class white	25.0	(2,001)	32.9	(3,287)	42.3	(3,318)	22.6	(1,980)
Lower-middle-class white	56.8	(3,977)	39.9	(2,373)	50.0	(3,353)	24.2	(2,080)
Upper-middle-class white	62.9	(1,397)	52.4	(2,704)	58.8	(3,287)	34.3	(2,271)
Upper-class white	64.5	(3,122)	70.2	(3,868)	62.8	(5,140)	57.5	(1,623)
Country vote[b]	54.4	(26,074)	45.6	(70,766)	46.5	(32,278)	29.6	(15,697)

[a](N) denotes the number of votes upon which the percentages are based.

[b]County-vote percentages are based on the total number of votes cast in the county.

lackluster leadership of the reactionary T. Coleman Andrews or, as in Mississippi and South Carolina, vicariously in the name of Harry F. Byrd.[10]

The Eisenhower-Stevenson contests of 1952 and 1956 are particularly revealing of political patterns and trends when the county behavior of Rim South North Carolina and Deep South South Carolina are compared, as in figures 4.2 and 4.3. Most striking is the degree to which traditional patterns held in North Carolina but were reversed in South Carolina. In North Carolina the Republicans built upon their traditional mountain base and extended their inroads into the Piedmont's urban-industrial corridor; the lowlands and tidewater in the east, where eleven counties contained black majorities, remained Democratic. But in South Carolina, where racial sensitivities and what V. O. Key called a "garrison psychology" had historically been more pronounced, the highlands remained predominantly Democratic, and the lowlands, where sixteen counties contained black majorities, surged toward the Republicans. Stevenson carried both states in both elections, but in South Carolina in 1956 his plurality of 136,372 was exceeded by the combined totals for Eisenhower (75,700) and Byrd (88,511). Although the dominant trend in presidential politics in the South reflected the erosion of Democratic strength in the Rim South, the evolution of partisan behavior in South Carolina suggested that a direct Republican appeal to the racial animosities of Deep South whites might be rewarding. Solidly Democratic in 1940, South Carolina's Democratic affiliation wavered in 1944 and crashed in 1948. By the 1950s the lowlands were going Republican, and Senator Strom Thurmond, having embraced two antagonistic parties, was beginning to consider a third.

With Eisenhower the Republicans had won 48.1 percent of the southern vote in 1952 and 48.9 percent in 1956, but the supreme test of Republican continuity and durability in the South was the 1960 election, when the G.O.P. did not have Eisenhower to grace the ticket.[11] Lacking Eisenhower's popular appeal and running against the charismatic John F. Kennedy, Richard Nixon carried Florida, Tennessee, and Virginia into the Republican camp for the third straight time but lost Louisiana and Texas, where the presence of a Roman Catholic and a Texan on the Democratic ticket had an obvious impact. The Republican share of the vote in Catholic Louisiana plummeted from 55.3 percent in 1956 to 24 percent in 1960, and in Mexican Texas from 52.4 percent to 39.5 percent. But otherwise Nixon

---

[10]See Bartley, *The Rise of Massive Resistance*, chap. 9.

[11]For a more detailed analysis of the election of 1956 in the South, see Donald S. Strong, *Urban Republicanism in the South* (University: Bureau of Public Information, University of Alabama, 1960). For the 1960 election, see Bernard Cosman, "Presidential Republicanism in the South, 1960," *Journal of Politics* 24 (May 1962): 303–22. A revealing case study of the development of the Republican party during the 1950s is Kenneth N. Vines, *Two Parties for Shreveport* (New York: Henry Holt & Co., 1959). See also the essays by Donald S. Strong, Philip Converse, and Robert Steamer, in *Change in the Contemporary South*, ed. Allan P. Sindler (Durham: Duke University Press, 1963).

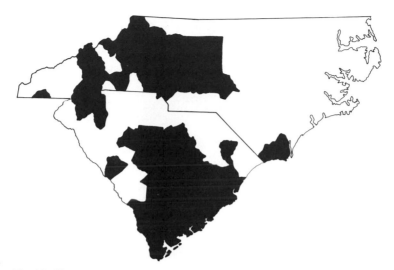

Fig. 4.2. North Carolina and South Carolina counties casting Republican majorities in the 1952 presidential election

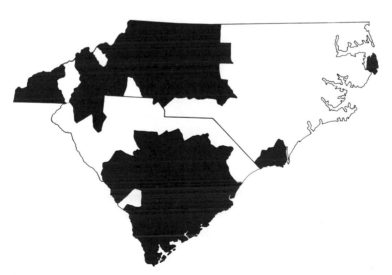

Fig. 4.3. North Carolina counties casting Republican majorities and South Carolina counties casting combined majorities for Eisenhower and Byrd in the 1956 presidential election

Table 4.5
Percentage of the Vote for Kennedy in 1960
in Mobile and Houston,
by Socioeconomic Class and Race

	Mobile		Houston	
Vote category	Percentage of vote received	$(N)^a$	Percentage of vote received	$(N)^a$
Black	72.2	(1,938)	85.3	(6,943)
Lower-class white	58.8	(2,728)	50.8	(6,342)
Lower-middle-class white	51.6	(5,125)	47.8	(6,241)
Upper-middle-class white	45.1	(2,943)	33.5	(7,260)
Upper-class white	36.2	(3,046)	16.7	(6,121)
County vote[b]	52.9	(55,267)	45.6	(325,399)

[a](N) denotes the number of votes upon which the percentages are based.

[b]County-vote percentages are based on the total number of votes cast in the county.

ran remarkably well in the South. His total of 46 percent of the regional vote strongly suggested that southern Republicanism had become institutionalized at the presidential level, and the high regional correlations between the elections of 1956 and 1960—.82 for the Democrats and .81 for the Republicans—reinforces the continuity of two-party presidential politics in the South.[12] Despite Eisenhower's strong showing among southern blacks in 1956 and his dispatch of federal troops to Little Rock in 1957, Kennedy's open appeal for the black vote was effective and played an important role in reducing the Republican share of the vote in metropolitan counties from 55.2 percent in 1956 to 50.0 percent in 1960.

Yet, as successful as the Republicans had been in achieving a presidential two-party system in the South, by 1960 there was almost no discernible coattail effect. The Republican House ratio remained 7 to 99, there were no Republican governors or U.S. senators, and the G.O.P. held only sixty of almost eighteen hundred seats in the southern legislatures. Theoretically, the presidential coattail effect should have been maximized in circumstances in which the gubernatorial candidates ran at the same time as the presidential candidate, and for a term of office of the same duration, and in which a solid base of mountain Republicanism existed to build upon. North Carolina best fit this model through 1960.[13] There G.O.P.

[12]The 1956–60 regional correlation omits Mississippi, again owing to the proliferation of state parties.

[13]Most southern states chose to shield their state politics from the impact of presidential elections and the national parties by holding gubernatorial elections either in odd-numbered years, as did Mississippi and Virginia, or only in the even-numbered nonpresidential years, as did Alabama, Georgia, South Carolina, Tennessee beginning in 1954, and Florida beginning

gubernatorial candidates had consistently received at least a quarter of the vote, and the combination of the mountain base, the growing suburban Republicanism in the twelve industrializing counties of the Piedmont crescent,[14] and the increasing pull of the presidential ticket produced in 1960 the closest general election for statewide office in the South since Republican Alf Taylor won the governorship of Tennessee in 1920.

If running in a presidential year was an advantage that Republican Robert Gavin possessed in 1960 and Ted Dalton had lacked in Virginia in 1953, Gavin in 1960 was denied the advantage of facing an opponent as

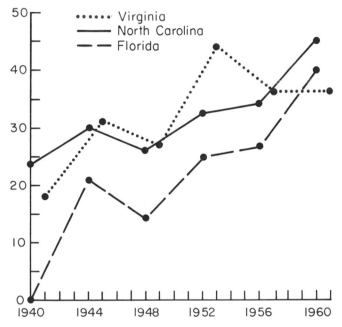

Fig. 4.4. The Republican vote cast for governor in Florida, North Carolina, and Virginia, 1940–61, in percent

in 1966 (previously Tennessee elected governors every even-numbered year, and Florida every presidential year). Only Louisiana and North Carolina elected governors exclusively in presidential years, though Louisiana followed the curious practice of nominating gubernatorial candidates in the late fall of the preceding year and electing them in the winter of the presidential year, and Arkansas and Texas elected them every two years throughout the postwar period. Among all Republican campaigns for statewide office in the period 1945–60, only the campaigns of Ted Dalton in Virginia in 1953 and Robert Gavin in North Carolina in 1960 reached the seriously threatening plateau of around the 45 percent mark, although George Peterson's 40.2 percent share of the vote against Farris Bryant in Florida in 1960 was a clear bellwether of Republican trends there to be capitalized upon in the late 1960s.

[14]These counties are, from east to west, Wake, Durham, Orange, Alamance, Guilford, Forsyth, Davie, Davidson, Rowan, Cabarrus, Mecklenburg, and Gaston, and the crescent contained the major cities of Raleigh, Durham, Greensboro, Winston-Salem, and Charlotte.

ineffectual as Dalton's opponent, Thomas Stanley, for Gavin, a relatively unknown Republican, was facing the popular Terry Sanford. Sanford had survived a strong runoff challenge by Lake, who had campaigned against school desegregation and the NAACP. Gavin might have been expected to appeal to the disgruntled supporters of the conservative Lake, but instead he avoided the race question and ran a progressive campaign, calling for a one-dollar-an-hour minimum wage, bond issues for highway construction, civil service for all state employees, and expanded efforts in education, industrialization, and per capita income to improve North Carolina's low national ranking in these areas.[15] Sanford also took the high road, concentrating on improved education. The results must have been particularly galling to Gavin, for although he edged Sanford in the mountains (53.7 percent), the Piedmont (51.8 percent), and metropolitan counties (51 percent), Sanford's hefty majorities in the eastern lowlands gave the Democrats a victorious margin of 54.4 percent. Sanford had his cake and ate it too, overwhelming Gavin not only among white voters in the black belt but also in the black precincts in the cities. Kennedy had accomplished the same feat, winning 76 percent of the vote in North Carolina's black belt, 60.9 percent in the white belt, and 95.5 percent in the selected black precincts in Charlotte, to carry North Carolina with 52.1 percent of the vote.

In Virginia and North Carolina the Republicans had taken their best shots at statewide office by running progressive campaigns free of race-baiting, and they had failed. The Rim South strategy was working well at

Table 4.6

Percentage of the Vote for Sanford and Gavin in 1960 in Charlotte

Vote category	Percentage of vote received		$(N)^a$
	Sanford	Gavin	
Black	91.8	8.2	(4,734)
Lower-class white	51.4	48.6	(5,306)
Lower-middle-class white	50.3	49.7	(2,328)
Upper-middle-class white	38.2	61.8	(4,291)
Upper-class white	34.9	65.1	(7,246)
Mecklenburg County[b]	50.6	49.4	(85,937)

[a](N) denotes the number of votes upon which the percentages are based.

[b]County-vote percentages are based on the total number of votes cast in the county.

[15]See Preston W. Edrall and F. Oliver Jones, "North Carolina: Bipartisan Paradox," in *The Changing Politics of the South*, ed. William C. Havard (Baton Rouge: Louisiana State University Press, 1972), especially pp. 382–87; and Terry Sanford, *But What About the People?* (New York: Harper & Row, 1966). Sanford won 56.1 percent of the runoff vote, narrowly losing to Lake in the black-belt counties but building up impressive majorities in the metropolitan (60.6 percent) and mountain (69.8 percent) counties.

the presidential level, but not below it, and the Democrats had recaptured the presidency again in 1960. As the Research Division of the Republican National Committee pointed out in a 1962 publication, the national Democratic party was strongly dependent on the South for its national majorities, and these majorities rested on "the support of an unnatural coalition— Negroes demanding change in the pattern of race relations and those most strongly opposed to departure from the pattern."[16] Impatient to speed the disruption of this unnatural coalition and mindful of the increasing tenacity of the Democratic black vote, and of the minority status of blacks in every southern state and congressional district, the Republican party gravitated rapidly toward, as Barry Goldwater aptly expressed it, "going hunting where the ducks are."[17]

Southern Republicans entered the decade of the 1960s with a dual legacy. The appeal of moderate conservatism had paid off fairly handsomely at the presidential level, especially in the peripheral South, but the coattail effect had been disappointing. The white majority of southern voters continued to behave paradoxically, voting for Democratic gubernatorial and senatorial candidates who often railed against the policies and nominees of the national Democratic party, while simultaneously voting for a Democratic presidency. Nixon had received only 33.4 percent of the vote in the black-belt counties in 1960, yet he was clearly more conservative, especially on racial matters, than was Kennedy. And the G.O.P.'s best efforts in statewide races in Virginia and North Carolina in the 1950s had rewarded progressive candidates only with respectable showings in defeat. In 1961, however, Republicans in Texas capitalized upon the paradox that was inherent in the Democratic support base and shattered the partisan unity of the southern Senate delegation for the first time since 1870.

Virtually unknown beyond the confines of Midwestern University in Wichita Falls, Texas, a thirty-four-year-old professor of government, John G. Tower, had resigned his academic post in 1960 to run as a Republican for the Senate seat of Lyndon Johnson. The diminutive Tower, an orthodox conservative who had married into wealth, attracted the active campaign support of Barry Goldwater, the arch-conservative senator from Arizona. Although considerable resentment had accumulated in Texas against Johnson's insurance tactic of simultaneously running for the Senate and the vice-presidency, few were prepared for Tower's surprising 41.1 percent of the vote in November 1960. Johnson carried the rural-small town counties handily enough, but Tower drew 45 percent of the metropolitan vote, even though he lost the urban black precincts to Johnson. Johnson successfully

---

[16]Research Division, Republican National Committee, *The 1962 Elections: A Summary Report with Supporting Tables* (Washington, D.C.: Republican National Committee, 1962), p. 38.

[17]As quoted in George B. Tindall, *The Disruption of the Solid South* (Athens: University of Georgia Press, 1972), p. 60.

held together the New Deal coalition of working-class white and black majorities; but in Houston, for example, Tower's majority among upper-middle-class whites was 60 percent, and among the upper class, 78 percent. The Republican inclinations of suburbanites in booming Texas was striking, and since the victorious Johnson had vacated the Senate seat, Tower moved aggressively toward the special election to determine Johnson's successor, scheduled for May 1961.

In the brief interim, the dominant conservative faction among Texas Democrats served the conservative Republicans well, as Governor Price Daniel appointed Democrat William A. Blakley to replace Johnson. The wealthy Blakley, who had failed in his effort to unseat Ralph Yarborough in 1958, stood ideologically to the right even of the staunchly conservative Tower, and liberal Texas Democrats were predictably appalled. Having rallied successfully around Ralph Yarborough in 1957 (to fill out the term vacated by Senator Price Daniel) and again in 1958 for a full term, liberal Democrats were thrown into disarray by the Blakley nomination. Many of the more militant liberals, contemptuously referred to as "Kamikazes" by loyal Democratic partisans, vowed to vote for Tower, preferring to vote for a conservative Republican rather than a reactionary Democrat, and thereby punish the dominant conservative Democrats. Others vowed to go fishing. The dilemma was particularly acute for black Democrats. In Houston, for instance, the Harris County Council of Organizations, representing approximately seventy black civic organizations, gave Blakley a tepid endorsement. Embarrassed by such support, Blakley attacked the candidacy of Robert C. Weaver for the top U.S. housing post and called for state control of all federal aid to education.

The result was a narrow (50.6 percent) but nevertheless stunning victory for Tower.[18] The turnout in this off-year election was low and thereby to the Republicans' advantage, and Tower cut heavily into the normal Democratic strength among working-class whites. The black precincts in Houston gave Blakley 73 percent of their vote, but it was 73 percent of a very small pie—only 827 votes in these selected black precincts in the runoff, whereas the same precincts had cast 1,724 votes in the preceeding special election, in which several candidates were attractive to blacks. As Johnson had the previous year, Blakley carried the rural and town counties of Texas, but with considerably reduced majorities, and Tower won the metropolitan counties with 56 percent of the vote. Tower's victory indicated that a decidedly conservative Republican could capitalize upon the growing Republican inclinations of the southern metropolis, and especially upon the weaknesses of the Democratic coalition, in a period of increasing

[18]Tower's slight majority was in the runoff election; in the preceeding special election he had led with 32.3 percent in a crowded and confused multipartisan field in which Blakley had received 18.8 percent and the votes of liberal Democrats had been distributed among such unsuccessful candidates as Henry Gonzales and Maury Maverick, Jr.

racial and social unrest. Yet generalizations from the Tower victory were constrained by the idiosyncrasies of Texas politics, where the left and right wings of the state Democratic party were locked in lusty combat. The conservative wing of the national Republican party had long held that, Eisenhower aside, Republican victories could best be achieved by opposing New Deal Democrats with an explicitly delineated conservative choice rather than the timid echo of the eastern Republican establishment. Tower fit the Republican mold, but Blakley was the antithesis of the Democratic one. Nevertheless, Tower had won, and conservative Republicanism stood an early chance of sounder testing in the South, as Senator Lister Hill was up for reelection in racially tense Alabama the following year, and in South Carolina Olin D. Johnston, who had retired "Cotton Ed" Smith and defeated Strom Thurmond and had twice before been elected governor, was also up for reelection.

Of the two incumbent senators, Johnston was less vulnerable to right-wing attack. A loyalist Democrat who had long opposed Dixiecratic tendencies in South Carolina, Johnston was nevertheless safely conservative on the race question and as governor had led South Carolina's attempts to avoid compliance with the *Smith* v. *Allwright* decision of 1944, which outlawed the white primary. In the Democratic primary in the spring of 1962, Johnston had been attacked as pro-labor by Ernest Hollings, who vowed to join the Senate's conservative bloc if elected. Nevertheless, Hollings lost by a two-to-one margin. But in the general election, the newly invigorated Republicans concentrated all of their fire on Johnston, leaving unopposed the winner of the Democratic gubernatorial primary, Donald S. Russell.[19] The Republican nominee, William D. Workman, Jr., was a veteran journalist but a political newcomer. He was the author of *The Case for the South*, a book supporting racial segregation, and his columns in the *Charleston News and Courier* had consistently reflected the views of the Citizens' Council movement. Since Johnston was not vulnerable on the racial question, Workman attacked him as a handmaiden of the Kennedys and intimated that a vote for Johnston was a vote for the invasion of Mississippi by federal troops. "The need of the hour," editorialized the *Charleston News and Courier*, "is to defeat Johnston, not simply because of his 'liberalism,' but because he is the man that the Kennedys want in the Senate."[20]

[19]The G.O.P. was inconsequential in South Carolina until 1952, when Eisenhower lost the state by less than 5,000 votes. In 1956, Stevenson was held to a plurality of 45.4 percent, as Republicans and defecting Democrats split their votes between Eisenhower and the independent Byrd. Previously, Republicans simply did not contest the election of U.S. senators in South Carolina. One Leon P. Crawford had challenged Johnston in the general election of 1956 and for his efforts had received 17.8 percent of the vote. There was no Republican gubernatorial candidate in modern South Carolina history until 1966.

[20]As quoted in the *New York Times*, October 19, 1963.

Although Workman carried only eight of South Carolina's forty-six counties, he won 53 percent in the metropolitan counties containing Charleston, Columbia, and Greenville and amassed an unprecedentedly respectable statewide total of 42.8 percent. Johnston carried rural-small town counties by sufficient margins to overcome Workman's lead in the cities, especially in Workman's home city of Charleston, where white support for Johnston fell to less than a third of the white voting electorate. Approximately nine out of ten blacks in Charleston voted for Johnston, however, as did the black precincts in Columbia, where blue-collar whites remained within the Democratic party in sufficient numbers to throw Richland County to the victorious incumbent.

If Johnston had survived what was by far the toughest general election of his career, his Senate colleague, Lister Hill of Alabama, was in greater peril, although the parallels between the two contests are striking. Both Hill and Johnston had been elected as New Deal Democrats during the tenure of Roosevelt; both had become more conservative in their Senate voting records during the late 1950s; both had amassed considerable seniority, had won renomination in the Democratic primaries with little difficulty, and faced well-financed and newly invigorated opposition from Republicans who attacked them from the right as handmaidens of the "Kennedycrat" national Democratic party. Further, the momentum of both Republican challengers was considerably accelerated when the Kennedy administration dispatched federal troops to quell the integration crisis at "Ole Miss" in September of 1962.

But Hill was a bit more vulnerable than Johnston on most points of comparison, especially in regard to Alabama's contiguity to Mississippi and hypersensitivity to events there and in the greater degree to which Alabama's Republican party was girded for warfare.[21] At the Republican state convention held in Birmingham on June 8, an insurgent group largely representative of the newer and younger urban business-professional wing of the party replaced the older chairman with John Grenier, an aggressive thirty-two-year-old Birmingham lawyer. As was the case in South Carolina, the party avoided the gubernatorial race and concentrated efforts on the Senate seat, nominating James D. Martin, an oil-products distributor from Gadsden and former president of the Associated Industries of Alabama. In his acceptance speech Martin set the tone of attack, calling for "a return of the spirit of '61—1861, when our fathers formed a new nation" to support their principles. "God willing," Martin concluded, "we will not again be forced to take up rifle and bayonet to preserve these principles. . . . Make no mistake, my friends, this will be a fight. The bugle call is loud and clear!

---

[21]For a penetrating analysis of the Alabama election, see Walter Dean Burnham, "The Alabama Senatorial Election of 1962: Return of Inter-Party Competition," *Journal of Politics* 26 (November 1964): 798–829.

The South has risen!"[22] Hill countered as best he could with appeals to fading memories of the "Republican depression" and Herbert Hoover and by emphasizing the New Deal's contribution toward alleviating the misery of depression and underdevelopment in Alabama, his own consistent support of TVA, and the advantages of his seniority.

When the returns were in, Hill had survived, but by the razor-thin margin of eight-tenths of one percent.[23] Like Tower in Texas and Workman in South Carolina, Martin had captured a majority (53.6 percent) of the vote in the metropolitan counties. In selected precinct returns from Birmingham, Mobile, and Montgomery, Hill did not muster a majority in any of the four socioeconomic classes of white voters—a dramatic indication of the disintegration of the class-based New Deal coalition in the face of racial unrest. Hill's share of the vote in the black precincts was overwhelming, but the black percentage of the Alabama vote in 1962 was still feeble.[24] Hill's majorities in the rural-small town counties of Alabama carried him through, but what is most striking about this remarkable election, a harbinger of the Goldwater phenomenon shortly to follow, is the extraordinarily high degree of discontinuity that emerges when it is compared with antecedent elections.

One arresting indication of this is the reversal of traditional friends-and-neighbors politics reflected in each candidate's loss of his home county. Hill was a native of Montgomery, and he had represented Montgomery County and south-central Alabama as congressman for the Second Congressional District for fifteen years prior to his election to the Senate in 1938. Yet in 1962 he lost Montgomery County, with only 42 percent of the vote. Similarly Martin, a prominent Gadsden businessman, lost Etowah County, for which Gadsden is the county seat, by an almost identical margin of 42.9 percent. This odd phenomenon reflected more than a mere political fluke, for the 1962 election overturned not only friends-and-neighbors traditions; it reversed the fundamental pattern in which highland north Alabama had historically proven more hospitable to Republican overtures, and the black belt downstate to Democrats. Figures 4.5 and 4.6 suggest the marked transition of Republican strength from north to south so accelerated by the climate of racial turmoil. Indeed, the ecological correlation between the Nixon vote in 1960 and the Martin vote in 1962 is a modest .53, whereas the correlation between Nixon in 1960 and Eisenhower in 1952 is .86. Projecting ahead, the correlation between Nixon in

[22]As quoted in *Congressional Quarterly Weekly Report* 20 (June 22, 1962): 1072.

[23]Hill received 201,937 votes, or 50.9 percent; Martin 195,134, or 49.1 percent.

[24]Just prior to the voting rights act of 1965, only 92,737 of Alabama's 481,220 voting-age blacks, or 19.3 percent were registered; 69.2 percent of Alabama's 1,353,122 voting-age whites were registered. In Lowndes and Wilcox counties, where blacks were heavily in the majority, no blacks were registered. See U.S. Commission on Civil Rights, *Political Participation* (Washington, D.C.: U.S. Government Printing Office, 1968), pp. 222–27.

1960 and Goldwater in 1964 in Alabama is a near random .26, whereas the correlation between Martin in 1962 and Goldwater in 1964 is a powerful .93.

Practical politics is the art of winning, of course, and in mounting their formidable and unprecedented challenges the Republicans in South Carolina and Alabama had lost. So, too, had the challenge of a third G.O.P. senatorial hopeful in Arkansas that year. There, despite the campaign assistance of Senators John Tower and Barry Goldwater, the campaign of Dr. Kenneth G. Jones, an ultraconservative Little Rock bone surgeon, against Senator J. William Fulbright never caught fire. Although Jones emerged with 31.3 percent of the votes, a total almost twice that achieved by previous Republican senatorial challengers, he nevertheless lost every county to Fulbright.[25]

Fig. 4.5. Alabama counties voting 40 percent or more for Nixon in the 1960 presidential election

[25]Similarly unsuccessful Republican candidates for southern Senate seats in 1962 were Taylor W. O'Hearn in Louisiana, who lost to Russell Long with 24.4 percent of the vote; Rupert H. Emerson in Florida, who lost to George Smathers with 30 percent; and Claude L. Greene in North Carolina, who lost to Sam Ervin with 39.6 percent. Democratic incumbent Senator Herman Talmadge was unopposed in Georgia.

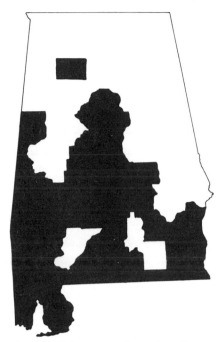

Fig. 4.6. Alabama counties voting 50 percent or more for Martin in the 1962 gubernatorial election

But in the southern House contests of 1962, the Republicans picked up
a net gain of four additional seats, all captured from Democrats by staunch
G.O.P. conservatives. In North Carolina's Ninth District (now the Tenth,
which harbors a large bloc of mountain Republicans), furniture executive
James T. Broyhill defeated an equally conservative Democrat, Hugh Q.
Alexander. In Florida's Eleventh, Winter Garden Mayor Edward T.
Gurney appealed to the growing conservatism of the Orlando-Cape
Canaveral area more effectively than did Democrat John A. Sutton. In
the Texas Sixteenth, which includes El Paso and in 1962 also included the
intensely conservative oil oases of Midland and Odessa, Goldwater Republican Ed Foreman successfully cashed in on the Billie Sol Estes scandal,
which touched many embarrassed Democrats who had benefited from
Estes's strategic campaign contributions, including the Sixteenth's incumbent, Democrat J. T. Rutherford. And in the Tennessee Third, the old
Chattanooga-based congressional district of Estes Kefauver, candy-manu-
facturer William E. Brock defeated a liberal Democrat, Wilkes T. Thrasher.
These gains represented a 36 percent increase in the size of the southern
Republican House delegation, the largest since Eisenhower's coattails
carried four new Republican congressmen to Washington in 1952. Electoral inactivity during 1963 belied the intensive and ultimately successful

efforts of conservative Republicans to line up state delegations behind the presidential candidacy of Senator Goldwater.

Only in Mississippi was a statewide general election held. There, in the emotional backwash of the previous year's violence at "Ole Miss," Democratic Lieutenant Governor Paul Johnson defeated former Governor J. P. Coleman in the runoff Democratic primary, in which Johnson featured the slogan "Stand Tall With Paul," in reference to his having stood in the schoolhouse door at "Ole Miss" the previous year to bar entrance to James Meredith. Given these excellent gubernatorial credentials and a history of no Republican opposition, under normal circumstances Johnson might well have regarded his runoff victory as tantamount to election. But these were not normal years, and the increasingly hungry Republicans mounted a powerful challenge even in Mississippi, nominating Rubel Phillips, a former Democratic public service commissioner, to oppose Johnson.[26] Both men ran less against each other than against the Kennedys, with Johnson engaging in wholesale racebaiting and Phillips urging voters to "KO the Kennedys." Although both candidates were conservatives on the segregation question, Phillips broadened his campaign appeal in a relatively progressive direction by calling for local option on liquor by the drink and a merit system in state employment. Johnson countered by equating the Mississippi Democratic party with the Mississippi way of life and warned that, should a two-party system evolve in Mississippi, white men would divide, and black men would hold the balance of power. Phillips carried only seven of Mississippi's eighty-two counties, but his 38.1 percent represented a quantum leap from the traditional moribund status of the Mississippi G.O.P., and in Jackson his majorities in black and upper-status white precincts resembled the coalition of blacks and suburbanites that had become so common in state Democratic factional politics.

Similarly, in neighboring Louisiana a newly energized state Republican party, characterized by a profoundly conservative consensus, moved to capitalize upon racial turmoil and popular discontent with the national Democratic party. Previously, Republicans in modern Louisiana history had never mounted a seriously threatening campaign for statewide office, preferring instead to concentrate on presidential elections and the dispensing of patronage that ensued from national victory. In 1952, moderate Republicans centered in New Orleans and, led by John Minor Wisdom, who was to become national committeeman, outmaneuvered the Old Guard delegation committed to Taft in a series of bitterly contested district and state conventions. The Wisdom delegation supported Eisenhower

---

[26]A useful state-by-state survey of southern Republican politics during the early and middle 1960s is a publication of the liberal Republican Ripon Society: John C. Topping, Jr., John R. Lazarek, and William H. Linder, *Southern Republicanism and the New South* (Cambridge, Mass., 1966).

in 1952, and subsequently Wisdom put together a biracial structure of state Republican leadership that was instrumental in carrying Louisiana for Eisenhower in 1956. Richard Nixon stood little chance against the Catholic Kennedy in Louisiana, and shortly after the 1960 presidential election, a group of well-financed and militantly conservative Republicans in Shreveport seized control of the state party from the moderate group.[27] Led by Charlton Lyons, the elderly but energetic owner of Lyons Petroleum Company, the new Republican leadership sought to take advantage of a divisive Democratic gubernatorial primary and runoff. Mayor deLesseps Morrison of New Orleans led the field of first-primary contenders and was thrown into the runoff against John McKeithen, public service commissioner in the northern Louisiana district that Huey Long once represented and long a protégé of Earl Long (his campaign was managed by Earl Long's widow, Mrs. Blanche Long).

In the runoff primary in early 1964, the politically adroit McKeithen managed to campaign simultaneously as a Long loyalist, a reformer who would clean up the mess in Baton Rouge, and a "100 percent segregationist," but not a "hater." Morrison was unable to exploit the contradictions inherent in McKeithen's stance, as the latter rode the strength of anti-black feeling among whites, anti-Catholicism in the Protestant north, and the pull of the Long connection to victory in the January 11 runoff election with 52.2 percent of the vote. Faced with McKeithen's political savvy, the sixty-nine-year-old Lyons called in outside support from Goldwater Republicans, and Louisiana was treated to visits from Ronald Reagan, Rubel Phillips, James Martin, and the Republican National Committee Chairman, Congressman William Miller. McKeithen responded, predictably, that "we Louisiana Democrats are determined to repel this second invasion by the carpetbaggers"[28] and repeatedly reiterated, with tongue heavily in cheek, his respect for his "honorable *elderly* opponent." Faced with such political acumen (Louisianans expected and often rewarded entertainment in their gubernatorial elections; indeed, the incumbent governor, Jimmie Davis, was chiefly famous for writing "You Are My Sunshine"), Lyons did well in the March 3 general election to accumulate 38.5 percent of the vote. As was the case with Phillips in Mississippi, Lyons's respectable showing had created a viable two-party option for statewide office in Louisiana for the first time, but like Phillips, he too had lost. Both contests clearly suggested that the racial unrest popularly associated with the civil-rights stand of the national Democratic party had thrown the Deep South into political turmoil.

---

[27]See Vines, *Two Parties for Shreveport*; Topping, Lazarek, and Linder, *Southern Republicanism and the New South*, pp. 68–74; and Perry H. Howard, *Political Tendencies in Louisiana* (Baton Rouge: Louisiana State University Press, 1971), pp. 379–97.

[28]As quoted in *New Orleans Times-Picayune*, February 4, 1964.

But the major ideological targets for conservative southern Republicans were not in the Deep South. These were liberal Democratic Senators Ralph Yarborough of Texas and Albert Gore of Tennessee, who were up for reelection in 1964, and with them Democratic Senate nominee Ross Bass of Tennessee, who was running in a special election occasioned by the death of Estes Kefauver and who had beaten previously undefeated Governor Frank Clement in the primary. The Texas battle was a classic donnybrook. Winning in the Republican primary the mandate to oppose the unapologetically liberal Yarborough was George Bush, a handsome and urbane Houston oil executive whose father, Prescott Bush, had been a senator from Connecticut. Bush declared his "enthusiastic support" for presidential nominee Barry Goldwater and established his credentials by campaigning against the 1964 Civil Rights Act, medicare, and attempts to solve the poverty problem through "left-wing spending programs."[29] In response to Kennedy's Bay of Pigs fiasco, Bush advocated recognition of an anti-Castro Cuban government in exile and stated: "When this government goes to liberate its homeland let's not be lacking in courage" but commit ourselves to "the support of it militarily and economically."[30] As the November general election neared and Goldwater's campaign outside the Deep South and his home state of Arizona was obviously collapsing, the rhetoric in the Texas Senate race grew nastier. Bush called Yarborough a "Reuther-controlled radical of the left" and a member of a "militant, mean little band of left wingers" in the Senate. Yarborough countered in fiery east Texas oratory that even though strontium 90 fallout was causing sterility and leukemia, Bush opposed the nuclear test ban treaty.

When the votes were counted, Bush had bettered Nixon's 1960 total in Texas by more than 12,000 votes and Goldwater's by greater than 175,000, but he nevertheless lost to Yarborough, whose 1,463,958 votes represented 56.2 percent of the Senate vote. (Johnson amassed 1,663,185 in overwhelming Goldwater in the president's home state.) Conservative Governor John Connally, cruising to reelection, refused to endorse Yarborough. The precinct returns from Fort Worth illustrated in figure 4.7 reflect Yarborough's success in holding together the New Deal coalition.

The same successful reconstruction of the New Deal coalition characterized the two Tennessee Senate races, although with a revealing wrinkle. There the Republicans could count on their mountain base in east Tennessee and the growing antipathy to Johnson's civil-rights policies in delta west Tennessee, in addition to the fact that Tennessee had not voted Democratic in a presidential election since 1948. Facing Gore was a Memphis executive for Proctor and Gamble, Dan H. Kuykendall, a largely unknown but aggressive Goldwater Republican who campaigned with surprising

---

[29]As quoted in Topping, Lazarek, and Linder, *Southern Republicanism and the New South*, p. 111.

[30]As quoted in *The Texas Observer*, October 30, 1964, pp. 4–6.

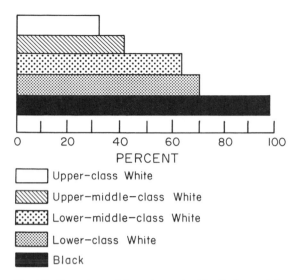

Fig. 4.7. Percentage of the vote received by Yarborough in Fort Worth in the 1964 senatorial election, by socio-economic class and race

vigor and effectiveness. Bass's opponent was Howard Baker, Jr., a thirty-eight-year-old Knoxville attorney whose Republican credentials were impeccable; both his father (1950–63) and his mother (1963–64) had served as Republicans in the House, and his father-in-law was Senate Minority Leader Everett McKinley Dirksen of Illinois. On election day both challengers left east Tennessee with hefty majorities, as Republican candidates have traditionally done in Tennessee; both took a severe beating in middle Tennessee, home of both Democratic nominees; and both scored well enough in racially sensitive west Tennessee to put a scare into Gore and Bass, but not enough to beat them. Even in defeat Kuykendall's 46.4 percent and Baker's 47.4 percent exceeded Goldwater's 44.5 percent and greatly surpassed the best efforts of all Republican challengers for statewide office in Tennessee since the 1920s.

What was most unusual about the Tennessee contest, however, was the unprecedented degree to which the class base of the New Deal coalition virtually disappeared in Memphis. The marked contrast between the pattern of white voter support which Albert Gore received in Nashville and that which he received in Memphis is clear from table 4.7. The same thing happened to Ross Bass and Lyndon Johnson in Memphis. Tennessee voting returns had long reflected strong tripartite sectional differences but rarely a phenomenon of this magnitude. The candidacy of Barry Goldwater essentially obliterated the traditional class differences among white voters in cities of the Deep South, which certainly includes Memphis, but not in cities of the Rim South, where racial fears were not strong enough to over-

Table 4.7

Percentage of the Vote for Gore in 1964
in Nashville and Memphis,
by Socioeconomic Class and Race

Vote category	Nashville		Memphis	
	Percentage of vote received	$(N)^a$	Percentage of vote received	$(N)^a$
Black	96.9	(10,600)	98.5	(11,986)
Lower-class white	68.2	(6,742)	35.0	(5,834)
Lower-middle-class white	67.4	(6,094)	34.3	(12,073)
Upper-middle-class white	60.7	(13,745)	36.2	(10,235)
Upper-class white	25.6	(25,121)	29.9	(12,607)
County vote[b]	64.9	(121,522)	52.9	(204,769)

[a](N) denotes the number of votes upon which the percentages are based.

[b]County-vote percentages are based on the total number of votes cast in the county.

come old New Deal loyalties among lower-income whites and strong reservations about Goldwater's hostility to TVA, social security, and other economic mainstays of the New Deal tradition.

Goldwater's appeal among white voters in the Deep South was so powerful that he reversed a century of history: he pulled all five Deep South states—Alabama, Georgia, Louisiana, Mississippi, and South Carolina—into the Republican column for the first time (excluding Louisiana, which had voted for Eisenhower in 1956) since Reconstruction. The black-belt counties of the South, which had cast 57.8 percent of their votes for Kennedy in 1960, cast 59.6 percent for Goldwater, although his extreme conservatism repelled the populist Republicans of the mountain counties, where the Republican majority of 56.5 percent in 1960 was reduced to a minority of 48.1 percent in 1964. The strange election of 1964 reflected that kind of trade-off all the way around, as the voting percentages in table 4.8 indicate. The parishes of Catholic Louisiana, for instance, having cast only 24.0 percent of their vote for Nixon in 1960, gave 47.3 percent to Goldwater; conversely, the counties of west Texas, which had voted 51.6 percent Republican in 1960, gave only 37.0 percent of their votes to Goldwater. The Southwide county correlations between successive pairs of Republican presidential votes, which registered a highly positive .83 for 1952–56 and .81 for 1956–60, fell to a near-random .21 for 1960–64.[31] Goldwater's most dramatic percentage gains over Nixon's performance

[31]The equivalent Democratic correlations reflected the same marked trend from high continuity to discontinuity: Pearson's r for the Democratic presidential vote in 1952 and 1956 was .84; for 1956 and 1960, it was .82; and for 1960 and 1964, it plummeted to .21.

were in the black belt and in Catholic Louisiana, but the relative contribution of these two categories of counties to the total two-party vote was small. He fell off substantially in the mountains and in south Florida, west Texas, and Mexican-American Texas and, most importantly, the Republican share of the South's metropolitan vote, which had soared since World War II and had not fallen below 50 percent since 1948, fell with Goldwater to 47.2. In the cities of the Deep South, Goldwater swamped Johnson with 60.6 percent of the vote, but in the peripheral cities, where more than twice as many votes were cast as in the Deep South cities (4,282,173 as compared with 1,275,958), Johnson crushed Goldwater with 56.6 percent of their heavier vote.

The Republicans paid the price of national disaster for Goldwater's Southern Strategy, of course, as Johnson's national majority of 61.1 percent was exceeded only by Roosevelt's triumph in 1936. Goldwater's alienation of black voters in the South clearly cost him the states of Arkansas, Florida, Tennessee, and Virginia, and apparently North Carolina as well, although white majorities in every southern state but Texas appear to have voted for Goldwater.[32] Furthermore, the ideological salience of the 1964 election increased voter turnout by approximately one-third in the Deep South and one-sixth in the Rim South. With so many new voters

Table 4.8

Percentage of the Vote for Nixon and Goldwater in 1960 and 1964, by Geographic and Demographic Category

	Percentage of the Two-party vote, 1964	Percentage vote for Nixon, 1960	Percentage vote for Goldwater, 1964	Percentage Republican Gain or Loss between 1960 and 1964
Geographic category				
White belt	32.5	43.2	50.9	+7.7
Piedmont	17.5	45.2	49.9	+4.7
Mountain	12.5	56.5	48.1	−8.4
West Texas	11.5	51.6	37.0	−14.6
South Florida	11.3	54.6	47.1	−7.5
Black belt	9.1	33.4	59.6	+26.2
Catholic Louisiana	3.8	24.0	47.3	+23.3
South Texas	1.8	39.5	30.8	−8.7
Demographic category				
Metropolitan	45.1	50.0	47.2	−2.8
Rural	40.8	42.4	49.1	+6.7
Urban	14.1	44.2	51.9	+7.7
Region	100.0	47.6	48.7	+1.1

[32]Southern Regional Council, "What Happened in the South?" (mimeographed).

Table 4.9

Percentage of the Vote for Goldwater in 1964
in Mobile and Jackson
by Socioeconomic Class and Race

Vote category	Mobile		Jackson	
	Percentage of vote received	$(N)^a$	Percentage of vote received	$(N)^a$
Lower-class white	80.1	(1,304)	93.7	(4,228)
Lower-middle-class white	81.6	(1,482)	95.6	(6,111)
Upper-middle-class white	81.1	(1,580)	93.5	(3,951)
Upper-class white	80.6	(1,436)	91.1	(5,170)
Black	.5	(747)	42.8	(1,508)
County vote[b]	70.7	(69,981)	87.9	(41,889)

[a](N) denotes the number of votes upon which the percentages are based.

[b]County-vote percentages are based on the total number of votes cast in the county.

flocking to the polls in the South, most of them white, established patterns of political behavior were shattered, and the sectional trade-offs were particularly dramatic in the contest for southern House seats. In Texas, the Republicans' two ultraconservative congressmen, Ed Foreman in El Paso and five-termer Bruce Alger in Dallas, were swamped in the Johnson landslide.[33]

In the Deep South, however, the Goldwater landslide swept into office seven new Republican congressmen, five in volatile Alabama, where they were the first Republican congressmen elected in the twentieth century, and one each in Georgia and Mississippi, in both cases the first since Reconstruction. An appreciation of the extreme racial polarization and the utter devastation visited upon the Democrats' New Deal coalition can be gleaned by an inspection of voting patterns in Mobile, Alabama, and Jackson, Mississippi. (Black precinct returns for Mobile are typical for the 1964 election, but in Jackson residential integration of the Old South type and continuing disfranchisement of most blacks made all-black precincts almost impossible to identify.) In such a lopsided partisan climate, the ranks of Alabama's all-Democratic, eight-man House delegation were decimated. Incumbents Bob Jones and George Andrews were fortunate enough to lack Republican opposition, and veteran Armestead Seldon managed narrowly to survive defeat by Republican challenger Robert French. But three

[33]Having been redistricted out of his conservative bastions in Midland and Odessa, Foreman lost to El Paso lawyer Richard White, a moderate Democrat. The reactionary Alger was defeated by former Dallas Mayor Earle Cabell, a conservative Democrat, who, unlike Senator Yarborough, enjoyed the active support of Governor John Connally.

other Democratic incumbents went under: George Huddleston was defeated by John Buchanan in Birmingham; George Grant of Troy lost to William Dickenson of Montgomery; and Kenneth Roberts of Piedmont lost to Glenn Andrews of Anniston. In one swoop the voters in these three Alabama districts wiped out fifty-two years of seniority in the House. Additionally, Republican Jack Edwards defeated Democratic nominee John Tyson of Mobile, and James E. Martin, having so narrowly lost to Lister Hill in the Senate race of 1962, easily defeated George Hawkins of Gadsden. In Mississippi, Republican Prentiss Walker defeated eleven-term incumbent W. Arthur Winstead, and in Georgia, Howard H. Callaway defeated former Lieutenant Governor Garland T. Byrd.

The Goldwater sweep of 1964 and the transformation of southern Republicanism that it signified should not be exaggerated. Lyndon Johnson won a smashing victory nationally and even a majority of the southern vote, and the major victims of the Republican's Southern Strategy of 1964, the seven hapless Democratic congressmen, were on the whole little less conservative than the men who displaced them. Also, the movement's major ideological targets in the South, Senators Yarborough and Gore and Democratic nominee Bass, were all elected, albeit for the last time.[34] Four conservative southern Democrats, Senators Harry F. Byrd of Virginia and Spessard Holland of Florida and Governors John Connally of Texas and Haydon Burns of Florida, rather easily turned back their conservative Republican challengers. And the two Republican challengers who were not conservatives, Winthrop Rockefeller in Arkansas and Robert Gavin in North Carolina, made impressive if losing races against Democrats Orval Faubus and Dan Moore, respectively. Even so, the racial turmoil and social unrest of the 1960s were making a shambles of the Democrats' New Deal coalition, and one-party politics was clearly coming to an end throughout the South. To survive this onslaught, the Southern Democrats were to devise a new tactic, or more precisely, to resurrect an old one, namely, the racebaiting that had so successfully destroyed the Populists and blunted Republican fusion in the 1890s. The combined efforts of the Southern Regional Council's Voter Education Project and the voting rights act of 1965 had prompted a surge of voter registration throughout the South that during the 1960s added an estimated six million new names to the rolls, of which roughly 30 percent belonged to blacks and 70 percent to whites,[35]

[34]Bass was defeated by Frank Clement in the Democratic primary in 1966, and Clement, looking a bit long in the tooth to an electorate that was tiring of the old war-horses, was in turn defeated by Republican Howard Baker in the general election. In 1970 Ralph Yarborough fell before conservative Democrat Lloyd Bentsen in the Texas primary, and in Tennessee Albert Gore was edged by Republican Congressman William Brock of Chattanooga.

[35]*Political Participation*; and Voter Education Project, "Voter Registration in the South: Spring-Summer, 1970" (mimeographed).

and majorities of both races continued to identify themselves as Democrats. Southern politicians were not unmindful of this arithmetic, and in response to it the threatened Democrats counterattacked with the newly enfranchised army of poor whites. To Charles Morgan, a white civil libertarian from Birmingham, the new message was clear: "My God. The galoots are loose."[36]

[36]As quoted in Marshall Frady, *Wallace* (New York: World, 1968), p. 177.

CHAPTER 5

THE POLITICS OF TURMOIL

The surging civil-rights movement, with its sit-ins, demonstrations, and protests that challenged the social status quo across the South, climaxed with passage of the 1964 civil rights law, which broke the back of Jim Crow and brought down the "White" and "Colored" signs that had adorned the public restrooms and drinking fountains across the region. Harried state legislators had hardly mapped redistricting plans to conform to the one man-one vote principle laid down by the U.S. Supreme Court in *Baker* v. *Carr* (1962) and *Reynolds* v. *Sims* (1964) before federal examiners arrived in fifty-eight southern counties to insure compliance with the 1965 voting rights act and to assist in opening the franchise to the sizable number of black southerners still barred from the polls. Not since Reconstruction had the federal government displayed such an active interest in social and political practices in the South.

One result of the heightening racial controversy was a vastly increased voter turnout, and survey data indicate that these new voters were over-whelmingly blacks and lower-status whites (see figure 5.1). Voter turnout during the 1950s demonstrated the traditional twentieth-century pattern of southern politics: the higher-status whites voted; the lower-status whites sometimes voted; and the blacks voted little at all. In presidential elections approximately eight out of ten of the better-educated whites cast ballots, and this turnout remained relatively consistent throughout the period. Black voter participation shot upward in the 1960s. Whereas less than a quarter of black respondents said they voted during the 1950s, in 1964, for the first time, more than 50 percent of black southerners went to the polls, and this figure continued to climb more rapidly than white turnout during the late 1960s. In terms of actual numbers of voters, however, the greatest increase in voter participation came from the less-educated whites. During the 1950s little better than half of the whites who had not finished high school turned out, but by 1964 the less-educated whites were almost as apt to cast ballots as the better-educated. Figure 5.1 divides whites according to education completed, and similar results are obtained by dividing them into blue- and white-collar occupation categories or into high- and low-income

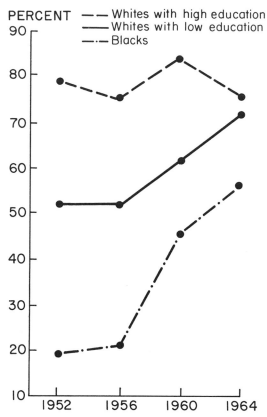

Fig. 5.1. Voter turnout in presidential elections, 1952–64, by race and education. Data are from the Survey Research Center, University of Michigan. Respondents were from Kentucky, Maryland, Oklahoma, West Virginia, and the District of Columbia, as well as from the eleven former Confederate states. See the Note on Methodology and Data Sources preceding the Bibliographical Essay.

groups. The white common folks, of limited education, blue-collar occupational status, and lower income, provided a majority of the votes that pushed voter turnout in the South to twentieth-century record levels during the heated political struggles of the late 1960s.

A favorite of these voters was Lester G. Maddox, whose reputation extended well beyond the boundaries of his home state of Georgia. Owner of the prosperous Pickrick restaurant in Atlanta, which specialized in fried chicken and a family atmosphere, Maddox had adamantly opposed the emerging civil-rights movement. He was active in a number of white-supremacy organizations, including the Citizens' Councils and Georgians Unwilling to Surrender (GUTS). He militantly turned back efforts by sit-in demonstrators to desegregate the Pickrick, on one occasion displaying a pistol to prevent blacks from entering his restaurant. He publicized his position by picketing the 1964 Democratic National Convention, the Atlanta federal court, and the White House. When the 1964 civil-rights bill became law, he refused to desegregate his restaurant, temporarily converting it into a curiosity shop specializing in the sale of items like axe handles, labeled "Pickrick Drumsticks," and ultimately selling it, still determinedly holding out against desegregation in any form.[1]

Maddox carried his personal vendetta against civil rights into the political arena. He made his first campaign in 1957, when he unsuccessfully attempted to dislodge William B. Hartsfield, the moderate mayor of Atlanta. Four years later, after Hartsfield announced his intention to retire, Maddox tried again, running second among five candidates and entering a bitterly contested runoff campaign with Ivan Allen, Jr., a businessman and the progressive former head of the city chamber of commerce. In his mayoral campaigns, Maddox fervently championed the virtues of segregation, free enterprise, and Protestant fundamentalism and often associated social and ideological change with communism. He won impressive majorities in white working-class precincts, but both Hartsfield and Allen combined solid black and upper-status white support for substantial majorities. But Maddox persisted. In 1962 he sought the Democratic nomination for lieutenant governor. He did well enough in the primary to force a runoff contest, where he made a respectable but unsuccessful showing against the veteran incumbent, Peter Zack Geer. Increasingly, however, Maddox's antics, inflammatory statements, and tendency toward bizarre behavior attracted the attention of the national media; by 1966, when he entered the Democratic primary for governor, he was one of the South's better-known exponents of white supremacy.

Few political observers considered Maddox a leading contender in the governor's race. Indeed, many found it difficult to take seriously the earnest little man with thick glasses, balding head, and rather flat, yet whiny voice who insisted that the 1964 Civil Rights Act was "inspired and supported by deadly and bloody communism."[2] His campaign was woefully financed, and he had virtually no organization in a state where county elites had traditionally played a prominent role in swaying the votes in rural-small town areas. Maddox traversed the countryside in a Pontiac station wagon, pasting on telephone poles, trees, and billboards small signs that read "THIS IS MADDOX COUNTRY" and defending God, liberty, free enterprise, and states' rights before any crowd he could attract.

[1]Bruce Galphin, *The Riddle of Lester Maddox* (Atlanta: Camelot, 1968), pp. 47–68.
[2]From the sign on the Pickrick announcing its closing in 1965. On this period of Georgia politics, see Numan V. Bartley, *From Thurmond to Wallace: Political Tendencies in Georgia, 1948–1968* (Baltimore: Johns Hopkins Press, 1970); and Galphin, *The Riddle of Lester Maddox.*

The opposition was formidable. Generally considered the man to beat was former Governor Ellis G. Arnall, past leader of the anti-Talmadge faction in state politics and a remarkably successful governor during the World War II years. Arnall had been driven into political inactivity after the Talmadge forces consolidated their control of state politics, and he watched from the sidelines during the 1960s while the federal courts declared the county-unit system unconstitutional, and almost half a million new voters, about a quarter of them black, added their names to the registration rolls. The biggest gains came in the cities: almost a hundred thousand in Fulton County and approximately sixty thousand in Dekalb County (the two counties containing the city of Atlanta).[3] The Talmadge faction's success in state politics had in part rested upon its ability to manipulate the race issue and the county-unit system. Progressive candidates had traditionally done well in the cities, and especially in urban black residential areas. Now the cities were freed from the shackles of the county-unit system, and the voter rolls were swelling with new names, a majority of them urban and a significant number belonging to blacks. Arnall launched a progressive—by Georgia standards downright liberal—campaign to take advantage of the new situation. His effort was well-financed, and his longstanding contacts in the counties provided him with a strong campaign organization.

The Talmadge-oriented leadership generally favored state Democratic Party Chairman James H. Gray, owner of a newspaper and a television station in Albany. Like Maddox, Gray had supported Goldwater in the 1964 presidential election, and he presented staunchly conservative views on major issues during the campaign. Of the other three candidates, James E. Carter, a moderately progressive state senator, possessed sufficient resources and voter appeal to be an important contender in the election. And looming over the campaign was a new and uncertain threat. Republican Congressman Howard H. "Bo" Callaway, the wealthy heir to a textile fortune who had been swept into the House of Representatives by the Goldwater tide, was energetically preparing a major effort against the Democratic nominee in November. "If the election were held today," the *Atlanta Journal* editorialized a few months prior to the Democratic primary, "Republican Rep. Bo Callaway would win in a walk."[4]

Arnall finished first in the primary balloting, but his 29.4 percent was a disappointment for the candidate widely considered the front runner. Maddox came in second, with 23.6 percent, narrowly beating out Carter, who polled 21 percent, and Gray, who got just less than 20 percent. In the runoff Arnall's exposed liberal flank made him vulnerable to Maddox's

[3]Registration statistics are from the office of the Georgia Secretary of State and from Voter Education Project, *V.E.P. News* 2 (April 1968).
[4]*Atlanta Journal*, May 25, 1966.

white common-man appeal. Arnall had run well in metropolitan counties, but in the 1966 primary elections a majority of the votes were cast in the hinterlands, and that was "Maddox country." When the ballots were in, Maddox had won a solid victory, with more than 54 percent of the vote. Arnall captured the cities, where he won virtually unanimous support in black precincts and solid majorities in affluent white neighborhoods. But Maddox won substantial majorities in lower- and middle-income white areas to hold Arnall's margins in the metropolitan counties to just under 60 percent (see figure 5.2). In the countryside he was impregnable, amassing a 64 percent majority.

The Republican camp was at first overjoyed with the results of the runoff election, since Maddox's erratic behavior still made it difficult for observers to take him seriously. Now the Democratic nominee for governor, Maddox had access to greater financial and organizational resources, and he had the support of the bulk of the county courthouses across the state, but he could still hardly match the generously financed, tightly organized Callaway campaign. Callaway took ultraconservative positions on social and economic issues, thereby avoiding the pitfall that had entrapped Arnall, that of being the liberal candidate in an election year when the race issue was paramount. But where Callaway interrupted his campaign to fly

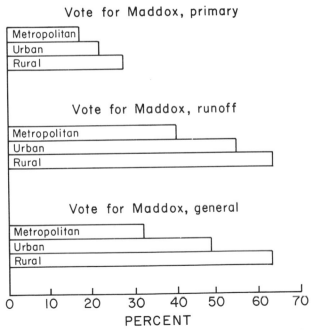

Fig. 5.2. Percentage of the vote received by Maddox in metropolitan, urban, and rural counties in Georgia in 1966

to Washington to vote against extension of the minimum wage act, Maddox identified with the workers and the common whites. Black and liberal white activists, appalled by the choice between Maddox and Callaway, organized a "Write-In, Georgia" campaign with Arnall as its candidate. The write-in movement attracted a sufficient number of votes, mainly in black areas, to deny either major party candidate a majority. Almost one million Georgians, approximately 40 percent of the voting-age population, cast ballots in the election, which in terms of total number of voters was an all-time high turnout for a Georgia state election, failing only to measure up to the turnout for the 1964 presidential contest. Callaway came in first, with a plurality of 46.5 percent; and Maddox was about three thousand votes behind, with 46.2 percent. Since Georgia had no provisions for a runoff contest in the general election, the solidly Democratic state legislature chose Maddox as governor.

Callaway's showing in the cities was impressive. He collected far more ballots than Arnall had won in the runoff, leading Maddox by better than two to one in metropolitan counties. In Atlanta and Macon, Callaway carried the black precincts, won heavily in affluent white neighborhoods, and even limited the expected Maddox majorities in lower-status white

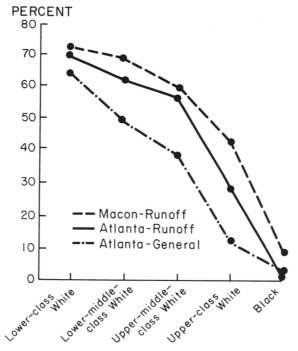

Fig. 5.3. Percentage of the vote received by Maddox in Macon and Atlanta in 1966, by socioeconomic class and race

areas. As before, Maddox demonstrated a magnetic appeal in the country-side, where he led Callaway by approximately 117,000 votes, just short of enough to offset the Republican's 120,000 margin in the cities and larger towns.

In the primary, runoff, and general elections, Maddox combined the rural-small town voters in the counties with working-class whites in the cities to win the Democratic nomination and, with aid from the state legislature, the governor's office. Such were the political alignments over much of the South. Passage of the epic civil-rights measures of 1964 and 1965 brought long-developing but conflicting trends into stark confrontation. The breakdown of disfranchisement, caste, and the one-party system combined with the continuing growth of urbanization and industrialization to create the conditions that some had hoped would be conducive to a politics of New Deal reform. But the social upheavals taking place in the region simultaneously fed "the darker strains in southern politics." While such progressive Democrats as Arnall sought to benefit from the burgeoning registration rolls and to orient politics in a more liberal direction, avid racists like Maddox seized upon the white reaction to rally the common whites, as had the demagogues of an earlier period.[5] And in the wings southern Republicans maneuvered to take advantage of the bitter divisions within the Democracy and to ride the long-heralded two-party trend to victory.

Symbolizing the white reaction was Governor George Corley Wallace of Alabama. First elected governor in 1962, Wallace made good his campaign promise to stand in the schoolhouse door, briefly blocking desegregation of the University of Alabama in 1963 in a televised charade that helped to establish Wallace's place as a leader of what nationally was being termed "the white backlash." In 1964 he carried his crusade against social and ideological change outside the South by entering the Democratic presidential primary elections in Wisconsin, Indiana, and Maryland, where he did surprisingly well and achieved massive publicity.[6] When the G.O.P. nominated Goldwater, Wallace reluctantly abandoned his plans for a third-party effort. As governor he presided over Alabama during the tumultuous civil-rights demonstrations in Birmingham and the Selma march to Montgomery, always condemning the demonstrators and sometimes publicly linking their activities to communist subversion. But while reactionary on social issues, the Wallace administration was relatively

[5]The political rhetoric was less inflammatory than it had been in the past. Serious candidates shunned the old style "niggerbaiting." Although many did defend segregation, they most frequently substituted attacks on the federal government and its social planners and "pointyheaded" bureaucrats, on communism and the alleged relationship between civil-rights agitation and subversion, and on liberalism and President Johnson's Great Society.

[6]Running against stand-ins for President Johnson, Wallace won approximately 34 percent in Wisconsin, 30 percent in Indiana, and 43 percent in Maryland.

progressive in economic matters, launching substantial programs for construction of junior colleges and vocational schools and generally increasing state spending for education, roads, and other state services. Wallace talked the language of the common white folks in Alabama, and his program provided them with some positive benefits.

The Alabama constitution did not allow a governor to succeed himself, and when a group of anti-Wallace state senators filibustered to prevent passage of a state constitutional amendment that would allow the governor to be reelected, Wallace announced that his wife, Lurleen Burns Wallace, would seek the Democratic nomination. Mrs. Wallace, who had never displayed any particular interest in political matters, dutifully made the race. On the campaign trail, she normally presented dignified, rather homey little talks and then turned the podium over to her husband, who continued to demonstrate an impressive ability to voice the hopes, fears, and prejudices of average white people in Alabama.

Mrs. Wallace had nine opponents. Attorney General Richmond Flowers campaigned as a liberal and vigorously sought the votes of the quarter-million registered blacks, a majority of whom were newly enfranchised.[7] Former Congressman Carl Elliott, a loyal New Deal-Fair Deal economic liberal who had lost his House seat in a confusing statewide at-large election in 1962, sought to restore the populist-New Deal voting alignments of the past. State Senator Bob Gilchrist, a leader in the filibuster that had prevented Wallace from directly making the primary campaign, took a moderately conservative position on most social and economic issues. The election offered voters a range of choices, encompassing the avid racism of the Wallaces, the moderate conservatism of Gilchrist, the older New Deal liberalism of Elliott, and the newer interracial liberalism of Flowers.

Voters turned out in record numbers to devastate the liberal-moderate cause. Mrs. Wallace swamped the field, winning a first-primary victory with 54 percent of the votes, a feat not accomplished since Folsom's first-primary triumph in 1954. The Wallaces overwhelmed the opposition in rural areas and even in the larger towns; only among metropolitan voters did they fail to win a majority. (Mrs. Wallace won majorities in the counties containing Mobile, Gadsden, and Tuscaloosa and pluralities in Montgomery, Birmingham, and Huntsville.) In the cities Mrs. Wallace ran up heavy majorities in lower- and middle-class white precincts. Flowers won the bulk of the votes in black districts, as well as majorities in two black-belt counties with large black registration, and finished second in the race with approximately 20 percent of the votes.

[7]V.E.P. News 2 (April 1968); Donald S. Strong, "Alabama: Transition and Alienation," in The Changing Politics of the South, ed. William C. Havard (Baton Rouge: Louisiana State University Press, 1972), pp. 442–58.

The Democratic primary dashed Republican hopes. Earlier, when Wallace was unable to push the gubernatorial succession amendment through the state legislature, 1966 appeared to be shaping up as a G.O.P. year in Alabama. Even after Wallace adopted the ploy of running his wife, Republicans could optimistically search for a negative voter reaction to such a transparent tactic. But after the primary election, few such hopes remained. The G.O.P. candidate was James Martin, who had carried the "spirit of 61" to near victory against Lister Hill and who now campaigned on the theme "Beat LBJ the Jim Martin Way."[8] But with the man who had vowed never to be "out-niggered" again spearheading the opposition, the "spirit of 61" paled into insignificance. Martin's cause was hopeless. The Wallaces won 63.4 percent of the votes and ravaged Republican ranks in the process. Senator Sparkman, who was considered vulnerable, cruised to an easy victory on the Democratic ticket over John Grenier, an adept organizer but an uninspiring campaigner. The Republicans saved three of the five congressional seats they had won in 1964, and they picked up a state senate seat, but every other G.O.P. candidate went down in flames, as the party lost all of the thirty-three local offices that it had captured in 1964.

The Wallaces won everywhere. They massively swept the rural counties and the larger towns, and they won in the cities by smaller though still substantial majorities. White working-class districts delivered whopping majorities, and the Wallaces even fared reasonably well in black neighborhoods, as Negro voters divided between a straight Democratic ticket, Martin, and an independent candidate. The beachheads Martin had established in the southern lowland counties in his 1962 race against Hill collapsed; he won less than one of every four votes cast in the southern half of the state. Martin ended up with 31 percent of the votes, well under half the Wallace total.

The Mississippi gubernatorial primary elections of 1967 were both a reflection and a parody of the political atmosphere prevailing over much of the South. One of the seven entries in the contest was former Governor Ross Barnett, who like Wallace had stood in the schoolhouse door at the state university and had achieved a deserved reputation for segregationist fanaticism, but by 1967 standards he appeared sometimes to border on moderation. Jimmie Swan, a Hattiesburg country-music singer, easily captured the position on the extreme right of the political spectrum. Making white supremacy virtually his only campaign issue, Swan promised to be "what Bilbo was to the State of Mississippi,"[9] and he quoted approv-

---

[8]"State of the Southern States: Alabama," *New South* 21 (Fall 1966): 97. On the election, see generally Marshall Frady, *Wallace* (New York: World, 1968).
    [9]As quoted in "State of the Southern States: Mississippi," *New South* 22 (Spring 1967): 98.

ingly from former Senator Theodore G. Bilbo's book *Take Your Choice: Separation or Mongrelization.*[10] Only slightly less reactionary was Citizens' Council stalwart John Bell Williams, a nominally Democratic Mississippi congressman who had been deprived of his seniority as punishment for his open support of Barry Goldwater in 1964.

While Barnett and Williams unsuccessfully competed with Swan for the extreme right in the campaign, state Treasurer William Winter projected a refreshingly moderate image. Almost 60 percent of Mississippi's voting-age population, a massive turnout by twentieth-century standards, gave Winter a plurality with something less than a third of the vote. Finishing second, Williams emerged as the strongest of the conservative candidates. In Jackson Winter won solidly in black precincts and carried upper-income white neighborhoods by pluralities, while Williams won pluralities in white working-class areas. Although Winter ran first in the primary, he was the underdog in the runoff, since Williams was in a favorable position to (and apparently did) pick up most of the votes cast for Swan and Barnett, who finished third and fourth, respectively. In the runoff, voter turnout was again impressive, as the campaign featured a clear choice between staunch social conservatism and moderation. As he had done in the first primary, Winter won handily in black neighborhoods and carried affluent white precincts. He also fared relatively well in heavily black Delta counties. But Williams, like Maddox and Wallace, swept lower-income white neighborhoods and most of the rural counties to win 54 percent of the votes (see table 5.1).

Table 5.1
Percentage of the Vote for Williams in 1967 in Jackson,
by Socioeconomic Class and Race

Vote category	Primary		Runoff	
	Percentage of vote received	$(N)^a$	Percentage of vote received	$(N)^a$
Lower-class white	39.7	(4,352)	70.9	(4,379)
Lower-middle-class white	40.1	(7,502)	64.9	(7,440)
Upper-middle-class white	32.5	(3,975)	52.6	(4,039)
Upper-class white	26.6	(6,224)	46.0	(6,523)
Black	13.1	(3,342)	21.6	(3,827)
Hinds County[b]	32.5	(53,505)	52.9	(55,469)

[a](N) denotes the number of votes upon which the percentages are based.

[b]County-vote percentages are based on the total number of votes cast in the county.

[10]Poplarville, Miss.: Dream House, 1947.

Swan's rabidly racist and unsuccessful campaign in Mississippi was similar to that of Congressman John R. Rarick in Louisiana. Rarick, who one Louisiana observer characterized as "against everything that's taken place in the world since the invention of the wheel,"[11] attempted to unseat Governor John J. McKeithen by portraying the governor as a moderate. McKeithen, whose segregationist campaign against Mayor Morrison of New Orleans in 1963 was justly regarded as something of a classic, wasn't vulnerable on the right, and he had won the support of New Orleans by trading his support for the construction of the "superdome" in exchange for New Orlean's support for a constitutional amendment permitting him to run for a second consecutive term as governor. He won renomination by a convincing margin. As the Swans and Raricks demonstrated, racism alone was insufficient for victory, but as the Arnalls and Flowerses and Winters also demonstrated, the absence of it was more often fatal during the political wars of 1966 and 1967.

In Arkansas former Citizens' Council leader and state Supreme Court Justice James D. Johnson won the Democratic nomination for governor. Orval Faubus decided to step down, at long last in the view of most of his prospective opponents, thus opening the way for a wide-open primary in 1966. Carrying the progressive banner was former Congressman Brooks Hays, an able and articulate spokesman for New South progressivism.[12] Hays had been dislodged from his House seat during the Little Rock desegregation crisis by school board member Dale Alford, who in turn surrendered the seat when he became odd man out in a redistricting plan following the 1960 census. Alford, who apparently liked impossible causes, had attempted to outflank Faubus on the racial issue in the 1962 gubernatorial primary and now sought to get to the right of the vigorously racist Johnson. The candidate of the Faubus camp was Jack Holt, who like Johnson was a former state supreme court justice.

Johnson ran sufficiently well in the rural counties of the southeastern lowlands to finish first in the primary election. Holt won a plurality in the mountains and came in second, well ahead of Hays and Alford. In the run-off Holt enjoyed strong organizational support, carrying such kept counties as Conway, Madison, and Newton by massive majorities, but Johnson won the bulk of the rural-small town counties and the election with 52 percent of the vote. In Little Rock Johnson carried the lower-income white precincts, though Holt won the city with huge majorities from black and affluent white precincts (see table 5.2).

Johnson's triumph proved to be short-lived, however, as Republican Winthrop Rockefeller won the general election. Rockefeller had made a

[11]"State of the Southern States: Louisiana," *New South* 21 (Fall 1966): 102, quoting former Congressman James E. Morrison.

[12]See Brooks Hays, *A Southern Moderate Speaks* (Chapel Hill: University of North Carolina Press, 1959).

Table 5.2
Percentage of the Vote for Johnson in 1966 in Little Rock,
by Socioeconomic Class and Race

Vote category	Primary		Runoff		General	
	Percentage of vote received	$(N)^a$	Percentage of vote received	$(N)^a$	Percentage of vote received	$(N)^a$
Lower-class white	18.5	(2,213)	54.3	(2,243)	54.0	(3,025)
Lower-middle-class white	20.5	(2,709)	56.9	(2,654)	46.4	(4,111)
Upper-middle-class white	11.3	(5,799)	41.5	(5,434)	32.4	(7,593)
Upper-class white	5.8	(3,266)	24.4	(3,243)	21.1	(4,828)
Black	9.9	(1,567)	22.2	(1,409)	19.0	(2,291)
Pulaski County[b]	13.5	(55,921)	40.3	(57,466)	35.1	(76,734)

[a](N) denotes the number of votes upon which the percentages are based.

[b]County-vote percentages are based on the total number of votes cast in the county.

creditable race for governor against Faubus two years previously and now commanded an efficient, well-financed organization. His relatively progressive position on race relations and other state problems generally contrasted with Johnson's reputation for colorful fanaticism. Not only did Johnson drive blacks, moderate whites, and even responsible conservatives into the Rockefeller camp, his free-swinging, vituperative attacks during the primaries on the Faubus administration, which was supporting Holt, and on his opponents (he called Holt a "pleasant vegetable") offended many of the party regulars and left the Democratic party in shambles.[13] Johnson's organizational weaknesses showed clearly in the returns from machine counties. He broke about even, for example, in Madison county, where as many as 104 percent of the eligible voters had cast ballots for Faubus in past primary elections. Johnson won a majority of the votes in rural-small town areas, but his margins even in the southeastern lowland counties were perilously thin, especially when compared with the massive support generated by Maddox and Wallace in kindred counties, which again testified to the differing political styles that prevailed from state to state. Rockefeller swept the cities and larger towns, winning more than three-quarters of the votes in affluent white precincts and doing even better in black districts in Little Rock, and won the election with a 54 percent majority. The G.O.P. also won the lieutenant governor's race, a congressional seat, and several local and state legislative contests.

[13]Richard E. Yates, "Arkansas: Independent and Unpredictable," in *The Changing Politics of the South*, ed. William C. Havard, pp. 275–85.

The Rockefeller victory in Arkansas was one of several breakthroughs, as Republicans made their most determined effort in the South in almost a century. Some G.O.P. candidates followed Rockefeller's example and campaigned as moderates. In Tennessee Howard Baker, Jr., won a U.S. Senate seat with a middle-of-the-road campaign, defeating Democratic Governor Frank Clement by a solid majority. Baker swept traditionally Republican east Tennessee and carried by a narrower margin the increasingly Republican western part of the state. Although black precincts remained heavily Democratic, Baker ran well among white voters generally in Memphis, and in Nashville he carried affluent white neighborhoods handily. In Mississippi Rubel Phillips, making his second gubernatorial campaign in 1967, uncovered considerably less support for moderate Republicanism, winning less than 30 percent of the vote, as Congressman John Bell Williams rode the ballots of rural and lower-income whites to an overwhelming victory.

But most G.O.P. candidates, emulating Callaway and Martin, sought to take advantage of voter disaffection with civil-rights legislation and Great Society liberalism by campaigning as hard-core conservatives. A mind-boggling example was Mississippi Congressman Prentiss Walker's 1966 campaign for the U.S. Senate. A poultry farmer swept into Congress by the Goldwater landslide, Walker attempted to unseat reactionary James O. Eastland, insisting that the incumbent senator was tainted with Great Society liberalism. Walker's valiant effort netted him little; he won hardly more than a quarter of the vote.

More serious was the Republican challenge in South Carolina. Senator J. Strom Thurmond had changed parties to campaign for Goldwater in 1964. Whether Dixiecrat, Democrat, or Republican, Thurmond was formidable at the polls in South Carolina, and with both U.S. Senate seats and the governor's office up for grabs in 1966, the G.O.P. grasped the opportunity and nominated strong contenders for a variety of state and local offices. With former Thurmond aide and state party chairman Harry Dent to plot strategy and Thurmond to grace the ticket, the Republicans named state Senator Marshall J. Parker as their candidate for the other Senate seat and state Representative Joseph O. Rogers, Jr., for governor. Like Thurmond, both were recent converts from the Democratic party. The Republican candidates took ultraconservative positions during the campaign, with Thurmond denouncing the Democratic party and calling President Johnson "a traitor to the South and to America."[14]

The Democrats were in their usual state of disarray. Donald Russell had resigned as governor to accept appointment to the Senate seat made vacant by the death of Senator Johnston. In the 1966 primaries, however,

[14]As quoted in "State of the Southern States: South Carolina," *New South* 21 (Fall 1966): 107. This election is ably analyzed in Donald L. Fowler, "Two-Party Politics: 1966," *University of South Carolina Governmental Review* 9 (May 1967).

former Governor Ernest F. Hollings defeated Russell to become Parker's opponent in the general election. State Senator Bradley Morrah, Jr., of Greenville, campaigning as a "South Carolina Democrat," downed a liberal challenger to win the dubious honor of opposing Thurmond for the other Senate seat. Lieutenant Governor Robert E. McNair, who became governor upon Russell's resignation, was the Democratic nominee for reelection. All the major Democratic candidates campaigned as conservatives, but none projected the hard rightwing image of their Republican opponents.

The election returns were a disappointment for the G.O.P. Senator Thurmond won reelection convincingly, and the Republicans retained their one House seat and increased their state legislative representation; nevertheless, the large majority of Republican candidates went down. Parker gave Hollings a close race for the other Senate seat, taking 48.7 percent of the votes, but Rogers lost substantially to McNair in the governor's race.

Table 5.3

Percentage of the Vote for Republican Candidates in 1966
in Charleston and Columbia,
by Socioeconomic Class and Race

Vote category	Thurmond		Parker		Rogers	
	Percentage of vote received	(N)[a]	Percentage of vote received	(N)[a]	Percentage of vote received	(N)[a]
Charleston						
Lower-class white	75.6	(1,331)	54.3	(1,400)	47.9	(1,408)
Lower-middle-class white	81.2	(1,474)	58.2	(1,384)	52.2	(1,380)
Upper-middle-class white	77.2	(2,017)	55.0	(2,032)	47.0	(2,036)
Upper-class white	85.9	(1,095)	64.6	(1,105)	56.1	(1,102)
Black	4.7	(1,710)	3.8	(1,729)	3.7	(1,735)
Charleston County[b]	63.5	(40,406)	47.9	(40,699)	43.5	(40,934)
Columbia						
Lower-class white	74.5	(2,074)	59.4	(2,073)	56.6	(1,939)
Lower-middle-class white	71.8	(3,651)	56.2	(3,647)	51.9	(3,647)
Upper-middle-class white	66.0	(2,614)	54.9	(2,671)	43.1	(2,627)
Upper-class white	76.7	(4,239)	60.9	(4,220)	46.9	(4,229)
Black	3.1	(1,453)	3.2	(1,455)	3.2	(1,488)
Richland County[b]	59.8	(38,507)	47.4	(37,990)	41.9	(38,108)

[a](N) denotes the number of votes upon which the percentages are based.

[b]County-vote percentages are based on the total number of votes cast in the county.

The Republicans failed to solidify white voters under their banner, but they did unify blacks behind the Democratic ticket, and blacks accounted for an estimated 20 percent of the heavy voter turnout in the 1966 elections.[15] Voting patterns in white precincts in Columbia and Charleston revealed little in the way of class cleavages. While Republican candidates generally did somewhat better in affluent districts and fared somewhat less well in working-class neighborhoods, the differences were small. Thurmond won heavily among white voters and lost overwhelmingly among blacks. Parker also won majorities in white precincts of all socioeconomic levels, but his majorities were adequate only to offset solid black opposition, permitting him to break approximately even in the cities (he carried Greenville and lost Charleston and Columbia) and to lose the election in rural areas. In the governor's race, McNair and Rogers fared about equally well in white neighborhoods, while black districts supplied the Democrat with handsome majorities. Republican candidates ran slightly better in the cities than in the countryside and slightly better in rural areas than in the larger county-seat towns but, for the most part, the G.O.P. campaign strategy divided the whites, solidified the blacks, and lost most of the contests.

Only in Florida did Republican conservatives score a major break-through, by turning the Democratic right flank. There the Democratic gubernatorial primary elections left the party bitterly divided, while producing the most liberal nominee Florida had seen in a state general election since the defeat of Claude Pepper. Governor Haydon Burns, whose two years in the statehouse had not been noted for high accomplishments, won only slightly more than a third of the votes in the Democratic primary and entered the gubernatorial runoff contest against Mayor Robert King High of Miami, his 1964 runoff opponent. For an incumbent governor, Burns's first-primary showing was hardly impressive, and in the runoff he became increasingly vituperative, attacking his archrival's "ultraliberal philosophy" and indebtedness to the "Negro bloc vote" and calling upon Floridians to "follow the lead of the people of Alabama," presumably offering himself as Florida's George Wallace.[16] High exploited Burns's mediocre record as governor and emerged victorious from the slugfest, winning just over 60 percent of the votes cast in the southern portion of the state and losing by about the same margin in the north, which netted a 54 percent advantage in the statewide vote.

The Republicans nominated Claude R. Kirk, Jr., of Jacksonville, a flamboyant campaigner who had run unsuccessfully for the U.S. Senate in 1964. Though eschewing outright racism, Kirk campaigned as a conservative and attempted to portray High as a Great Society liberal. The election

[15]Fowler, "Two-Party Politics: 1966," p. 4; Southern Regional Council, "What Happened in the South, 1966" (mimeographed), p. 2.

[16]"State of the Southern States: Florida," *New South* 21 (Summer 1966): 91–92.

returns gave Kirk a solid 55 percent victory margin. Kirk ran well almost everywhere, carrying both sections of the state and winning in most rural as well as urban counties. In his home city of Jacksonville, Kirk won more than two-thirds of the votes in white precincts of all socioeconomic levels, while he lost well over 90 percent of the votes in black precincts. In High's home city of Miami, Kirk did not fare so well, though he won in affluent Protestant neighborhoods and made a good showing in Protestant white districts generally. Kirk's conservative strategy apparently attracted the bulk of the voters who had supported Burns in the runoff election.[17]

Overall in the South in 1966, the G.O.P. elected or reelected two governors (in Arkansas and Florida) and three U.S. senators (in South Carolina, Tennessee, and Texas) and added seven new House seats, giving the party 23 of the 106 southern positions in the lower house of Congress. In Texas Senator John Tower won reelection easily, as the Democratic primary again produced a staunch conservative in Waggoner Carr, and the "Kamikaze liberals" again displayed little enthusiasm for the Democratic cause. In North Carolina a little-known conservative Republican, John S. Shallcross, won a respectable 44 percent against Senator B. Everett Jordan. Virginia Republicans failed to take advantage of the deep splits that developed in the Democratic party as the Byrd organization declined, and G.O.P. contenders fared poorly in two Senate races. Republican candidates lost far more contests than they won, but they also made breakthroughs, and the two-party trend made significant if limited progress.

The outpouring of new voters and the increasingly competitive two-party system brought the South closer to national political norms. Yet, southern voters had difficulty fitting into a two-party model. The lower-income whites demonstrated a frequent fondness for segregationist conservatives, especially those like Maddox and Wallace. Affluent urban and suburban whites normally supported moderate candidates in Democratic primaries and then shifted to Republicanism in general elections. Blacks usually supported the most liberal alternatives available, though they favored the Democratic party in general elections. These differing political inclinations among major groups of southern voters found outlet in the presidential election of 1968.

In the South the presidential election of 1968 was a closely contested three-way race, and the voter turnout, by southern standards, was massive.[18] The number of people voting in 1968 was almost three times what it

[17]This point is analyzed in Galen A. Irwin, "Florida Gubernatorial Election of 1966: A Look at Transitions," *Florida State University Governmental Research Bulletin* 5 (January 1968).

[18]Calculated from Richard M. Scammon, comp., *America Votes: A Handbook of Contemporary American Election Statistics*, 10 vols. (Washington, D.C.: Governmental Affairs Institute, 1956–73), vol. 9, p. 11; Research Division, Republican National Committee, *The 1968 Elections: A Summary Report with Supporting Tables* (Washington, D.C., 1969), p. 13; and from election returns.

had been two decades before. Although the southern population had increased by only 34 percent since 1948, the increase in voter turnout was 183.6 percent. In the wake of the voting rights act of 1965, abolition of the poll tax, legislative reapportionment, and the sharp political competition in the region, almost two-thirds of the southerners of voting age were registered in 1968, and some 14.8 million, approximately 51 percent of the voting-age population, cast ballots. Despite the fact that this performance was still beneath national norms and far behind other Western democracies, it was impressive when compared with southern political participation in the early post-World War II period.

Republican Richard Nixon finished first in the South, with 34.7 percent of the votes, narrowly beating American Independent George Wallace, who won 34.3 percent; Democrat Hubert Humphrey ran third with 31 percent. Despite the usual state-to-state variations, voting patterns were remarkably consistent over the region. Nixon ran best in higher-prestige neighborhoods, where his economic conservatism and law-and-order defense of social stability appealed to affluent urban and suburban whites throughout the region. Post-election survey data reveal that a majority of white voters of white-collar occupational status in the southern and border states cast ballots for the Republican candidate. These votes combined with the ballots from Republican mountain redoubts to give Nixon pluralities in Florida, North Carolina, South Carolina, Tennessee, and Virginia. Wallace, whose white common-man campaign style, populist economics, and social reaction appealed to the whites of the countryside and the working-class districts in the cities, won a plurality of the votes cast by blue-collar whites. His success among lower-status whites won him Alabama, Arkansas, Georgia, Louisiana, and Mississippi. The Southwide Wallace vote by county correlated positively with the 1964 vote for Goldwater (.57), since both did best in the states of the southern heartland, and both tapped a similar strain of white backlash. But Wallace's appeal to the common whites attracted a basically different, though sometimes overlapping, constituency than had Goldwater's business-oriented individualism. Humphrey was the candidate of blacks and other minority groups. His welfare economics and social liberalism made him the virtually unanimous choice in black neighborhoods and attracted solid majorities in Jewish and Chicano precincts—a coalition which provided Humphrey with a plurality only in Texas. In an occasional peripheral South city, the white working-class districts that had once been Democratic citadels offered grudging support for the Democratic ticket, but, for the most part, southern whites voted for Nixon or Wallace. Nixon was the favorite of the affluent and did best in the rim states; Wallace was the choice of rural and lower-income voters, especially in the Deep South.

Figures 5.4 and 5.5 display the votes for Nixon, Wallace, and Humphrey in three Louisiana and three North Carolina cities. In Louisiana

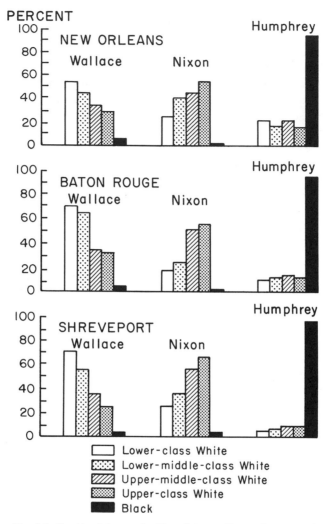

Fig. 5.4. Presidential vote in New Orleans, Baton Rouge, and Shreveport in 1968, by socioeconomic class and race

Wallace won 48.3 percent, a substantial plurality. In North Carolina Nixon finished first with just under 40 percent. The voting alignments in Louisiana are representative of returns throughout the southern heartland. Humphrey won black precincts massively and had little appeal in white neighborhoods. Wallace and Nixon had even less support among blacks, as they split whites along class lines. The returns reflect intrastate sectional differences. In Catholic New Orleans Humphrey's better than nominal showing in white precincts and his solid black following gave him a plurality. In upstate Baton Rouge and Shreveport Wallace's massive support in lower-income white districts netted him pluralities in the parishes containing the two cities. Wallace did not fare so well in North Carolina urban areas, polling less than a quarter of the ballots in metropolitan counties. Nixon did far better. In the burgeoning New South city of Charlotte his solid appeal to upper-income white voters netted a majority of the votes cast in the county. In Wake (Raleigh) and Guilford (Greensboro) counties Nixon won pluralities. Nixon's impressive showing among white voters generally in upper South urban areas cut into the Wallace following; nevertheless, the American party candidate still fared best in working-class white districts, while Humphrey, though doing better among white

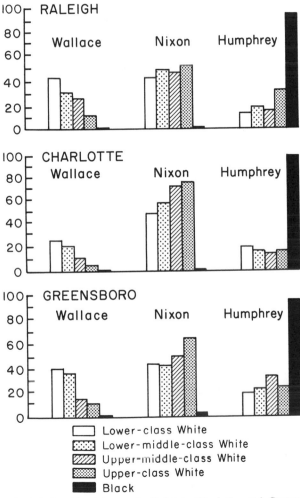

Fig. 5.5. Presidential vote in Raleigh, Charlotte, and Greensboro in 1968, by socioeconomic class and race

voters in North Carolina than in the states to the south, still relied primarily on black support. Only along the southern fringe, in cities like Fort Worth, Waco, Norfolk, and Miami, did remnants of the class-based New Deal voting alignments of past partisan competition survive. In the South as a whole, Nixon won a plurality in metropolitan counties, while Wallace won pluralities in the countryside and larger towns.

The Democratic party fared considerably better in state politics than it did at the presidential level. The G.O.P. again made gains, winning a U.S. Senate seat in Florida and adding three members in the lower house of Congress to give the Republicans 26 of 106 southern House seats. The party registered a net gain of nine in southern state legislatures, even winning control of the lower house in Tennessee. But in local politics the G.O.P. remained very much the minority party; in 1968 its candidates won only 240 of more than 1,800 southern state legislative seats.

Generally the Wallace voters, after registering their displeasure with the national Democrats, tended to shift back into the Democratic fold in other contests on the ballot. The patterns were often chaotic, however, as ticket splitting and shifting electoral alignments abounded. In Arkansas voters gave a plurality to Independent George Wallace while reelecting Democrat William Fulbright to the Senate and Republican Winthrop Rockefeller to the statehouse. North Carolina election returns exemplified the instability of partisan voting alignments. In Guilford County, for example, Nixon won 46.2 percent, and the G.O.P. candidates for governor and senator each won approximately 44 percent. These returns in the aggregate suggest continuity; but when divided into socioeconomic group-ings, they illustrate the instability of southern partisan voting behavior. As figure 5.6 indicates, substantially different alignments within the electorate supported the G.O.P. candidates in each of the three elections on the same ballot.

To be sure, the citizens of Greensboro and High Point, the two cities in Guilford County, demonstrated considerable logic and political aware-ness in their choices. The G.O.P. gubernatorial candidate was Congress-man James C. Gardner, a Goldwater Republican who campaigned as a law-and-order segregationist and an adamant opponent of all programs remotely associated with Great Society liberalism. His opponent was Lieutenant Governor Robert Scott, son of W. Kerr Scott and an associate of former Governor Terry Sanford. Scott was the candidate of the pro-gressive wing of the Democratic party, but he ran a conservative cam-paign in both the Democratic primary and the general election, though he appeared somewhat moderate in comparison with the rightwing Gardner. In the Senate race the Republicans chose Robert V. Somers to oppose incumbent Sam J. Ervin, Jr. Although Ervin's record for conservatism and hostility to Negro rights was unassailable, Somers attacked from the right, "promulgating a philosophy," a Ripon Society publication observed, "that

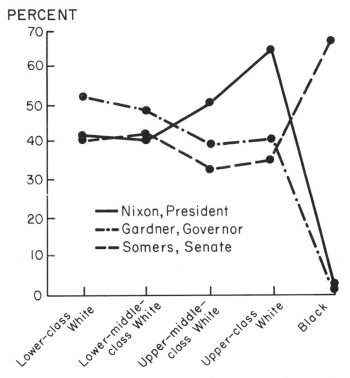

PERCENT

Fig. 5.6. Republican vote in Greensboro in 1968, by socioeconomic
class and race

made Jim Gardner sound like a progressive. . . ."[19] Guilford county voters
responded with considerable ideological consistency. In the presidential
race affluent whites supported the conservative moderation of Nixon; in
the gubernatorial and senatorial elections they supported the conservative
moderation of Democrats Scott and Ervin. Working-class whites divided
the bulk of their votes between the socially conservative Nixon and the
socially reactionary Wallace; they also gave relatively strong support to
the segregationist Gardner and Somers. Blacks voted overwhelmingly for
Humphrey and Scott, but they rejected Ervin's negative record on civil-
rights legislation in the Senate to back Somers. Thus, all three Republican
candidates received a similar share of the votes. Nixon won a plurality in
the county almost entirely on the basis of white votes, especially those of
affluent whites. Gardner won just over 44 percent, also by appealing to
white votes, but his appeal was essentially to lower-income whites. Somers
won 44 percent by winning substantial support in black precincts while
making a creditable showing in working-class white districts.

[19]Michael S. Lottman, "The G.O.P. and the South," *Ripon Forum* 6 (July-August 1970),
p. 57.

Both Gardner and Somers sought to combine economic and social conservatism to unite the Nixon and Wallace voters into a winning combination, a point Gardner made rather explicit by endorsing both Nixon and Wallace as his choices for the presidency. It was a widely utilized strategy by the G.O.P. in the South, and, for the most part, it proved lacking, as in North Carolina. Gardner made a strong race, tallying 47.3 percent against Scott, but Somers managed only 39.4 percent against Ervin, slightly less than Nixon won in the three-way presidential race. The lowland counties in the eastern part of the state that delivered pluralities to Wallace also cast substantial majorities for the Democratic state ticket. The lowland county-seat elites who were not willing to go out of their way to benefit Humphrey and the national Democrats were by no means reconciled to G.O.P. control of the statehouse and Senate patronage. Gardner, who represented a congressional district that included a number of lowland counties, fared better in the eastern part of the state than past Republican candidates had done; nevertheless, the votes for both Gardner and Somers correlated positively with the vote for Nixon (.75 and .95, respectively) and negatively with both Humphrey (−.86 and −.75) and Wallace (−.55 and −.84).

Similarly, in South Carolina, as in most of the rest of the South, Humphrey's blacks and Wallace's rural and low-income whites both generally supported the Democratic candidate in state politics. In 1966 Republican Marshall Parker had given Democrat Ernest Hollings a close race in the contest to fill Senator Johnston's unexpired Senate term. Encouraged by his strong showing, Parker tried again when the seat came up for a full term in 1968. This time Hollings won easily. Nixon carried South Carolina with 38.1 percent, which was precisely the percentage received by Parker in the Senate election. As in North Carolina, the votes for Nixon and Parker were not identical; nevertheless, the returns clearly implied that the bulk of the citizens who cast ballots for either Humphrey or Wallace also voted for Hollings.[20] Parker's poor showing was reflected in local elections, as G.O.P. membership in the state legislature dropped sharply.

Republican efforts to outflank the Democrats on the right worked best, logically enough, when the G.O.P. was able to find a Democrat vulnerable to charges of liberalism. And such was the case in the senatorial election in Florida, as it had been in the gubernatorial contest two years before. Leroy Collins, after a successful six-year stint in the statehouse during the 1950s, had moved to national politics, serving on the Community Relations Service in the Johnson administration and becoming associated with Johnson's civil-rights policies. When incumbent Senator George A. Smathers retired in 1968, Collins sought his seat. His chief opponent in the

---

[20]This election is analyzed in greater depth in Donald L. Fowler, "The 1968 General Election in S.C.," *University of South Carolina Governmental Review* 9 (May 1969).

Table 5.4

Percentage of the Vote for Nixon and Wallace
and for Gurney in the 1968 General Election in Jacksonville,
by Socioeconomic Class and Race

Vote category	Percentage of vote received by Nixon	Percentage of vote received by Wallace	(N)[a]	Percentage of vote received by Gurney	(N)[a]
Lower-class white	23.3	53.9	(4,014)	63.4	(3,567)
Lower-middle-class white	24.0	60.3	(4,410)	69.5	(3,950)
Upper-middle-class white	34.2	46.7	(4,287)	67.0	(3,974)
Upper-class white	48.8	29.9	(5,718)	68.1	(4,631)
Black	2.5	2.8	(3,633)	2.7	(3,125)
Duval County[b]	30.9	36.3	(166,978)	56.1	(152,927)

[a](N) denotes the number of votes upon which the percentages are based.

[b]County-vote percentages are based on the total number of votes cast in the county.

Democratic primary was Attorney General Earl Faircloth. In bitterly contested primary and runoff elections, Faircloth attacked Collins's work in civil rights and condemned his "dangerous attitude" toward law and order. Collins narrowly survived the runoff election, with 50.2 percent. Two-thirds of the voters in north Florida and in rural areas supported Faircloth; however, Collins won heavily in south Florida's cities to salvage the Democratic nomination. As in 1966, the Democratic primaries had left the party deeply divided and had produced a progressive nominee. The G.O.P. nominated Edward J. Gurney, a staunchly conservative congressman. Against Collins, Gurney accomplished what the Gardners and Parkers had been unable to do, the fusion of the economically conservative and Republican-oriented affluent whites with the socially conservative and Wallace-inclined rural and lower-status whites. Gurney's vote correlated positively with the vote for Wallace (.63 at the county level of analysis); he won in northern and southern as well as rural and urban areas of the state to carry the election with 56 percent of the votes.[21]

In Texas liberal Democrats threatened but failed to overturn the hegemony of the Democratic conservatives. Governor John Connally, who had dominated Lone Star State politics during most of the 1960s, stepped down, making the 1968 gubernatorial primary a wide-open affair. Liberal Don Yarborough finished first in the primary, while the runoff candidate from the sharply divided conservative camp was Lieutenant Governor Preston Smith, a lackluster west Texas conservative who was not the

[21]See Elston Roady, "The 1968 Election in Florida," *Florida State University Governmental Research Bulletin* 6 (January 1969).

favorite of the Connally-oriented leadership in the state. Nevertheless, Smith ran strongly in the western part of the state and defeated Yarborough with relative ease with 55 percent of the vote. New Deal voting alignments held together in Texas, more so than anywhere else in the South. Yarborough won heavily in black precincts and carried white working-class districts in the cities, but affluent whites overwhelmingly supported Smith, and lower-status whites did not provide Yarborough with the hefty margins liberals had often received in the past.

The Republicans in their primary nominated Paul W. Eggers, a relatively unknown Wichita Falls lawyer generally regarded as a member of the moderate wing of the party. In the general election, Eggers's campaign was vigorous, but it never developed a theme, as the candidate seemed to vacillate between a strategic desire to reach out for the Kamikaze Texas liberals on the one hand and to appease the conservative Goldwater Republicans in his own ranks on the other. Preston Smith roved through the small towns of the Texas countryside shaking hands, espousing a bland conservatism, and awaiting that peculiar inversion of voting patterns that had carried conservative Democrats to victory so often in the past. Predictably on election day, the upper-income precincts that had voted for Smith in the runoff switched to Eggers, while the black and lower-status white districts shifted to Smith, who swept the rural-small town counties and cruised to an easy victory.[22] Eggers appealed best to the same voters who had supported Nixon; his vote correlated negatively with that for Humphrey and Wallace.

Southern politics was in turmoil during 1966, 1967, and 1968. The galoots were loose over much of the region, as the Maddoxes and Wallaces rode the votes of an expanded white electorate to victory. Conservative Republicans sought gain from the disrepute of national Democratic policies, but, for the most part, Democratic primaries produced mainly conservative Democrats who were relatively immune to assaults from the right. Efforts by liberal Democrats to harness the expanded electorate to a politics of progressivism proved notably unsuccessful. Moderate Republicans did record occasional victories, but, generally, conservatism was in the ascendency. Yet, the economic conservatism of the affluent whites was substantially different from the social conservatism of the common white folks, a division clearly etched by voting patterns in the 1968 presidential elections, which divided southern voters more rationally than did the two-party politics so long desired by southern progressives.

Within a year after the 1968 election, Kevin P. Phillips published *The Emerging Republican Majority*,[23] which included a vigorous defense of the

---

[22]Jerry D. Conn, *Preston Smith: The Making of a Texas Governor* (Austin: Pemberton, 1972), is an interesting "insider's" account that focuses on the 1968 campaign.
[23]New Rochelle: Arlington House, 1969.

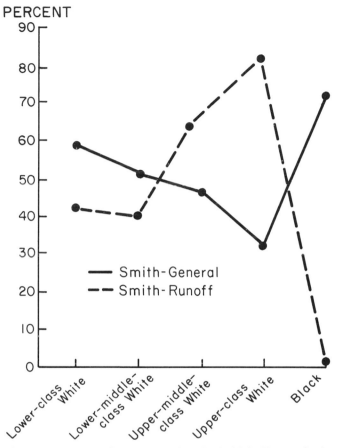

Fig. 5.7. Percentage of the vote received by Smith in Houston in the 1968 runoff primary and general elections, by socioeconomic class and race

Southern Strategy. By remaining true to conservatism, Phillips argued, Republicans would inherit the support of the economically conservative Nixon voters and the socially conservative Wallace supporters. As the first Reconstruction was followed by the reign of the Bourbon Democrats, the Second Reconstruction would usher in the age of Bourbon Republicanism. But whatever the long-term validity of Phillips's analysis, the response of the southern electorate during the campaigns of 1969 and 1970 surely must have unnerved its adherents.

CHAPTER 6

THE AMBIGUOUS RESURGENCE
OF THE NEW SOUTH

The 1968 presidential election left the South in political disarray, and its backwash posed unanswered questions. New Deal voting alignments lay in wreckage, and the constituent logic of an election in which blacks could vote for Humphrey, suburbanites for Nixon, and working-class whites for Wallace was apparent. Yet the poor showing of American independent candidates in state and local races suggested that the Wallace appeal was basically a protest against national trends largely confined to presidential politics. Where the Wallace voters would come to rest within the still maturing southern two-party system was by no means certain.

Survey research data make clear that the southern electorate was undergoing sweeping attitudinal change. On the fundamental matter of party identification, massive numbers of white southerners abandoned the Democratic party during the 1960s, while growing numbers of blacks joined. Most of these southern whites did not, however, shift their loyalty to the Republican party; instead they identified themselves as independents. Figure 6.1 illustrates changes in party identification by blacks, lower-income whites, and higher-income whites in the southern and border states during the years 1952–70. The bulk of respondents in all three groups identified themselves as Democrats in 1952, and substantial majorities continued to do so for more than a decade. But during the 1960s blacks and whites diverged radically. The exodus of black southerners into the Democratic camp reached a flood-tide 91.9 percent in 1968, after which it subsided to approximately 80 percent. White southerners drifted away from the party after 1964 to the point that by 1970 a majority of both affluent and unaffluent whites no longer counted themselves Democrats.

Republicans benefited little from the white flight from the Democracy. In 1970 only 6.5 percent of blacks, 15.6 percent of lower-income whites, and 20.9 percent of higher-income whites identified themselves as Republicans, leaving the G.O.P. in about the same place as it had been throughout the postwar period, in possession of little in the way of a substantial base

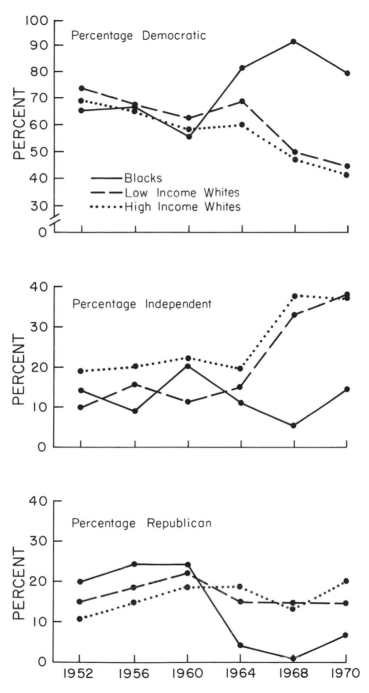

Fig. 6.1. Party identification in the southern and border states, 1952–70, by race and income

of reliable partisan followers. The bulk of the white defectors from Democratic partisanship classified themselves as independents, and their numbers shot upward from less than 20 percent in 1964 to 38 percent in 1970, with almost the identical percentage among both lower- and higher-income whites. Aggregate voting data clearly indicate that in practice many among the burgeoning number of white independents of higher socioeconomic status supported Republican candidates, suggesting that affluent whites may have been using partisan independence as a halfway house on the road to identification with the Republican party. If a similar assumption could be drawn from the political behavior of the lower-status white independents, then the South would be well on the way toward a fundamental partisan realignment. In this regard it is no doubt significant that the basic factor determining the trend lines in figure 6.1 appears to be skin color; whites, whether of high or low income, shifted their partisan identifications in a similar manner and behaved significantly different from black southerners.

This growing attitudinal divergence along racial rather than class lines was also evident in regard to other issues. Crucial, of course, was the matter of race relations. Figure 6.2 records the percentage of blacks, blue-collar whites, and white-collar whites questioned who favored the active involvement of the federal government in public-school desegregation. Although the wording changed between the 1960 and the 1964 surveys, the two queries apparently measured similar attitudes. In 1956 approximately the same minority of southerners, regardless of occupational status or race, favored a more active federal involvement in the school-desegregation controversy; of those questioned, a majority of whites, especially blue-collar whites, preferred federal nonintervention, while blacks were roughly equally divided between governmental intervention, nonintervention, and undecided. But as the school-desegregation issue became increasingly salient, blacks rallied to support an active federal involvement, while whites moved away from that position. By the end of the 1960s, most whites no longer offered positive support for segregation, but they also did not endorse federal integrationist policies. In 1970 approximately one-fourth of blue-collar whites and one-fifth of white-collar whites favored an active governmental integrationist policy—a difference that pales when compared with the 83.8 percent of blacks in favor of governmental intervention.

The pattern of response was somewhat different when pollsters inquired about the federal government's role in insuring fair treatment for blacks in employment. Again the wording of the questions changed between 1960 and 1964, and the nonthreatening terminology of the 1956–60 query may account for the higher than expected percentage of favorable responses. But in any case, blacks during the 1956–68 period overwhelmingly endorsed federal guarantees of fair treatment, while sharply declining numbers of whites, whether of low or high income, did not. As

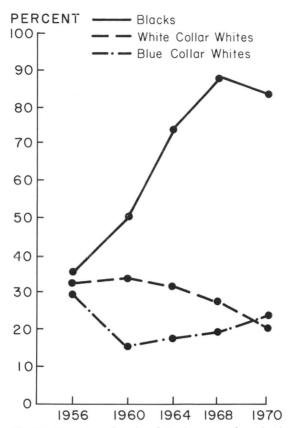

Fig. 6.2. Percentage favoring federal support for school
desegregation, 1956–70

figures 6.2 and 6.3 illustrate, the gap between the overwhelming black
preference for active federal support for civil rights and the increasingly
limited support offered by whites represented an attitudinal difference of
massive proportions.

When one considers that New Deal voting alignments rested upon
common bonds of self-interest of poor whites and blacks, figure 6.4 is particularly arresting. In 1956 the bulk of blacks and a heavy majority of low-
income whites favored the proposition that the federal government ought
to guarantee jobs to anyone who wanted work. Only among higher-income
whites did a majority disagree. But by 1968 southern white support for such
governmental intervention had virtually collapsed, while 80 percent of
black southerners still found the proposition meritorious.[1]

[1]Again the wording of the question changed between 1960 and 1964. See the Note on
Methodology and Data Sources preceding the Bibliographical Essay for a discussion of the
questions asked, the size of N, and other information.

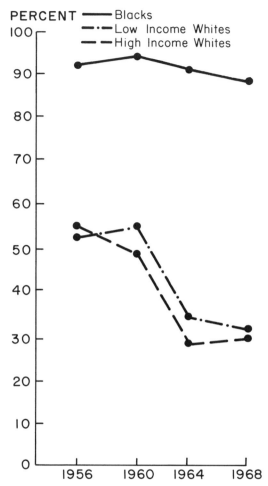

Fig. 6.3. Percentage favoring federal guarantee of fair-employment opportunities for blacks, 1956–68

By 1970, survey research data revealed an American society sharply polarized over fundamental questions of social and economic policy, a society in which southern blacks generally occupied the most liberal position, nonsoutherners hovered in the middle, and southern whites anchored the conservative stance. For example, 97.1 percent of the southern blacks polled agreed that blacks should have a right to open housing; 78.5 percent of nonsoutherners agreed, as compared with only 46.2 percent of southern whites. Similarly, 60.5 percent of southern blacks endorsed government medical insurance, as against 30.1 percent of nonsoutherners and 15.5 percent of southern whites. On the Vietnam issue, 59.4 percent of southern blacks agreed that the United States should pull out, as compared with only 29.8 percent of southern whites. Conversely, 56.9 percent of southern whites disapproved of protest marches, as compared with 45.4 percent of nonsoutherners and 22.7 percent of southern blacks.

In the South, the lower-income whites were much closer attitudinally to the more affluent whites than they were to the still liberally inclined blacks. The vast and generally growing differences between blacks and lower-status whites over such matters as partisan identification, the federal government's role in minority rights, and New Deal-type welfare measures seemed to offer little foundation for the resurrection of the alliance of have-nots across color lines. But the real test as to whether traditional partisan patterns were disintegrating and new ones evolving would be at the polling places, and in 1969 Virginia stood alone in the spotlight.

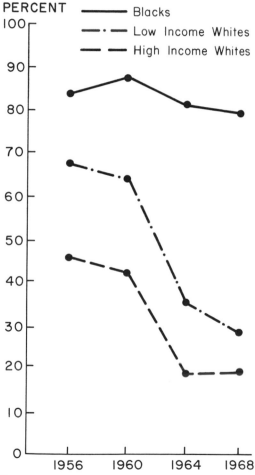

Fig. 6.4. Percentage favoring federal guarantee of employment for all who wish to work, 1956–68

Virginia politics was symptomatic of the demolition of the old one-party South. The Byrd organization was crumbling. Its legatee as governor, the old massive resister Mills Godwin, had abandoned the sacred canons of the dying founder, Harry Flood Byrd, and in a surprising accommodation to the tides of change had presided over the passage of sales taxes and a bond issue for schools, liquor by the drink, and constitutional reform. Liberal Democrat George C. Rawlings had retired Judge Howard Smith, a member of the Byrd organization's inner circle, in the 1966 congressional primary only to fall victim in the general election to conservative Republican William L. Scott. That same year Democrat William B. Spong, a forty-five-year-old Portsmouth state senator, defeated the seventy-eight-year-old incumbent, A. William Robertson, in the Senate primary and then defeated Republican James P. Ould to join Harry Byrd, Jr., in the Senate.[2] For almost half a century the Byrd organization had dominated Virginia politics, and its collapse made the 1969 gubernatorial scramble a wide-open and revealing contest.

The Democratic primary for the gubernatorial nomination was a hotly contested three-man race. Remnants of the Byrd organization attempted to rally around the ultraconservative lieutenant governor, Fred G. Pollard, who ran a poor third with 23.3 percent of the votes. Finishing second was Henry E. Howell, Jr., an unapologetic liberal state senator from Norfolk. Running on the slogan "keep the big boys honest," the aggressive Howell demanded protection for consumers and attacked high insurance rates and the sales tax on food. In both the primary and the runoff campaigns, Howell effectively sought to forge an urban coalition of blacks and lower-status whites and by populistic appeals to attract George Wallace's rural constituency. Occupying the middle position in the primary was William C. Battle, the moderately conservative son of a former governor. Battle came in first in the primary, edging Howell 38.9 percent to 37.8 percent. In the runoff Battle benefited from the active support of Governor Godwin and the organization regulars, as the Democratic party polarized around the sharply contrasting styles and programs of the runoff contestants.

[2]On the apparent assumption that the Spong-Robertson victor would be more vulnerable than Harry Byrd, Jr., Virginia Republicans nominated Ould, the mayor of Lynchburg, for the full Senate term and selected little-known Lawrence Traylor, an attorney from the Northern Neck area, to run for the remainder of the retired Byrd, Sr.'s term. Ould ran an essentially conservative campaign against the moderately progressive Spong and carried only 33.5 percent of the total votes. Traylor, on the other hand, courted black and labor support in an aggressive campaign against Byrd and emerged with 37.5 percent of the total vote and 41.2 percent of the two-party vote. (Conservative candidates in both Senate contests attracting roughly 60,000 of the approximately 730,000 total votes.) On Virginia politics during the period, see J. Harvie Wilkinson III, *Harry Byrd and the Changing Face of Virginia Politics, 1945–1966* (Charlottesville: University of Virginia Press, 1968), pp. 247–304; Virginius Dabney, *Virginia: The New Dominion* (Garden City: Doubleday, 1971), pp. 552–76; Michael S. Lottman, "The G.O.P. and the South," *Ripon Forum* 6 (July–August 1970): 81–86; and Ralph Eisenberg, "Virginia," in *The Changing Politics of the South*, ed. William C. Havard (Baton Rouge: Louisiana State University Press, 1972), pp. 39–91.

Howell ran extremely well in the cities, where insurgent candidates had traditionally fared best in Virginia. He won a comfortable plurality in metropolitan counties in the first primary and a majority in the runoff, and his appeal in the cities was attractive to blacks and lower-status whites. Despite all the evidence suggesting the breakdown of New Deal voting alignments, Howell's frankly liberal campaign was generally successful in the cities. As figure 6.5 indicates, Howell carried black precincts by overwhelming margins, ran well ahead in lower-income white districts, and fared poorly in upper-income white neighborhoods. He carried middle-income areas in his hometown of Norfolk and won majorities in lower-

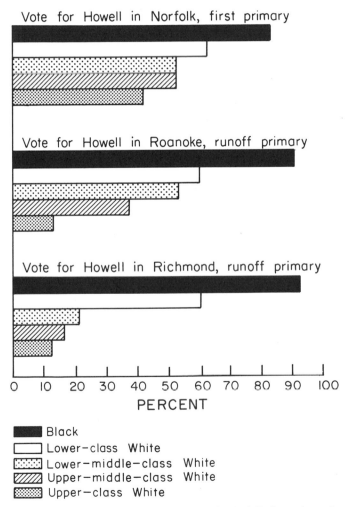

Fig. 6.5. Percentage of the vote for Howell in Norfolk, Roanoke, and Richmond in 1969, by socioeconomic class and race

middle-class precincts in Roanoke in the runoff, but in Richmond middle-income areas went heavily against him. Battle won the runoff election by sweeping almost 60 percent of the ballots cast in rural-small town counties. Howell broke even in the black belt, but in the nonmetropolitan counties of the Virginia uplands Battle built up majorities sufficiently hefty to offset Howell's advantages in the cities and to give Battle a 52.1 percent majority and the nomination.

The state Republican convention unanimously selected A. Linwood Holton of Roanoke as its gubernatorial nominee. A loyal Republican, Holton had been state campaign manager for G.O.P. gubernatorial nominee H. Clyde Pearson in 1961, and in 1965 Holton had run a creditable if losing campaign against Democrat Mills Godwin. Sandy-haired and square-jawed, a church elder and Sunday School teacher, father of a handsome brood, graduate of Washington and Lee and Harvard Law School, and a captain in the Naval reserves, Holton was a winsome candidate. Central casting could scarcely have improved upon his image. But in the eyes of conservative Republicans, Holton was suspect, especially on racial matters (a consistent critic of massive resistance, Holton had once paid for a newspaper advertisement urging his fellow Virginians to "Keep Your Schools Open"). Conservative Republicans were assuaged by the nomination for attorney general of Richard S. Obenshain, a staunch Goldwater Republican from Richmond who had narrowly lost his bid for a U.S. House seat in 1964. Rounding out the Republican ticket was H. D. Dawbarn, nominee for lieutenant governor, a moderately conservative state senator from Waynesboro who proved ineffective as a campaigner.

Republican Holton and Democrat Battle did not differ fundamentally on mainstream issues, and the contest was not characterized by heated charges or inflated rhetoric. Holton inherited a number of advantages, which he exploited through a highly organized and well financed campaign. The two heated primary battles had seriously split the Democratic party; while Governor Godwin supported Battle in the general election, Howell remained aloof. The Virginia AFL-CIO and the Crusade for Voters, the state's largest black political organization, both endorsed Holton, apparently owing less to enthusiasm for the Republican candidate than to eagerness to deliver the *coup de grace* to the Byrd organization. The election was reminiscent of Ted Dalton's campaigns during the 1950s, when the Republicans stood to the left of the Democrats. But unlike the 1950s, Holton had by election time convinced a majority of 52.5 percent of the voters that it was indeed time for a change. Holton swept the metropolitan counties and the traditionally Republican counties of the Shenandoah Valley and the highlands by identical 55.9 percent margins. In the cities he ran well among white voters generally; in Richmond and Roanoke he carried white precincts of all socioeconomic categories, and in Norfolk he lost only the low-income white districts. Holton also cut into Democratic

strength in black neithborhoods, carrying the black precincts in Richmond
and winning almost 40 percent in Roanoke, though getting only 20 percent
in black areas of Norfolk. Holton's ticketmates, Dawbarn and Obenshain,
did not fare so well; both were trounced by attractive young Democrats.
State Senator J. Sargeant Reynolds, the thirty-three-year-old heir to the
Reynolds Metals Company fortune whose rising star in Virginia politics
was abruptly snuffed out less than one year later by a brain tumor, and
Andrew P. Miller, son of Democratic insurgent Francis Pickens Miller who
had crusaded against the Byrd machine a generation earlier, won the
offices of lieutenant governor and attorney general, respectively.

The first Republican governor of Virginia in the twentieth century,
Holton was elected with a Democratic lieutenant governor and attorney
general. All three were relatively young men of progressive inclinations
who rejected the racial emotionalism breathed by the war-horses of the
recent past; in response, journalists unearthed that much abused rubric,
"New South" and, echoing the post-Reconstruction rhetoric of Henry
Grady, began to refer to such appealing new faces as politicians of the
progressive New South. In the wake of the series of manic state campaigns
that had featured the likes of George Wallace, Lester Maddox, Jim
Johnson, John Bell Williams, Strom Thurmond, and other old faces
fiercely defending the social distinctions of the ancient regime (and a
presidential campaign that had presented three rather too-familiar faces
as well), a wave of attractive, moderate candidates, who were for the most
part youthful and relative newcomers to politics, swept to election successes throughout the South during the early 1970s.[3]

In Florida two virtually unknown state senators, forty-one-year-old
Reubin Askew of Pensacola and forty-year-old Lawton Chiles of Lakeland, overwhelmed veteran Democrats in primary contests and then
defeated Republican opponents in November 1970 general elections. Cut
from the same strait-laced cloth, Askew and Chiles were boyishly handsome, low-keyed in style, and conspicuously lacking in both observable
vices and pronounced ideologies. Since neither possessed well-heeled
campaign chests, they both shunned the customary media-oriented campaigns. Chiles, in his quest for the Senate seat being vacated by retiring
incumbent Spessard Holland, walked the thousand-mile length of Florida

[3]Thoughtful discussions of this phase of southern politics are James Clotfelter, William
R. Hamilton, and Peter B. Harkins, "In Search of Populism," *New South* 26 (Winter 1971):
6–15; and James Clotfelter and William R. Hamilton, "But Which Southern Strategy?"
South Today 2 (April 1971): 1–7. Handy guides to recent political developments in individual
southern states are the appropriate chapters in Havard, *The Changing Politics of the South*;
and Michael Barone, Grant Ujifusa, and Douglas Matthews, *The Almanac of American
Politics: The Senators, the Representatives—Their Records, States Districts, 1972* (Boston:
Gambit, 1972). For the states of the lower South, see Neal R. Peirce, *The Deep South States
of America: People, Politics, and Power in the Seven Deep South States* (New York: W. W.
Norton, 1974).

in an effort to get acquainted with the average voters. Askew campaigned for the statehouse on the populist conviction, if without the populist style, that corporate tax reform was long overdue.

The Democratic primary campaigns in both the gubernatorial and senatorial contests attracted crowded fields of candidates. Askew drew a sufficiently strong friends-and-neighbors vote in the panhandle counties of north Florida to win a spot in the runoff with Attorney General Earl Faircloth, who had narrowly lost to LeRoy Collins in the 1968 senatorial primary. Chiles ran best in the central Florida counties around his hometown of Lakeland and finished second behind former Governor Farris Bryant. Neither Chiles nor Askew projected a detectable class or racial appeal in either Miami or Jacksonville. In the runoff campaigns, Faircloth and Bryant, who were better known and had access to greater financial resources than their opponents, were the early favorites, but by election day the initiative had clearly passed to the young challengers. Askew won the gubernatorial nomination by a hefty 57.5 percent majority, and Chiles did even better, besting Bryant by almost two to one. The victors ran strongly virtually everywhere, erasing the usual north-south split in Florida Democratic primary contests. Neither attracted a consistent class following, although they generally fared best among voters of higher education and status.[4] Chiles swept precincts of every socioeconomic category in Miami, running best in upper-income white Protestant neighborhoods. In Jacksonville he carried white precincts of all socioeconomic levels—this time running best in lower-income white areas—and lost in black neighborhoods by substantial margins. Askew broke about even in Dade county, winning in upper- and upper-middle-class Protestant and Jewish areas. In Jacksonville Askew ran slightly ahead in lower- and middle-income white neighborhoods and slightly behind in upper-income white districts, losing the county by finishing well behind in black precincts.

Florida Republicans were ill prepared to face the Democrats' newly found champions. Although G.O.P. candidates had carried the state in four of the last five presidential elections and had won the most recent gubernatorial and senatorial elections, the party was deeply divided in 1970, something of a role reversal for Florida Republicans who in the past had taken advantage of divisions within Democratic party ranks. President Nixon had asked Republican Congressman William Cramer to give up his safe St. Petersburg seat of sixteen years and run for the Senate. But Republican Governor Claude Kirk, who in characteristically flamboyant style had unsuccessfully sought the G.O.P. vice-presidential nomination in 1968 and then had thrown his support behind the Rockefeller forces at the Republican convention at Miami Beach, induced, with the alleged assis-

    [4]Robert S. Erikson and William James Zaviona, "Issues and Voters in the 1970 Florida Election," *Florida State University Governmental Research Bulletin* 8 (November 1971): 1–4; and Larry Vickers, "Askew of Florida," *South Today* 4 (November 1972): 1–4.

tance of Senator Edward Gurney, Nixon's rejected Supreme Court nominee J. Harold Carswell to abandon his federal district judgeship and enter the primary against Cramer. The embittered Cramer easily demolished the hapless Carswell in the primary, but Kirk was forced into a runoff by millionaire drug-chain owner Jack Eckerd, who, coincidentally, came from Cramer's home district in St. Petersburg. Torn by factional feuding and trailing the Democrats by a margin of almost three to one in registration, the Republicans anticipated facing the battle-scarred Faircloth and Bryant. Instead Askew and Chiles presented the veteran Republicans with no apparent vulnerabilities.

Both Kirk and Cramer sought to take advantage of the storm over busing, promising an unstinting defense of neighborhood schools from the diabolical bus. But against Chiles, who dubbed himself a "progressive conservative" and received the endorsement of the eminently safe Senator Holland, Cramer was unable to make stick his charges that Chiles was a radical and a busing candidate. Similarly, Kirk enjoyed limited success in directing attention away from his own erratic performance as governor. Askew and Chiles benefited from support emanating from the Democratic county courthouses, whose occupants had learned the sacrifices in patronage and influence that resulted from Republican control of the statehouse, a Senate seat, and the White House. The Democratic candidates crushed their Republican opponents by convincing margins, sweeping black, Jewish, and working-class white precincts in the cities and carrying every county category except rural south Florida.

Another fresh new Democratic face surfaced to tumble the old-guard veterans in Arkansas. Republican Winthrop Rockefeller, the incumbent governor, had lost to Orval Faubus in 1964 but, following the retirement of Faubus, had defeated James Johnson in 1966, turned back Marion Crank in 1968, and in 1970 was gearing up to run for a third two-year term. Among his prospective opponents was the restive sixty-year-old Faubus, now sporting a new mod haircut, a new thirty-one-year-old wife, a slimmed-down profile, and a network of courthouse loyalties nourished during his twelve years in the statehouse. Entering the lists against Faubus in the Democratic primary were seven aspirants of lesser age and stature, including Attorney General Joseph Purcell, Arkansas House Speaker Hayes McClerkin, and the eighth candidate to sign on, Dale Bumpers, a forty-four-year-old lawyer from the small hill town of Charleston (population 1,353). Since Bumpers had only once before sought elective office, unsuccessfully running for the Arkansas house of representatives in 1962, he was even less associated with old political ties than Holton, Askew, and Chiles had been.[5] Yet like them, he was relatively young, a solid family

[5]Bumpers had held public office as a member of the Charleston school board and for eighteen years was Charleston city attorney, the latter reflecting the fact that he was Charleston's only attorney.

man, untouched by political strains, and possessed of a handsome and disarming face and an earnest flair for low-keyed oratory. Even his name suggested unpretentious integrity.

Bumpers narrowly edged Purcell (20.5 percent to 19.3 percent) in the crowded Democratic primary to make the runoff against Faubus, who led with 37.3 percent. Aided by the powerful and liberal *Arkansas Gazette*, Bumpers soon had Faubus on the defensive, swinging wildly and calling his opponent a "country clubber, a tuxedo boy, a highball-to-highball type." Faubus had used the same type of attack against Rockefeller in 1964 and to rather good effect, accusing the Republican millionaire of being an outsider, a boozer, and a sissy pants, and a divorced one at that. But it was Faubus who now stood guilty of the sin of divorce, and besides, Charleston didn't even have a country club. In the runoff Bumpers devastated Faubus, carrying every category of county except the black belt.

The subsequent Bumpers-Rockefeller campaign was, for the Arkansas of the Faubus era, a novel, gentlemanly affair, with both candidates agreeing that Arkansas's industry and its public sector should grow, that racial discrimination should stop, and that the winner should continue the policy begun by Rockefeller of appointing blacks to public agencies. Originally primed to combat Faubus, the sixty-eight-year-old Rockefeller could not match the fresh appeal of Bumpers, who enjoyed strong support from Senator William Fulbright, and Rockefeller went under in a dignified landslide as the Democrat garnered 61.7 percent of the vote.[6] In the runoff and general elections, Bumpers employed a tactic similar to the gambit successfully exploited by the conservative Democrats in Texas and Virginia who marshaled middle- and upper-class white votes in the cities to ward off black and working-class-backed threats from the left in the primaries and then solidified lower-class Democratic support to outvote the Republican suburbanites in the general elections. In the runoff primary Bumpers fared best in the cities and larger towns; in Little Rock he constructed a coalition of blacks and affluent whites to defeat Faubus. Then in the general election he rallied rural and working-class Democrats to offset black and affluent white losses to Rockefeller (see table 6.1).

In Georgia the popular revolt against the political establishment propelled James E. "Jimmy" Carter into the governor's office. Although a veteran state legislator, Carter had made only one other statewide campaign, finishing third behind Ellis Arnall and Lester Maddox in the 1966 gubernatorial primary. In that campaign Carter had projected a progressive "go forward" image. But in 1970 Carter's chief opponent and the clear favorite in the Democratic primary was former Governor Carl Sanders, whose generally successful administration during 1963–67 had been marked by a dignified moderation in racial matters and whose political

---

[6]*Arkansas Gazette*, June 26–July 12; November 7–8, 1970.

Table 6.1
Percentage of the Vote for Bumpers
in the 1970 Gubernatorial Runoff Primary and General Election,
by Rural, Urban, and Metropolitan Counties in Arkansas and
by Socioeconomic Class and Race in Little Rock

Vote category	Runoff		General	
	Percentage of vote received	(N)[a]	Percentage of vote received	(N)[a]
Statewide				
Rural	55.7	(288,217)	64.6	(381,926)
Urban	61.6	(76,772)	57.3	(111,519)
Metropolitan	67.3	(75,867)	56.0	(115,753)
Little Rock				
Lower-class white	50.7	(2,060)	67.0	(3,050)
Lower-middle-class white	56.5	(2,808)	72.7	(3,772)
Upper-middle-class white	71.6	(4,057)	57.9	(5,699)
Upper-class white	72.1	(2,103)	48.6	(4,609)
Black	60.4	(1,725)	50.7	(1,856)
Pulaski County[b]	64.6	(51,763)	53.4	(80,658)

[a](N) denotes the number of votes upon which the percentages are based.

[b]County-vote percentages are based on the total number of votes cast in the county.

courage had been affirmed by his vigorous support of Lyndon Johnson in the 1964 presidential election. Sanders was well known, and he possessed ample campaign funds, but in 1970 those advantages were of dubious value. Carter's pollsters detected basic weaknesses in the former governor's popular image; many Georgia whites viewed Sanders as the establishment candidate, a "limousine liberal" too closely associated with the federal government and the "Atlanta bigwigs"—an image reinforced by the enthusiastic support given to Sanders by the Atlanta daily press. Carter tailored his campaign to exploit these weaknesses. A forty-four-year-old peanut farmer from the small south Georgia town of Plains, Carter labeled Sanders "Cufflinks Carl" and portrayed himself as the common-man candidate. One of Carter's more effective television commercials pictured the door to a country club and contained a message that began: "This is the door to an exclusive country club, where the big-money boys play cards, drink cocktails and raise money for their candidate: Carl Sanders. People like *us* aren't invited. We're busy working for a living. That's why our votes are going for Jimmy Carter. . . ."[7] Although eschewing outright race-

[7]As quoted in Clotfelter and Hamilton, "But Which Southern Strategy?" pp. 6–7. The discussion of the Carter campaign is based primarily on a series of articles by Bill Shipp, entitled "How He Won," in the *Atlanta Constitution*, November 8–11, 1970.

baiting, Carter struck hard at busing, identified himself with the Maddox administration—unable to succeed himself as governor, Maddox ran for and won the lieutenant governor's office—and promised to invite George Wallace to visit Georgia.

Carter's campaign strategy was eminently successful. He almost won a majority in the first primary, carrying the rural counties and larger towns and sweeping the lower-status precincts in the cities. Sanders's strength in black and upper-status white neighborhoods was sufficient, however, to net the former governor a plurality in metropolitan counties and to force a runoff contest. Carter finished with 48.6 percent in the first primary, as compared with 37.8 percent for Sanders, with the remaining votes divided among seven other candidates. In the runoff Carter's rural and working-class support proved decisive, overwhelming Sanders's metropolitan coalition of blacks and affluent whites and providing Carter with just under 60 percent of the total vote. Carter appealed to the same voting groups which had made Maddox the Democratic nominee for governor in 1966 and for lieutenant governor in 1970 and which had delivered Georgia's electoral vote to Wallace in 1968. The vote for Carter in the runoff election correlated with the Wallace vote at the .95 level, with ecological categories as the units of analysis.

Carter's Republican opponent in the general election was Atlanta television news commentator Hal Suit, who had defeated the favored James L. Bentley in the Republican party's first Georgia primary contest. An attractive conservative candidate, Suit was little known outside the Atlanta area, and even in a year generous toward political newcomers, he was no match for the peanut farmer from Plains. Carter once again combined his rural-small town constituency with urban working-class whites and even substantial black support to swamp Suit by approximately the same margin as that by which he had defeated Sanders six weeks before. In his inaugural address Carter echoed the more consistent rhetoric of Askew and Bumpers, calling for a "time for truth and frankness" and affirming "that the time for racial discrimination is over."[8]

In South Carolina the "New South" candidate for governor, Democrat John Carl West, did not represent a fresh young face. Forty-seven years old in 1970, West looked even older, more in the image of a stocky, round-faced banker with thinning grey hair and conservative demeanor. More than any of the new breed of New South politicians, West had moved in a traditional fashion through the dominant Democratic establishment. His political career started as highway-commissioner, included twelve years as state senator beginning in 1954, led in 1966 to his election as lieutenant governor under Governor Robert E. McNair, and culminated in an unopposed gubernatorial nomination in 1970. Raised by his mother on a

[8]As quoted in the *New York Times*, January 17, 1971.

modest farm outside Camden—when he was eight months old his father had perished in a fire attempting to rescue his mother—West graduated from the Citadel, rose to the rank of army major in World War II, and subsequently earned his law degree from the University of South Carolina. Throughout his political career the soft-spoken West had largely avoided exploiting racial animosities—in 1958 he quarreled publicly with the local Ku Klux Klan—and had concentrated on the bread-and-butter issues of industry-building and improving South Carolina's meager investment in health and educational facilities. In 1968 he supported Hubert Humphrey, who came in third in South Carolina behind Wallace and the winner, Nixon, and that same year in South Carolina West addressed an NAACP testimonial dinner in behalf of Roy Wilkins.

West's opponent in 1970 was Republican Congressman Albert Watson, who had been elected to represent the Columbia-based Second District in 1962 as a Democrat but who had supported Goldwater in 1964 and as a result had been stripped of his congressional seniority, together with Mississippi's John Bell Williams, by the Democratic congressional leaders. In response Watson resigned his seat and was reelected to it as a Republican in 1965. A Nixon supporter in 1968, Watson's chief sponsor in 1970 was Senator Strom Thurmond, who nominated Watson at the Republican state convention. Watson's Goldwater credentials were authentic and consistent. A tall, assertive man whose wavy dark hair and tub-thumping oratory contrasted sharply to the bland style of the older West, Watson's speeches rang with outrage at the behavior of hippies, civil-rights and anti-war protestors, school integrationists, campus radicals, criminals, and even the subversive degradation of modern art.

On two occasions during the campaign, Watson's enthusiasm backfired. In a speech at Lamar in February, he urged the crowd to "use every means at your disposal" to fight school integration, and nine days later in Lamar a mob of whites attacked a school bus loaded with black children. Then as the election contest heated up in the fall, Watson's campaign introduced a five-minute television commercial showing five-year-old scenes of blacks rioting against police and asking, "Are we going to be ruled by the bloc? Look what it did in Watts . . . in the nation's capital." West's criticisms of such tactics were echoed even in conservative Republican circles. Republican Mayor Cooper White of Greenville accused Watson of running a campaign that was "polarizing the races," and the conservative *Greenville News* editorialized that "the Republican campaign has to be regarded as racist to a disturbing degree." Stung by such charges, the Watson campaign dropped the television spot after one week and imported David Eisenhower, Harry Dent, and Vice President Agnew to bolster the candidate's image. But as the campaign closed, it was the fire-breathing Watson rather than the low-keyed West who was on the defensive. Nevertheless, West was sensitive to charges that he was playing for the black vote, and when in July federal officials brought pressure to bear in a number of school-integration suits in South Carolina, West condemned the "social experimentation" by the Department of Health, Education, and Welfare and urged that South Carolinians "must continue to fight to prevent the massive disruption of our public schools."[9] In response, the black United Citizens Party nominated a black attorney, Thomas Broadwater, as a write-in candidate for governor. And on Watson's right an offshoot to the Wallace movement, the Independent party, nominated A. W. Bethea.

When the final returns were in, West had defeated Watson by 51.6 percent to 45.7, with Broadwater and Bethea splitting a meager 2.7 percent. West ran well generally, winning by about the same margin in rural as well as urban counties, although doing somewhat better in the Piedmont than in the lowlands. In the four metropolitan counties containing Charleston, Columbia, Greenville, and Spartanburg, which contributed one-third of the total vote, West lost only Greenville. Precinct returns indicated that

Table 6.2

Percentage of the Vote for West and Watson
in the 1970 Gubernatorial General Election in Columbia and Charleston,
by Socioeconomic Class and Race[a]

Vote category	Percentage of vote received		(N)[b]
	West	Watson	
Columbia			
Lower-class white	40.0	56.2	(3,897)
Lower-middle-class white	40.8	56.4	(2,906)
Upper-middle-class white	47.5	49.6	(3,621)
Upper-class white	48.9	49.5	(4,105)
Black	93.9	1.1	(2,902)
Richland County[c]	53.9	43.1	(46,328)
Charleston			
Lower-class white	32.8	65.4	(1,544)
Lower-middle-class white	41.3	57.4	(1,207)
Upper-middle-class white	40.6	58.0	(3,023)
Upper-class white	36.2	62.0	(1,605)
Black	95.3	4.3	(2,739)
Charleston County[c]	52.2	45.9	(45,950)

[a]Votes for Broadwater and Bethea are excluded.

[b](N) denotes the number of votes upon which the percentages are based.

[c]County-vote percentages are based on the total number of votes cast in the county.

[9]As quoted in Jack Bass, "John C. West of South Carolina," *South Today* 3 (July–August, 1972): 9.

neither candidate projected a strong class appeal, although West's solid support in black districts was clearly crucial to his victory. In Columbia Watson's support among whites decreased with socioeconomic class, a pattern consistent with Watson's record in past congressional elections in the city. Watson carried only six counties, all but Greenville in or adjacent to his old congressional district.

In the gubernatorial contest in Tennessee the fresh new face belonged not to a Democrat but to a Republican dentist, Dr. Winfield Dunn of Memphis. Although his father had served one term (1935–37) as a Democratic congressman from Mississippi, Dunn had switched to the Republican party in 1960, and a decade later the forty-three-year-old dark horse candidate won a surprise victory in the Republican primary. Aided by White House staffers anxious to exploit a trend toward Republicanism in Tennessee by capturing the statehouse and retiring their vexing nemesis, Senator Albert Gore, Dunn enjoyed a well-financed and highly organized campaign that capitalized upon his appealing personal qualities and lack of political taint and was characterized less by occasional controversial allusions to his opponent's "socialist views" than by such charming observations as that should the amiable dentist be elected governor, he would have to learn how to operate from behind a desk.[10]

His opponent, Nashville attorney John Jay Hooker, was a handsome and wealthy Democrat of liberal persuasions and Kennedy connections who had lost to Governor Buford Ellington in the 1966 primary and who in 1970 had struggled through a six-man primary with a plurality of 44.7 percent (Tennessee had no provision for a runoff primary). Hooker was plagued throughout the campaign by a speculative collapse in the Minnie Pearl fried chicken franchise business that had added to his wealth and to the wealth of his close friends but had enmeshed a larger number of later participants and smacked less of scandal than of poor business judgement.

Although overshadowed by the nationally publicized campaign to oust Albert Gore, the Dunn-Hooker race reflected many of the same dynamics: burgeoning Republicanism in the suburbs, especially in the booming port city of Memphis; popular disenchantment with the reform, protest, and turmoil associated with the Democratic party in the 1960s; and the alienation of the state's Wallace voters, who had cast 34 percent of the total in 1968, compared with 37.8 percent for Nixon and 28.1 percent for Humphrey. Dunn's advantages were formidable, as he was in a position to gang up on Hooker's home base in middle Tennessee by combining the votes of Republican east Tennessee with his Memphis hometown. And that is precisely what he did, carrying the counties containing Knoxville (63.6 percent) and Chattanooga (58.7 percent) in the eastern grand division and Memphis (55.4 percent) in the west, while holding Hooker's margin in

[10]*Nashville Tennessean*, November 7–8, 1972.

Nashville to only 51.9 percent. The precinct returns dramatically illustrate how the New Deal coalition that Hooker barely held together in Nashville utterly crumbled in Memphis (see table 6.3).

Even Mississippi was engulfed in the unexpected surge of racial moderation. A field of seven candidates entered the Democratic gubernatorial primary to fill the office being vacated by the still defiantly segregationist John Bell Williams. On the right in the campaign was Hattiesburg country-music singer Jimmy Swan, a pronounced segregationist of the Bilbo school who had run a strong race in the 1967 gubernatorial primary and was regarded as a major contender in 1971. But the old pitch didn't sell, and Swan finished a distant third. Lieutenant Governor Charles L. Sullivan came in first with 37.8 percent of the votes and entered the runoff with William L. Waller, who won just under 30 percent. A forty-four-year-old former district attorney from Jackson, Waller was once known as a strong segregationist but more recently was remembered for having twice attempted and failed to convict Byron de la Beckwith for the murder of NAACP state field secretary Medgar Evers. Both candidates voiced their staunch opposition to busing but otherwise generally avoided racial issues, encouraged perhaps by the relatively recent accumulation of approximately 300,000 blacks on the voter rolls, up from 185,000 when Williams won four years earlier. In the rather bland campaign, Sullivan stressed his conservative credentials, while Waller clothed his campaign in the common-man rhetoric characteristic of other New South moderates. Waller won by a comfortable 54 percent majority, running well everywhere except in Sullivan's home bailiwick in the Mississippi delta. In Jackson Waller carried every category of voters, faring somewhat better

Table 6.3

Percentage of the Vote for Hooker in the
1970 Gubernatorial General Election in Nashville and Memphis,
by Socioeconomic Class and Race

	Nashville		Memphis	
Vote category	Percentage of vote received	$(N)^a$	Percentage of vote received	$(N)^a$
Lower-class white	52.7	(7,403)	29.0	(6,164)
Lower-middle-class white	51.9	(5,678)	28.3	(10,766)
Upper-middle-class white	44.5	(13,815)	19.0	(6,484)
Upper-class white	21.3	(20,446)	14.3	(10,941)
Black	96.8	(5,165)	98.0	(9,869)
County vote[b]	51.9	(130,622)	42.8	(202,963)

[a](N) denotes the number of votes upon which the percentages are based.

[b]County-vote percentages are based on the total number of votes cast in the county.

in white working-class districts than in upper-income or black precincts. The Republicans chose not to nominate a gubernatorial candidate, leaving Mayor Charles Evers of Fayette, a black independent contender, as Waller's major opponent in the general election. The Democratic nominee largely ignored the race question, pledging instead to involve "all people" in government, to improve Mississippi's tarnished image, and to restore working relationships with the national Democratic party.[11] Waller won overwhelmingly with approximately 77 percent of the votes.

One week later Louisiana held its gubernatorial primary. Governor John McKeithen's prestige had declined precipitously during his second term in the statehouse as charges of corruption and maladministration mounted. With the incumbent administration in disrepute, seventeen candidates responded to the vacuum in the November 1971 gubernatorial primary. Included were such veterans as former Congressman Gillis Long, former Governor Jimmie Davis, and, representing the arch-segregationist sentiment, Lieutenant Governor C. C. Aycock. But symptomatic of the New South mood, the top two vote-getters to enter the runoff primary were newcomers to statewide campaigns. The leader in the crowded first-primary field was forty-four-year-old Edwin W. Edwards, a Cajun Congressman from Acadia parish in Catholic Louisiana who had been elected to the House in a 1965 special election. Facing Edwards in the runoff was thirty-nine-year-old J. Bennett Johnston, a state senator from Shreveport. Both men were moderates, and during the campaign they publicly differed very little over issues, jousting with a decorum that seemed alien to Louisiana politics. Johnston's Baptist religion (even though his wife and children were Roman Catholic), north Louisiana background, and past association with segregationist school boards in Shreveport did, however, contrast with Edwards's Catholicism and south Louisiana Cajun heritage.[12]

The election provoked relatively sharp cleavages along religious, racial, and to some extent even class lines as Edwards won a razor-thin 50.2 percent majority to become the first south Louisiana Democratic gubernatorial nominee in three decades. Edwards won more than two-thirds of the votes cast in the towns and parishes of the Catholic South, while Johnston swept the predominately white Protestant parishes by margins almost as great (see figure 6.6). The Protestant black-belt parishes were divided somewhat more evenly, since Edwards collected a solid majority of the ballots cast by black voters. The three non-Catholic parishes that he carried were black-belt counties with high black registration. In the cities Edwards's majorities in black districts ranged from 55 percent in Shreveport to 81 percent in Baton Rouge.

[11]Jack E. White, Jr., "Kluxer's Nightmare Runs for Governor," *Race Relations Reporter*, September 21, 1971, p. 3.
[12]Ferrell Guillory, "Edwards of Louisiana," *South Today* 4 (April 1973): 5–7.

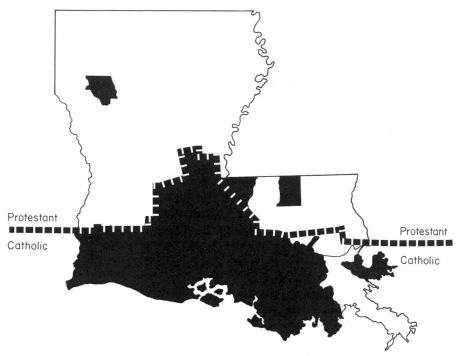

Fig. 6.6. Louisiana parishes voting 50 percent or more for Edwards in the 1971 gubernatorial runoff primary

The Democratic nominee's ability to combine Catholic and black votes was reminiscent of Mayor Morrison's campaigns of the early 1960s, and the vote for Edwards and for Morrison in the 1960 and 1964 runoff contests correlated positively (at the .90 and .76 levels, respectively). Morrison lost and Edwards won primarily because far more blacks voted in 1971 than had done so a decade before. But the differences between the appeals of Morrison and Edwards were also substantial. Unlike the late New Orleans Mayor, Edwards ran better in the countryside than in metropolitan parishes, and in the cities he fared better in white working-class districts than in upper-income white areas. Although Johnston carried every category of white voter in Shreveport, Baton Rouge, and New Orleans, Edwards made respectable showings in lower-income areas, and that, combined with his black support, held Johnston's lead in the metropolitan counties to a 54.3 percent majority.

In the general election in February 1972, Edwards faced David C. Treen, an energetic New Orleans attorney. Observers expected Treen to conduct an its-time-for-a-change-type campaign to take advantage of the apparent mood of southern voters and the fact that Louisiana's attorney general had recently been convicted of perjury, the state director of public works had just been indicted, and other Democratic Louisiana public servants were under investigation. But Treen chose to build his campaign around his own hard, rightwing ideological stance, assaulting the federal medicare program, attacking organized labor, and generally upholding an uncompromising social, economic, and philosophical conservatism.[13] Treen won solidly in the predominately white and Protestant upland parishes, and he carried most white precincts in the cities, running best in upper-income areas and doing far better in Shreveport in the north than in his hometown of New Orleans to the south. The Republican campaign solidified Edwards's Catholic and black support, however, and the Democratic candidate won an easy victory with more than 57 percent of the total vote. Edwards was virtually the unanimous choice in urban black precincts, and he collected more than three-fourths of the votes cast in rural Catholic parishes.

The public demand for refreshing faces transcended ideological concerns. The epic campaign for Albert Gore's seat in Tennessee and the defeat of Ralph Yarborough in Texas suggested that the incumbents, whether old-guard conservatives or old war-horse liberals like Gore and Yarborough, surrendered the advantage to their younger challengers, regardless of party or political philosophy. Albert Gore was nationally regarded as the number one target of the Nixon administration's Southern Strategy in 1970. A veteran of thirty-two years on Capitol Hill, the last eighteen in the Senate, Gore had defeated the Crump-allied McKeller in 1952 and, together with his senior colleague Estes Kefauver, had kept the New Deal torch burning, consistently sundering the defensive unity of the South's Senate delegation throughout the years of the Second Reconstruction.[14] Gore's refusal to participate in southern filibusters against civil-rights proposals, his support of TVA and public power, and his efforts on behalf of tax reform had angered conservatives of both parties over the years, and his hostility to the Vietnam war and his opposition to the Supreme Court nominations of Haynsworth and Carswell had especially rankled the Nixon administration.

The Republican campaign to retire Albert Gore was carefully planned and abundantly financed. A full fifteen months prior to the election, Kenneth Rietz, a senior associate of Harry Treleaven, whose political consulting firm had directed the public relations of the 1968 Nixon campaign, was dispatched to Tennessee to plan the attack. (No pauper himself, Gore subsequently countered by signing on Charles Guggenhcim, whose media expertise was often employed by liberal Democrats.) Against the sixty-two-

[13]David Snyder, in *New Orleans States-Item*, February 3, 1972; and Charles E. Grenier and Perry H. Howard, "The Edwards Victory," *Louisiana Review* 1 (Summer 1972): 31–42.

[14]See generally Joseph Bruce Gorman, *Kefauver: A Political Biography* (New York: Oxford University Press, 1971); and Albert Gore, *Let the Glory Out* (New York: Viking Press, 1972).

year-old, silver-haired Gore the Republicans nominated thirty-nine-year-old William Brock III, scion of the Brock Candy fortune and since 1962 the representative from the Chattanooga-based Third Congressional District. Like Winfield Dunn's father, Brock's grandfather had once sat as a Democrat in the U.S. Congress. Brock's hard-line speeches, delivered with uninspiring flatness and unrelenting purpose, were vintage Agnew, in content if not in flair. Unlike Kefauver, Gore had never generated an intense personal following in Tennessee, and his vulnerability to charges of being remote from Tennessee and too liberal for his constituency was reflected in his narrow victory in the primary over the relatively unknown Hudley Crockett, a former news commentator and press secretary to Governor Buford Ellington. By contrast, in the Republican primary Brock defeated country-music singer Tex Ritter by a margin of three to one.

By August Gore's chances looked hopeless. But "the Old Gray Fox of Carthage" was not beaten. Sensitive to the charge that he no longer represented the views of the average Tennessean, Gore began barnstorming the hustings, appearing in shirt-sleeves at supermarkets and factory gates, while Brock played to the receptive junior chambers of commerce. Gore proclaimed that he had grown up "with Tennessee dirt on my hands, not Chattanooga chocolate," that he and a majority of Tennessee's congressional delegation had voted for fifty bills that involved federal aid to Tennessee while Brock had voted against all fifty. When the Republicans brought Vice-President Agnew to Memphis, Gore crashed the public reception. When wealthy Nashville Republicans staged a "Fox Hunters' Ball" fundraiser for Brock, Gore staged a hilarious "one-gallused luncheon." In Chattanooga he even broke out his hoedown fiddle, and by late October the appreciative local politicians were guessing that he might be pulling it out, especially with the crucial Wallace voters, of whom Gore reckoned two-thirds would be needed to win.[15]

Then Brock unleashed his eleventh-hour media blitz, focused directly on the Wallace constituency and hammering with telling effect on four points: busing, gun registration, school prayer, and the nominations of Haynsworth and Carswell. Gore had voted for busing and gun registration and against school prayer and the nominations of Haynsworth and Carswell, and Brock had opposed him on all four. The charges were not new, but the massive media exploitation of their emotional content was. Gore had attempted to clarify the contextual distortions of their thrust before; indeed, he had momentarily waffled a bit on his anti-Vietnam stand, much as he had retreated on the civil-rights question when running in 1964 against a Goldwater candidate, Memphis Congressman Dan Kuykendall.

---

[15]Among numerous post-mortems of the campaign are David Halberstam, "The End of a Populist," *Harper's*, January 1971, pp. 35–45; Richard Harris, "Annals of Politics: How the People Feel," *The New Yorker*, July 10, 1971, pp. 35–54; and Gene Graham, "Gore's Lost Cause," *New South* 26 (Spring 1971): 26–34.

Fig. 6.7. Tennessee counties voting 50 percent or more for Dunn in the 1970 gubernatorial election

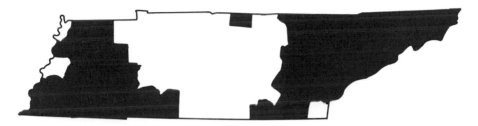

Fig. 6.8. Tennessee counties voting 50 percent or more for Brock in the 1970 senatorial election

But the blitz was too much and, for Gore, too late. Brock might well have won without it, but when the votes were counted, he had downed Gore by a margin of 52.1 percent to 47.9. Brock came out of the east Tennessee mountains with a 60 percent edge, and Gore countered with a 62 percent margin in middle Tennessee. Then Brock, like Dunn, sealed his Democratic opponent's doom in west Tennessee, carrying Shelby County (Memphis) by 55 percent and the western grand division by the same margin. (The conservative coalition of the eastern and western grand divisions against the middle, which was reminiscent of the Crump era, is reflected in Figure 6.8.) Gore had run a stronger race than Hooker, but, as in the case of Hooker, while his New Deal coalition had held up in Nashville, it had disintegrated in Memphis. He had enticed substantial numbers of Wallace voters to return to the Democratic fold, but not quite enough.

A similar fate befell Ralph Yarborough in Texas, albeit in the Democratic primary, where the sixty-seven-year-old incumbent was challenged by Lloyd M. Bentsen, Jr., a forty-nine-year-old banking and insurance millionaire from Houston. At the age of twenty-seven, Bentsen had been elected to Congress to represent the lower Rio Grande Valley, but in 1955 he had retired to pursue his business career. Bentsen was a conservative Democrat of the Connally persuasion who attacked Yarborough for his dovishness on Vietnam and his unsouthern votes against the confirmation of Haynsworth and Carswell. Bentsen's television spots suggested that the chaos at the 1968 Democratic convention in Chicago was a function of the permissiveness with which Yarborough's liberalism was suggestively

Table 6.4

Percentage of the Vote for Gore in the
1970 Senatorial Election in Nashville and Memphis,
by Socioeconomic Class and Race

	Nashville		Memphis	
Vote category	Percentage of vote received	(N)[a]	Percentage of vote received	(N)[a]
Lower-class white	59.9	(7,287)	27.3	(5,838)
Lower-middle-class white	60.4	(5,850)	36.2	(7,112)
Upper-middle-class white	50.2	(13,321)	23.7	(7,804)
Upper-class white	31.3	(18,209)	20.5	(11,013)
Black	97.5	(4,988)	98.3	(8,273)
County vote[b]	57.3	(130,776)	45.2	(197,927)

[a](N) denotes the number of votes upon which the percentages are based.

[b]County-vote percentages are based on the total number of votes cast in the county.

linked. Yarborough responded, as he always had, in vibrant, even dogmatic defense of liberalism's challenge to the vested interests, which certainly included Houston millionaires. But the smooth Bentsen was no Blakley, and Yarborough's campaign was late-starting, disorganized, and, as ever, underfinanced.[16] In the four of Texas's 254 counties that contained 41 percent of its population, the old warrior ran close behind Bentsen, carrying Harris County (Houston) while losing Dallas, Tarrant (Forth Worth), and Bexar (San Antonio). Yarborough held together his New Dealish coalition of blacks and lower-status whites, although his margins in working-class white districts were less impressive than they had been in previous elections. But the countryside belonged to Bentsen, who won hefty majorities not only in west Texas but in the east Texas towns and counties that had once been Yarborough country as well. Yarborough carried only the heavily Chicano south Texas region, to lose statewide with 46.9 percent of the vote.

The general election in November was anticlimactic. Bentsen faced a fellow Houston conservative millionaire, three-term Republican Congressman George Bush, who had carried 43.6 percent of the vote against Yarborough in 1964. Bush agreed with Bentsen that the Nixon position on Vietnam was prudent, that gun registration was threatening to constitutional liberties, that the oil depletion allowance should not be modified, that price controls on natural gas were unwise, that NASA and the F-111 fighter-bomber, being heavily Texas-based, should be pushed, and that the SST, being Seattle-based, should be blocked. Bentsen did attack the Nixon administration on inflationary economic policies, and his modest post-

[16]E. Larry Dickens, "Microcosm in Texas: An Achilles Heel for a Liberal Coalition," *New South* 26 (Summer 1971): 10–18.

primary gestures in the direction of the left wing of the party, partly at the urging of Lyndon Johnson, did bring tepid endorsements from the Texas AFL-CIO and from black state Senator Barbara Jordan and San Antonio Congressman Henry Gonzalez. But predictably, a faction of Kamikaze liberals formed the Democratic Rebuilding Committee in support of Bush. In any event, Bentsen's eventual 53.5 percent victory margin over Bush was partly a function of the fortuitous coincidence that two constitutional amendments—one to legitimize liquor by the drink and one to tax as farmland all undeveloped Texas land—brought rural voters out in droves, and their tendency to support conservative Democrats carried Bentsen through.[17] Bentsen once again demonstrated the classic and ironical

Table 6.5

Percentage of the Vote for Bentsen in the
1970 Senatorial Primary (against Yarborough) and
General Election (against Bush) in Houston, Waco, and Fort Worth,
by Socioeconomic Class and Race

Vote category	Primary		General	
	Percentage of vote received	(N)[a]	Percentage of vote received	(N)[a]
Houston				
Lower-class white	45.2	(2,290)	52.6	(4,981)
Lower-middle-class white	48.0	(2,539)	46.0	(5,436)
Upper-middle-class white	62.2	(2,924)	32.0	(7,089)
Upper-class white	76.7	(3,378)	22.2	(8,091)
Black	2.7	(3,578)	83.0	(4,367)
Harris County[b]	43.7	(174,687)	39.7	(358,150)
Waco				
Lower-class white	39.3	(3,126)	69.5	(4,200)
Lower-middle-class white	46.1	(1,672)	64.3	(2,598)
Upper-middle-class white	63.3	(3,162)	57.3	(4,850)
Upper-class white	75.6	(3,887)	44.5	(5,112)
Black	14.1	(1,965)	90.8	(2,356)
McLennan County[b]	50.0	(22,219)	63.4	(33,121)
Fort Worth				
Lower-class white	38.2	(2,789)	65.5	(5,674)
Lower-middle-class white	47.8	(3,553)	60.3	(6,598)
Upper-middle-class white	72.3	(3,651)	42.3	(8,103)
Upper-class white	75.9	(5,775)	31.0	(11,178)
Black	3.4	(1,629)	92.0	(2,368)
Tarrant County[b]	54.1	(64,724)	50.1	(133,771)

[a](N) denotes the number of votes upon which the percentages are based.

[b]County-vote percentages are based on the total number of votes cast in the county.

[17]*Houston Post*, May 5–7; November 6–9, 1970.

ability of conservative Texas Democrats to appeal to the affluent whites in the primary and then to rally the New Deal coalition against a Republican in the general election.

To be sure, not all veteran politicians went under. In 1970 Mississippi Senator John Stennis won reelection without opposition. Virginia Senator Harry Byrd, Jr., running for reelection as an independent, demonstrated both the magic of his name and the rapid disintegration of the party structure in the Old Dominion, as he trounced both the ineffective and sacrificial Republican nominee, Ray Garland, and the liberal Democrat, George Rawlings. (The liberals struck back in 1971, however, when Henry Howell, also running as an independent, won the special election to fill the lieutenant governor's office made vacant by the death of Reynolds.)

Democratic Governor Preston Smith of Texas remained in office by again defeating Republican Paul Eggers, a former counsel to the Treasury Department in the Nixon administration who had carried 43 percent of the vote against Smith in 1968 and who lost with just over 46 percent in 1970. Smith, an amiable but overwhelmingly bland gentleman whose positions on the issues remained as unclear as his differences with Eggers, highlighted the campaign with an appearance at the University of Houston, where activist students hooted him off the stage with a chant of "Free Lee Otis," referring to the draconian sentence of black militant Lee Otis to thirty years in prison on a marijuana charge. The bewildered Smith explained that he thought the students were shouting "frijoles," and exclaimed following the encounter, "I wonder why they were yelling about beans."[18] To liberal Democrats, the incident was monumental testimony to the governor's remoteness from the concerns of oppressed minorities; but to many in the larger electorate, it no doubt appeared that anyone routed by student radicals couldn't be all bad, and Preston Smith was reelected with a whoop.

The dramatic surge of New South politicians following hard upon the explosive thrust of the Maddoxes and Wallaces of the late 1960s left political pundits groping for explanations. As previously suggested, the phenomenon did not seem to be directly related to specific issues, such as the Wallace-Maddox explosion had been to racial matters. A survey research study conducted by the Institute for Social Research at Florida State University found that "issues played a negligible role in the Democratic primary victories of Askew and Chiles, and were only of slight importance in the general election."[19]

Aggregate data demonstrate that the South's newly found moderation did not rest on a common base of voter support. Voting patterns varied widely in the Democratic primaries. In Louisiana Edwin Edwards's coali-

[18]As quoted in the *New York Times*, November 5, 1970.
[19]Erickson and Zavoina, "Issues and Voters in the 1970 Florida Election," p. 1.

tion of Catholics, blacks, and lower-status whites resembled national New Deal voting patterns. Virginia's Henry Howell attracted solid support from urban blacks and working-class whites, but his populist rhetoric netted him little in rural areas. Dale Bumpers in Arkansas also won in black precincts, but against Faubus he ran better in higher-status white districts than in black or white working-class areas. Against Republican opposition in general elections, New South Democrats, like others of their party, normally ran best in rural and lower-status white and black urban areas, but even here patterns were irregular, as evidenced by West's support in South Carolina. Successful Republican moderates like Holton or Dunn relied upon the usual G.O.P. constituency of none-too-prosperous white Republicans of the mountains and prospering whites of the suburbs, but, as in the case of Memphis, these patterns were not always consistent. There clearly seemed to be an underlying antiestablishment tone to voter behavior during the period, however, as there had been to the Wallace-Maddox upsurge that preceded it.

CHAPTER 7

THE 1972 ELECTIONS

As the 1972 presidential election approached, the ambiguities that marked the resurgence of the New South remained. Amidst the regional mood of racial moderation, the South's foremost congressional liberals, Gore and Yarborough, fell victims to the Social Issue, and the supreme symbol of southern resistance, George Corley Wallace, sustained and enhanced his political base. At a time when many of the old faces associated with the diehard resistance were falling by the wayside, the nationally preeminent veteran of southern resistance regained the Alabama statehouse, from where he soon launched a crusade that was to have substantial repercussions in southern as well as national politics.

Wallace emerged victorious from the 1970 Alabama gubernatorial primary elections in the face of formidable obstacles. Governor Lurleen Wallace had died of cancer in 1968 and had been succeeded by Lieutenant Governor Albert P. Brewer, a former Wallace protégé whose genteel style and Big Mule affiliations contrasted more sharply with Wallace's populism than did his rather similar racial convictions. His threat to depose Wallace excited the enthusiasm of the national Republicans and the national media more than his modest accomplishments would seem to have warranted. Vice-President Agnew, Interior Secretary Walter Hickel, and Postmaster General Winton Blount, a native Alabamian, visited the state to dispense kind words for Brewer, whose fortunes were not unrelated to Republican hopes of destroying Wallace's base for the presidential politics of 1972.

Brewer ran ahead of Wallace in the May 1970 Democratic primary. He won a plurality in the metropolitan counties, carrying the blacks, who were voting against Wallace, and the affluent whites, who objected both to Wallace's populism and to his explicit racism, or at least to Alabama's national and indeed international reputation as a primitive and racist state. Wallace did well in the Alabama countryside and in white working-class districts to finish close behind with 40.8 percent, as compared with Brewer's 42 percent. Most of the remaining votes went to Charles Woods, a Dothan businessman-turned-populist who campaigned against the sales tax on food and medicine, the high price of milk, and Brewer's support of tax breaks for utilities and other industries. Wallace's populist appeal placed him in a favorable position to attract these voters in the runoff. Wallace also once again moved rightward on the race question, attacking Brewer as the candidate who had sold out for the black "bloc vote."[1] Brewer's moderate coalition of blacks and affluent whites carried the metropolitan counties but not by sufficient majorities to overcome Wallace's majorities in the towns and counties, and Wallace won the nomination with a 51.6 percent majority.

The Republicans, having been devastated by the Wallace landslide of 1966, carefully avoided naming a gubernatorial nominee, thus insulating their local candidates from charges of being anti-Wallace in the campaign. Wallace therefore faced several minor candidates, including a candidate of the Whig party and Dr. John L. Cashin, a Negro dentist from Huntsville and the nominee of the predominately black National Democratic Party of Alabama. Precinct returns in Birmingham dramatically illustrated the tripartite electoral divisions that had marked the 1968 presidential contest. Lower-income whites voted heavily for Wallace, and blacks for Cashin, but Birmingham's upper-class whites, repelled by Wallace and appalled by Cashin, cast a solid majority of their votes for minor candidates, especially

Table 7.1

Percentage of the Vote for Wallace and Brewer in the
1970 Gubernatorial Runoff Primary and for Wallace, Cashin,
and Other Candidates in the
1970 Gubernatorial General Election in Birmingham,
by Socioeconomic Class and Race

	Runoff Primary			General Election			
	Percentage of vote received			Percentage of vote received			
Vote category	Wallace	Brewer	(N)[a]	Wallace	Cashin	Other	(N)[a]
Lower-class white	64.0	36.0	9,874	84.9	2.8	12.3	7,943
Lower-middle-class white	59.5	40.5	12,477	80.1	2.2	17.7	10,276
Upper-middle-class white	42.5	57.5	12,808	68.3	3.9	27.7	10,036
Upper-class white	18.3	81.7	12,029	39.8	5.0	55.1	9,143
Black	1.9	98.1	10,613	4.4	84.5	11.1	5,498
Jefferson County[b]	39.4	60.6	190,730	58.9	21.2	19.9	141,920

[a](N) denotes the number of votes upon which the percentages are based.

[b]County-vote percentages are based on the total number of votes cast in the county.

[1]*Montgomery Advertiser*, May 3-8, June 4-6, 1970; Ray Jenkins, "Standing for it Again in Alabama," *New South* 25 (Summer 1970): 26-30.

Independent A. C. Shelton. Wallace waltzed to an easy victory with approximately 77 percent of the votes.

Having consolidated his power base in Alabama, Wallace turned his attention to national politics, entering the March 1972 Florida Democratic presidential primary. With ten other contenders, including all the major Democratic presidential hopefuls, Wallace's campaign was initially given limited prospects for success. Most Florida political leaders either remained neutral in the contest or endorsed Senators Hubert Humphrey, Edmund S. Muskie, or Henry M. Jackson, at the time considered among the leading prospects for the nomination. But the Wallace campaign rapidly gained momentum; on the eve of the election, campaign aides in the Jackson, Humphrey, and Muskie camps were lamenting that "we've got all the officials, and, off the record, Wallace has got all the voters."[2] Wallace hammered away at the evils of busing and attacked high taxes, big government, and other national trends that he associated with the Democratic "establishment" candidates.

The returns gave Wallace a stunning 41.5 percent plurality, far ahead of Humphrey's meager 18.6 percent and Jackson's 13.5 percent. (No other candidate received as much as 10 percent of the vote.) Wallace won pluralities in every county in the state, but, as figure 7.1 indicates, his basic

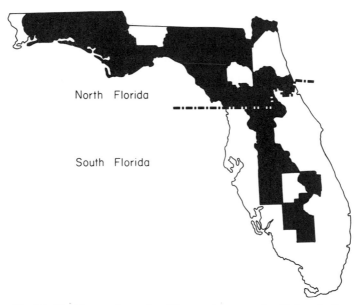

North Florida

South Florida

Fig. 7.1. Florida counties voting 60 percent or more for Wallace in the 1972 presidential primary

[2]As quoted in the *Miami Herald*, March 13, 1972. See the reports in the *Miami Herald*, March 12–16, 1972, and the analysis by Otis Perkins, in the *Jacksonville Times-Union*, March 15, 1972.

appeal was to voters in north Florida and in the rural counties in the central part of the state. In the south Florida cities his pluralities were narrow; in Miami Humphrey carried black and Jewish precincts, and Jackson ran well in upper-income white Protestant neighborhoods to limit Wallace to 27 percent of the vote. But in the north Florida countryside, the Alabamian tallied massive majorities, and in Jacksonville he won majorities in every category of white precincts, taking almost two of every three votes cast in lower- and lower-middle-income white areas and winning about 55 percent in upper- and upper-middle-status neighborhoods. Wallace received virtually no black votes, which held his Duval county total to a 46 percent plurality.

On the same ballot were three referenda soliciting voter preference for or against "forced busing," a return to a segregated public-school system, and prayers in public schools. In a display of unusual political courage, Governor Askew campaigned against the antibusing amendment and for the antisegregation measure. But despite Askew's efforts, a solid 74 percent majority recorded opposition to forced busing, as white Protestant voters massively endorsed the measure, while black and Jewish voters divided. But an even greater majority of almost 79 percent voted against a return to segregation in the schools, and almost 80 percent supported the reestablishment of prayer in the schools. Florida voters favored George Wallace, prayers, and integrated schools but not the use of buses to achieve integration. Both the balloting and survey data suggested that southern whites had conceded defeat on the segregation issue, but at the same time, underlying the region's newly found racial moderation was a continuing commitment to social conservatism.

Less than two months later, Wallace swept the Tennessee presidential primary with more than two-thirds of the votes, and on the same ballot approximately eight of every ten voters endorsed a referendum measure opposing the use of busing to achieve racial integration in the schools. Wallace's substantial victory in Tennessee attracted limited national attention and a low voter turnout, since other Democratic candidates conceded the state to the Alabamian and presented no organized opposition.[3] But immediately afterward Wallace faced a major challenge from a fellow southerner in the North Carolina presidential primary. Terry Sanford, a popular former governor who possessed a well-established network of political friends across the state as well as the support of Governor Robert Scott, conducted a vigorous campaign that appealed to homestate loyalties and racial moderation. Wallace insisted that Sanford, who was president of Duke University, was a front for ultraliberals attempting to derail his presidential effort and continued his assault on "the pointy-headed professors, the welfare loafers, the Rockefellers, the tax chiselers, the no-

[3]*Nashville Tennessean*, May 5, 1972.

win war, the elitists, the sophisticates, the noisemakers and the faceless bureaucrats in Washington who bus your children all over creation."[4] Black Congresswoman Shirley Chisholm also campaigned actively, while Senators Muskie and Jackson, whose names appeared on the ballot, ignored the contest.

Again Wallace made an impressive showing, winning the election with a 51 percent majority and finishing well ahead of Sanford, who polled approximately 37 percent. Wallace carried the rural-small town counties, especially those in the lowlands in the eastern part of the state, and in the cities he swept the lower- and lower-middle-status white precincts by heavy majorities. Sanford ran slightly ahead of Wallace in higher-status white neighborhoods and about even with Chisolm in black districts. But while boosting Wallace's national effort, North Carolina's Democratic voters also favored progressive Congressman Nick Galifianakis over conservative incumbent Senator B. Everett Jordan and moderate Hargrove Bowles, a close political friend of Sanford, over Lieutenant Governor Pat Taylor. Both Galifianakis and Bowles won near majorities in the first-primary elections and one month later overwhelmed their opponents in the runoff contests by solid majorities.[5]

The nomination of the vigorous forty-three-year-old Galifianakis over a seventy-six-year-old Senate veteran testified to the continuing vitality of New South moderation, and similar trends were evident in primary contests in Texas and Arkansas. The electorate's tendency to throw the rascals out was reinforced in Texas by a massive banking stock scandal that ensnared Governor Preston Smith, Lieutenant Governor Ben Barnes, and numerous other state governmental officials. Prior to the scandal, Barnes, the articulate thirty-four-year-old protégé of Lyndon Johnson and John Connally, generally had been considered the rising star in Texas politics. Both Barnes and Smith entered the Democratic gubernatorial primary but soon found themselves on the defensive, as lesser known candidates capitalized on the corruption-in-government issue.

On the left in the campaign was state Representative Frances T. "Sissy" Farenthold, who in addition to being a woman, a Catholic, and an enthusiastic supporter of the presidential efforts of Senator George S. McGovern was a plain-spoken liberal who met the Social Issue head-on by advocating liberalization of laws governing abortions, reduction of penalties for possession of marijuana, gun-control legislation, and other matters considered explosive in the Lone Star State. Although a leader of the liberal forces in the state legislature, Farenthold attracted limited aid from organized labor, which concentrated its financial and organizational re-

[4]As quoted by Carl Bernstein, in the *Washington Post*, May 7, 1972.
[5]Linda Charlton, in the *New York Times*, May 6–8, 1972; Marjorie Hunter, in ibid., June 3–5, 1972.

sources behind Ralph Yarborough's campaign to return to the U.S. Senate. But Farenthold's charismatic frankness attracted an army of volunteer workers whose efforts catapulted her into the position of a major contender in the race. Her chief opponents were the "two contaminated candidates," as she chose to describe Smith and Barnes, and "a big bowl of pablum," by which she meant Dolph Briscoe.[6] A gentleman whose overwhelming blandness rivaled Preston Smith's, Briscoe was a west Texas banker and rancher whose holdings reputedly made him Texas's largest landowner. Briscoe projected a staunchly conservative image, although he promised little beyond restoration of integrity in state government and opposition to any new tax measures.

Briscoe finished first in the primary, while Farenthold easily outdistanced Barnes and Smith to win a spot in the runoff. The second primary was a sharp and sometimes antagonistic liberal-conservative clash. Farenthold held together the New Deal alignments in the cities. In Houston she won just above 90 percent of the votes cast in black precincts, slightly more

Table 7.2

Percentage of the Vote for Farenthold and Yarborough
in the 1972 Runoff Elections in Houston and Waco,
by Socioeconomic Class and Race

Vote category	Farenthold		Yarborough	
	Percentage of vote received	(N)[a]	Percentage of vote received	(N)[a]
Houston				
Black	90.3	(2,990)	93.9	(2,603)
Lower-class white	54.2	(3,448)	54.4	(3,277)
Lower-middle-class white	58.2	(3,163)	49.5	(3,025)
Upper-middle-class white	48.0	(5,862)	40.8	(5,641)
Upper-class white	45.7	(5,704)	31.8	(5,479)
Harris County[b]	60.9	(255,521)	52.8	(250,153)
Waco				
Black	77.5	(2,263)	84.4	(2,218)
Lower-class white	42.5	(4,387)	56.4	(4,361)
Lower-middle-class white	38.5	(3,062)	54.2	(3,229)
Upper-middle-class white	32.9	(4,804)	44.6	(4,773)
Upper-class white	27.4	(4,976)	32.7	(4,981)
McLennan County[b]	39.4	(35,536)	51.3	(34,993)

[a](N) denotes the number of votes upon which the percentages are based.

[b]County-vote percentages are based on the total number of votes cast in the county.

[6]As quoted in the *Houston Post*, June 4, 1972. On the campaigns, see the accounts by Martin Waldron, in the *New York Times*, May 6–8, June 3–5, 1972.

than 75 percent in the Chicano districts, and above 55 percent in lower- and lower-middle-income white areas. Even in Waco, heartland of east-central Texas Baptist country, Farenthold won more than three-quarters of the vote in black neighborhoods and 42.5 percent in lower-income white precincts. But if the election results suggested a growing maturity in Texas factional politics in the cities, the returns also clearly indicated that rural-small town voters were not quite ready for a liberal, Catholic lady to direct matters of state. Briscoe swept the countryside and the election with more than 55 percent of the vote.

At the same time, Ralph Yarborough failed in his attempt to recapture a U.S. Senate seat. Barefoot Sanders, a moderately conservative former assistant U.S. attorney general during the Kennedy-Johnson years (whose unusual first name testified to his Indian ancestry), attacked Yarborough as an ultraliberal advocate of school busing in the runoff to win the senatorial nomination and complete the rout of the liberals for major offices (in the first-primary contest Texas voters had expressed opposition to enforced busing by more than a three-to-one majority).

In Arkansas Senator John L. McClellan, a seventy-six-year-old veteran of three decades in the Senate, narrowly survived the hotly contested Democratic primary. David H. Pryor, a thirty-seven-year-old representative from the Fourth District, in the southern part of the state, conducted an aggressive campaign, countering McClellan's senatorial seniority with charges that the incumbent used his congressional power for the benefit of "the arrogant rich." When McClellan raised the busing issue, Pryor announced his opposition to busing, but he gave equal emphasis to condemning politicians who used racial issues for "inflaming emotions of the people."[7] McClellan finished ahead in the primary, but his approximately 44 percent of the vote was well short of a majority, and Pryor was close behind with 42 percent. Liberal lawyer Ted Boswell, who took most of the remaining votes, promptly announced support for Pryor in the runoff. Jolted by the first-primary results and now in the unaccustomed role of something of an underdog, McClellan took full advantage of the two weeks of campaign time between the first and second primaries. The conservative incumbent conducted an energetic campaign, branding Pryor the candidate of "out-of-state labor bosses" (Pryor had received contributions from national labor unions) and hammering hard on the school busing issue.[8] With support from former Governor Faubus and other old-line Arkansas Democratic leaders, McClellan squeezed by in the runoff with approximately 52 percent of the vote.

Wallace's formidable performance at the polls rested on his established constituency of working-class and rural-small town whites, but in other

[7]As quoted by Roy Reed, in the *New York Times*, June 1, 1972.
[8]Ibid., June 13, 14, 1972.

major contests voter alignments remained relatively fluid. Farenthold appealed to a New Dealish urban constituency, while she attracted little support in the Texas countryside. Voting returns in North Carolina indicated no detectable class bias at the base of Galifianakis's primary victory, except that he won the bulk of votes cast in black precincts. In the Arkansas runoff primary Pryor also swept the black districts in Little Rock, and he ran somewhat better in lower-status white neighborhoods than he did in upper-income white areas, although McClellan ran first in a majority of the rural-small town counties. The surprisingly strong showings by Wallace in the presidential primary elections on the one hand and by such candidates as Galifianakis, Farenthold, and Pryor on the other evidenced the ambivalent tendencies in southern politics.

Elsewhere in the South, Democratic primary elections tended to reward those candidates who best accommodated voters who seemingly approved of George Wallace and antibusing statements and who still showed a fondness for fresh new faces and progressive policies. In South Carolina state Senator Eugene N. Zeigler, an articulate and erudite Harvard Law School graduate who had actively supported Kennedy, Johnson, and Humphrey in successive presidential campaigns, adopted a strong law-and-order defense of social conservatism in his campaign for the Democratic senatorial nomination. Since the Republican opponent in the general election would be Senator Thurmond, most of the state's better-known Democrats, such as former Governor Robert McNair, concluded that Thurmond could not be unseated and abandoned the contest to Zeigler and perennial liberal contender John Bolt Culbertson. Although fifty-one years old, Zeigler was otherwise in the New South tradition; a relatively new face in state politics, a close political friend of Governor John West, and a progressive in the state legislature, he was, as one journalist described him, an "Ivy League populist."[9] But in 1972 Zeigler combined his populism with a generally Wallacite stance that emphasized social conservatism. Zeigler easily defeated Culbertson for the senatorial nomination.

In Georgia Sam Nunn, an unknown south Georgia state representative with four rather undistinguished years in the legislature, won the Democratic nomination for the Senate seat made vacant by the death of Senator Richard B. Russell. During the early part of the campaign Nunn was listed with the fourteen minor candidates who were expected to flounder in the wake of the two favorites, moderate Atlanta lawyer David Gambrell, whom Governor Carter appointed to the Senate following Russell's death in early 1971, and former Governor Ernest Vandiver, long considered a power in state politics. But the youthful Nunn adopted as his campaign slogan "Get Tough in Washington" and combined an attractive fresh face with a strong

[9]Jack Bass, in the *Atlanta Journal and Constitution*, November 14, 1971, and in the *Washington Post*, November 7, 1972.

antiestablishment, law-and-order, antibusing social conservatism to win a spot in the runoff with Gambrell, while Vandiver, who in his last campaign a decade and a half before had won the gubernatorial nomination with more than 80 percent of the votes, finished a weak third. The runoff against Gambrell was a replay of the 1970 gubernatorial campaign, as Nunn, like Jimmy Carter two years before, attracted the Talmadge-Maddox-Wallace constituency of working-class and rural-small town whites to swamp Gambrell's moderate coalition of metropolitan blacks and affluent whites.[10] Similarly, Tennessee Democrats nominated lame-duck conservative Congressman Ray Blanton for a Senate seat; and in Louisiana J. Bennett Johnson, the runoff opponent of Governor Edwards in the gubernatorial primary earlier in the year, inherited the senatorial nomination when his only major opponent, veteran Senator Allen J. Ellender, died prior to the election but after the filing deadline.

Although the deaths of Senators Russell and Ellender and the defeat of Senator Jordan in North Carolina further diminished the southern old guard in the Senate, James Eastland of Mississippi and John Sparkman of Alabama won renomination with relative ease. Eastland brushed aside minor opposition in the Democratic primary to become the Democratic nominee for the seat that he had occupied for almost three decades. In Alabama Sparkman faced a more substantial challenge. Among his six primary opponents were State Auditor Melba Till Allen, whose anticorruption campaign in state government had made her well known, and Mobile Mayor Lambert C. Mims, a Baptist lay leader. Sparkman nevertheless won a first-primary victory.

The prospect that Wallace might mount a third-party effort in the 1972 presidential campaign terminated at a Maryland campaign rally in May with an assassin's bullets, which left Wallace grievously wounded. The Democratic party's reformed delegate-selection process benefited minority and liberal groups in the South as elsewhere in the nation and resulted in alienating numerous Democratic conservatives and ultimately in the nomination of Senator George McGovern as the Democratic presidential candidate. Reminiscent of the Eisenhower years, some conservative Democrats turned to presidential Republicanism; former Governor John Connally of Texas became national head of Democrats for Nixon, and such conservative stalwarts as former Governor Mills Godwin of Virginia played active roles in the effort to reelect the president. With Wallace out of the race and Nixon facing the unabashedly liberal McGovern, the time for the testing of the Southern Strategy seemed to have arrived, in a year in which ten southern Senate seats and three statehouses were up for grabs.

As usual, the results of the elections were inconclusive. Nixon carried the Solid South, which voted as a bloc for the first time since 1944, by a

[10]*Atlanta Constitution*, August 1–10, 1972.

greater margin than any other region. He took 70.5 percent of the vote, while McGovern fared more poorly than even Humphrey had done in 1968. Nixon won virtually all of the voting groups that had supported either Nixon or Wallace in 1968, which meant that the vast bulk of white Protestants, as well as most white Catholics, voted Republican in the presidential race. As table 7.3 indicates, the Republican presidential ticket swept every demographic category, most by remarkable margins, and Republican gains over 1968 paralleled very closely the 1968 vote for Wallace. In the South as in the nation Nixon ran better in the towns and counties of the countryside than he did in the cities, but even in metropolitan counties he won more than two of every three votes. In the cities the New Deal alignments that had collapsed in the Deep South in 1964 and throughout the region in 1968 were further obliterated in 1972. Table 7.4 illustrates the votes by socioeconomic and racial categories for Nixon and Wallace in 1968 and for Nixon in 1972 in three selected southern cities. In Charlotte, North Carolina, Nixon ran extremely well in 1968, while Wallace fared rather poorly. In New Orleans Nixon and Wallace split white voters along class lines in 1968. Macon, Georgia, was a Wallace stronghold in 1968, and Nixon did well only in upper-income neighborhoods. But in 1972 Nixon swept white precincts of every socioeconomic category in all three cities. Presumably the bulk of the Wallace voters rallied to Nixon, a

Table 7.3

Percentage of the Vote for Nixon and Wallace in 1968 and for Nixon in 1972, by Geographic and Demographic Category

Vote category	1968		1972	
	Percentage of vote received by Wallace	Percentage of vote received by Nixon	Percentage of vote received by Nixon	Republican gain from 1968 to 1972
Geographic category				
White Belt	38.6	30.8	71.0	40.2
Black Belt	47.2	19.6	67.1	47.5
Piedmont	41.7	32.6	72.2	39.6
Mountains	29.3	45.9	73.0	27.1
Catholic Louisiana	44.0	25.6	73.8	48.2
South Florida	22.4	45.2	71.3	26.1
West Texas	16.4	43.1	68.8	25.7
South Texas	8.6	36.8	57.6	20.8
Demographic category				
Metropolitan	26.1	39.2	67.8	28.6
Urban	40.7	32.7	74.0	41.3
Rural	41.3	30.4	72.7	42.3
Region	34.3	34.7	70.5	35.8

Table 7.4

Percentage of the Vote for Nixon and Wallace in 1968
and for Nixon in 1972 in Charlotte, New Orleans, and Macon, Georgia,
by Socioeconomic Class and Race

Vote category	1968			1972	
	Percentage of vote received by Wallace	Percentage of vote received by Nixon	$(N)^a$	Percentage of vote received by Nixon	$(N)^a$
Charlotte					
Lower-class white	28.4	49.7	(4,215)	70.6	(4,215)
Lower-middle-class white	21.8	58.8	(8,614)	77.3	(8,173)
Upper-middle-class white	11.3	71.8	(8,039)	79.4	(10,217)
Upper-class white	6.1	75.7	(7,819)	79.9	(8,662)
Black	.1	1.3	(7,418)	6.2	(5,284)
Mechlenburg County[b]	18.7	52.4	(107,497)	68.5	(113,176)
New Orleans					
Lower-class white	53.2	25.4	(4,976)	77.1	(3,855)
Lower-middle-class white	43.1	39.8	(5,862)	81.0	(5,077)
Upper-middle-class white	33.8	44.8	(4,020)	75.5	(3,618)
Upper-class white	28.6	54.3	(4,964)	78.7	(4,961)
Black	5.5	1.1	(3,272)	12.8	(4,254)
Orleans Parish[b]	26.7	32.7	(178,668)	55.5	(158,676)
Macon					
Lower-class white	59.9	28.6	(4,869)	86.9	(3,828)
Lower-middle-class white	57.8	27.0	(6,839)	88.3	(5,173)
Upper-middle-class white	51.4	35.6	(5,564)	82.5	(5,028)
Upper-class white	28.4	56.1	(6,447)	87.0	(4,948)
Black	7.6	5.8	(2,313)	16.4	(2,089)
Bibb County[b]	41.9	32.6	(41,397)	72.9	(37,603)

[a](N) denotes the number of votes upon which the percentages are based.
[b]County-vote percentages are based on the total number of votes cast in the county.

supposition that cannot be precisely proven because of the aggregate nature of the data used here but one that certainly seems warranted by the consistency with which the combined Nixon-Wallace vote of 1968 equals the Nixon vote in 1972 (see tables 7.3 and 7.4) and by the negative correlations in every geographic and demographic category of counties between the Wallace vote in 1968 and the McGovern vote in 1972 and the corresponding positive county correlations between Wallace in 1968 and Nixon in 1972.

Like Humphrey four years before, McGovern fared well only among minority voters. He won the bulk of the votes cast in predominately Negro precincts in the cities and did better in black-belt counties than in surrounding areas. Similarly, he won hefty majorities in Chicano precincts, although not by sufficient majorities to outvote the Anglos in southern Texas.[11] Jewish precincts in Miami, especially the lower-income Jewish precincts, also turned in substantial Democratic majorities. But Chicano votes were influential only in Texas, and Jews were numerous only in south Florida. Throughout most of the South, McGovern's support, like Humphrey's, rested on a base of black voters. If the presidential election returns seemed to confirm the validity of the Southern Strategy (at least when utilized against Senator McGovern), state election results were considerably less conclusive.

The G.O.P. did make gains in the South, winning 5 of the 10 Senate elections and 1 of 3 gubernatorial contests and increasing its southern House delegation from 27 of 106 seats to 34 of 108. But given the magnitude of the Nixon landslide, southern Republicans, like Republicans elsewhere in the nation, found the Nixon coattails difficult to grasp. The party that had taught southern voters to split their tickets during the Eisenhower years became the proponent of the straight party vote, as Republican state and local candidates sought to tie themselves to Nixon and attempted to identify their opponents, no matter how conservative, with McGovern. Democratic candidates with some success frantically disassociated themselves from the national ticket, often identifying with the Wallace wing of the party; Wallace reciprocated by endorsing Zeigler in South Carolina, Nunn in Georgia, and Sparkman in Alabama.

The Republicans made their biggest breakthrough in North Carolina, capturing the statehouse and a Senate seat. The gubernatorial contest was a relatively bland affair. Republican James E. Holshouser, a thirty-eight-year-old state representative from a mountain district, differed little from Democratic Hargrove Bowles over significant issues. Both were moderates who promised economy and efficiency in government and attention to the problems of racial minorities. A wealthy Greensboro businessman, Bowles possessed an abundant campaign chest and was generally regarded as the favorite in the election. Holshouser was not only hard pressed financially, but as a result of a hotly contested Republican primary contest between Holshouser and veteran campaigner James Gardner, he headed a divided party. But the youthful Holshouser proved to be an attractive candidate in a state where Nixon won majorities in all one hundred counties, and it was enough to carry him through to a narrow victory.

Overshadowing the gubernatorial contest in the national media was the bitter ideological clash between progressive Democrat Nick Galifianakis and Republican Jesse A. Helms, whose political views were ultraconservative if not downright reactionary. For twelve years a television and radio editorialist, Helms in his commentaries had raged against the com-

---

[11]On this point, see the results of a CBS News survey analysis reported by Stephen Isaacs, in the *Washington Post*, November 9, 1972.

munist-socialist-anarchist forces behind federal governmental support for integration, social-welfare measures, trade with communist nations, foreign aid, and other acts of appeasement abroad and creeping socialism at home. During the campaign Helms sought to moderate his image by identifying himself with Nixon while seeking to tie Galifianakis to McGovern. Galifianakis staffers attained copies of Helms's old editorials and constantly embarrassed the Republican candidate by releasing old texts that contradicted his newly found moderation, especially editorials that described major Nixon initiatives as "almost laughable" and "socialistic."[12] Helms countered by calling Galifianakis "McGovernGalifianakis" and portraying the contest as a clear choice between McGovernite liberalism and Nixonian conservatism.

Helms won a convincing 54.3 percent majority, while Holshouser edged past Bowles with 51 percent. Helms ran well generally, carrying every area of the state and, in tandem with Nixon, becoming the first modern Republican to sweep the Wallacite stronghold in the eastern lowlands. He fared better in the towns and counties of the countryside than in the metropolitan areas, but even in the latter counties Helms ran slightly ahead of Galifianakis. The race-conscious lowland whites who supported Nixon and Helms cast majorities against Holshouser in the gubernatorial contest, where traditional partisan alignments reappeared as Holshouser, with his moderate stance and mountain residency, solidly carried the Republican highland redoubts, ran well ahead in the Piedmont, and lost

Table 7.5

Percentage of the Vote for Helms and Holshouser
in the 1972 General Elections in Charlotte,
by Socioeconomic Class and Race

	Helms		Holshouser	
Vote category	Percentage of vote received	(N)[a]	Percentage of vote received	(N)[a]
Lower-class white	53.8	(3,849)	55.1	(4,003)
Lower-middle-class white	56.8	(7,548)	60.1	(7,733)
Upper-middle-class white	58.9	(9,573)	64.1	(9,931)
Upper-class white	60.5	(8,119)	64.6	(8,371)
Black	10.2	(3,548)	11.4	(4,067)
Mecklenburg County[b]	54.1	(100,793)	56.4	(105,805)

[a](N) denotes the number of votes upon which the percentages are based.

[b]County-vote percentages are based on the total number of votes cast in the county.

[12]Gene Marlowe, in the *Atlanta Journal and Constitution*, October 15, 1972; and Jack Scism, in the *Greensboro Daily News*, November 8, 1972.

black-belt and coastal areas to the east. Neither Helms nor Holshouser projected a consistent class appeal in the cities. In Greensboro the two Republicans did best in upper- and lower-status white precincts, while their Democratic opponents fared relatively well in middle-income white neighborhoods. In Charlotte the Republicans won majorities in every white socioeconomic category, drawing somewhat greater support in upper-income neighborhoods than in lower-income ones. But in any case, class divisions in the cities were not sharp. Helms and Holshouser both won the counties containing Charlotte and Raleigh by sweeping the white districts, while they lost heavily in black neighborhoods; both lost by relatively narrow margins most of the other metropolitan counties, again running well in white precincts and losing the black ones. Although the moderate Holshouser ran slightly ahead of the conservative Helms in the cities, the class and racial base of their urban support was similar.

The senatorial election in Virginia, like the one in North Carolina, was a relatively sharp moderate-conservative ideological clash that resulted in a significant Republican victory. Senator William B. Spong, the Democratic incumbent, had during his six years in the Senate compiled a generally moderate record, normally standing somewhere between the policies of the Nixon administration and its liberal critics, a position exemplified by his support for the confirmation of Haynsworth as a Supreme Court justice and his opposition to the confirmation of Carswell. Spong's opponent was William L. Scott, a staunchly conservative northern Virginia congressman. Scott was a man who, as a Virginia journalist observed, tended to be "there when the lightning struck."[13] When Scott decided to seek his congressional seat in 1966, he had little trouble winning the Republican nomination, since the Democratic nominee was expected to be Howard W. Smith, a thirty-six-year veteran in the House of Representatives whom few Republicans cared to challenge. But Smith was upset in the Democratic primary by a far more vulnerable liberal contender, whom Scott then defeated in the general election.

In 1972 Scott captured the Republican senatorial nomination without opposition, since most observers considered Spong unassailable. Shortly afterward, however, Virginia Democrats became embroiled in another intraparty bloodletting that resulted in the pro-McGovern liberals winning control of the state Democratic convention. While the delegates at the meeting did not promise, as one bemused participant quipped, "to bus everyone to Canada for free abortions and infusions of marijuna," they did present a party image that was "going to be hard to explain to the folks back home in the Third district."[14] But despite a divided party and McGovern at the head of the ticket, Spong seemed to be safely ahead until

---

[13]Wayne Woodlief, in the *Norfolk Virginian-Pilot*, November 8, 1972.
[14]As quoted by Helen Dewar, in the *Washington Post*, June 18, 1972.

the closing weeks of the campaign, when the national Republican party channeled staffers and finances to bolster Scott's foundering efforts. The Scott campaign began a television-radio blitz that linked Spong to gun control, busing, and George McGovern and pictured Scott firmly on the side of patriotism and Richard Nixon.

The returns gave Scott a solid victory. The Republican won a 53.7 percent majority and a lead of almost ten percentage points over Spong, since a third-party candidate drained off a small share of the votes. Like Helms in North Carolina, Scott won everywhere, carrying the past Democratic strongholds in the black-belt and tidewater counties by even greater margins than he won in the traditionally Republican mountain region. He ran better in the towns and hinterlands than in metropolitan counties, but he carried even the latter by comfortable majorities. In the cities the basic division was between Democratic blacks and Republican-trending whites, although New Deal voting alignments held up somewhat better in Virginia than they had in North Carolina. In Richmond Spong swept the black precincts, won handily in lower-income white areas, and carried the lower-middle-status whites while losing in upper-income areas. But in the white precincts in Norfolk Spong ran best in lower- and upper-income areas, while Scott swept the middle-income white neighborhoods. For the most part, in both North Carolina and Virginia Helms and Scott fared remarkably well in the bailiwicks that had once been Democratic preserves.

Republican breakthroughs on the state level were confined to North Carolina and Virginia, but three incumbent Republican senators won reelection, all by substantial majorities. In Tennessee Senator Howard Baker easily turned back Democratic Congressman Ray Blanton. Baker won just under 62 percent of the vote, running only six percentage points behind Nixon and carrying all three grand divisions by comfortable majorities. In South Carolina the venerable Strom Thurmond cruised to another victory, despite early forecasts that the veteran senator might be in serious political trouble. Democrat Eugene Zeigler, who bore George Wallace's endorsement, conducted a vigorous campaign, attacking Thurmond's "negative" record in the Senate and reminding voters that Thurmond had campaigned actively against Wallace in 1968. But Zeigler was no match for "ole Strom." Thurmond added a black aide to his staff, announced a series of federal grants for South Carolina projects, a number of which were of particular benefit to black citizens, and publicized his role in accomplishing textile import agreements limiting foreign competition and protecting the jobs of white South Carolina textile workers.[15] Most important, the sixty-nine-year-old senator's twenty-six-year-old wife, a former Miss South Carolina, gave birth to their second child, effectively spiking any suggestion that the old-guard legislator was losing any of his legendary vigor. In Columbia

[15]Jack Bass, "Thurmond Thawing?" *South Today* 2 (May 1971): 3–7.

and Charleston, Thurmond lost the black precincts by overwhelming margins as usual, but he countered by amassing huge majorities in white precincts of all socioeconomic levels. Thurmond won the bulk of votes cast by whites and the election in a state that Nixon carried with approximately 71 percent of the vote.

Senator John Tower again won reelection in Texas. For the first time Tower faced a Democratic candidate (Barefoot Sanders) who was both popular with the conservative Democrats and acceptable to the liberals. As the campaign developed, however, much of the conservative Democratic establishment followed the lead of former Governor Connally in directing their efforts toward the Democrats for Nixon campaign, and the liberals, while supporting Sanders, were unwilling to make any great sacrifices for the man who had beaten Ralph Yarborough. Tower, on the other hand, monopolized the resources of the state Republican party. The Republican candidate won a formidable 55 percent majority, running best in western Texas but carrying every area of the state. New Deal voting alignments continued to hold up better in Texas than anywhere else in the region, but even here the strains were apparent. In Waco Tower did terribly in black precincts and well in upper-income white areas, but he won 45 percent in lower-income white districts and 47 percent in lower-middle-status white areas, far better than Republicans normally fared. Similarly, in Fort Worth Tower lost overwhelmingly in black neighborhoods and ran superbly in affluent white districts, but he took almost half of the votes of lower-income whites and a majority in lower-middle-income white areas. Compared with past performances, the New Deal coalition appeared intact in a state where Nixon won a two-to-one majority and Tower carried the rural counties and broke almost even in white working-class districts only when compared with other southern states.

Perhaps the most revealing Texas election was the gubernatorial contest between Dolph Briscoe and Republican Henry C. Grover. A former Harris County schoolteacher, Grover had an undistinguished career in the state legislature before winning the Republican gubernatorial nomination. With the Tower forces controlling the state Republican party, Grover set out on a rather lonely campaign. The conservative Democrats worked for Nixon, the Republicans worked for Tower, and Grover, underfinanced and generally unknown, plodded along, espousing views toward governmental issues that made the conservative Briscoe seem progressive. But Briscoe had made something of a name for himself before the television cameras as a delegate to the national Democratic convention by endorsing and voting for Wallace, then shifting his vote to McGovern, and during the campaign disavowing any association with McGovern. Adding to Briscoe's problems was the La Raza Unida party and its candidate, Ramsy Muniz. Muniz drew over 6 percent of the votes, votes that presumably would have gone to the Democratic candidate. Grover's plurality in the metropolitan counties was sufficient to make the election a down-to-the-wire contest. Only Briscoe's solid support in rural areas salvaged a Democratic victory. The conservative Briscoe won black precincts overwhelmingly, and he carried the working-class white districts. But with many Chicanoes defecting to Muniz and with Grover, like Tower, not only sweeping the upper-income precincts but also competing for lower-status white votes, Briscoe just managed to squeak by with a narrow plurality.[16]

The most notable Republican failure came in Georgia. Republican Congressman Fletcher M. Thompson had structured an immaculately conservative record in the House of Representatives since his election from an Atlanta district in 1966. Thompson had seized the busing issue, addressing rallies in Georgia to ban the use of buses to achieve integration. During his senatorial campaign, Thompson sometimes seemed to be running less against his Democratic opponent, Sam Nunn, than against school buses, McGovern, and actress Jane Fonda and former Attorney General Ramsey Clark, both of whom had visited North Vietnam and whom, according to Thompson, should be charged with treason. Visits by President Nixon, Vice-President Agnew, Senator Goldwater, and others evidenced the concern of national Republican leaders for Thompson's campaign. But Nunn was virtually invulnerable on the Social Issue. Not only had the Democratic candidate received George Wallace's endorsement in the campaign, but Senator Herman Talmadge, who feared a Thompson victory might tip the Senate to Republican control and terminate his chairmanship of the agricultural committee, led a concerted effort by the state Democratic leadership. While Thompson hardly suffered from lack of financial resources, the Republican could not match the organizational superiority that the Democratic county courthouses and the Talmadge network of political friends provided for Nunn.[17]

Since political observers and the national Republican leadership had rated Thompson's chances as rather good, his 46 percent showing was noticeably unimpressive, especially since Nixon won three of every four votes in the presidential election. But from the perspective of post-World War II Georgia partisan politics, Thompson did not fare quite so badly as first impressions indicated. In a state that had never veered from the Democratic party in presidential elections until the 1964 Goldwater victory and one where the Republican party had not even fielded a senatorial or gubernatorial candidate until 1966, Thompson ran more strongly than any other Georgia Republican, except for Bo Callaway, who polled a fraction of a percentage point better in the 1966 gubernatorial contest. Thompson carried the metropolitan counties, but he ran far more poorly in the cities than had Callaway in 1966 and even failed to match the metropolitan

[16]Sam Wood, in the *Waco News-Tribune*, November 9, 1972, is an incisive account of the campaign.
[17]Maurice Fliess, in the *Atlanta Journal*, November 8, 1972.

vote that Republican Hal Suit had received in the 1970 gubernatorial election, in part because black voters were more united in opposition to Thompson than they had been to either Callaway or Suit. But if Thompson's avid social conservatism, which bordered on outright racism, failed unduly to impress urban voters, it was no doubt a factor in his relatively strong showing in rural counties, where he won more than 40 percent of the vote, substantially better than Georgia Republicans had done in the past. In Atlanta, most of which was within his old congressional district, Thompson carried white precincts of all socioeconomic levels by approximately the same majorities, completely annihilating the New Deal patterns that had existed in past statewide partisan contests, though not in a number of local races or in Thompson's previous congressional contests. Table 7.6 compares the Republican votes in Atlanta in the 1966 and 1970 gubernatorial campaigns with the 1972 senatorial returns. Thompson did considerably worse in Macon, which was adjacent to Nunn's home county of Houston, than in Atlanta. Like Grover in Texas, Thompson carried a solid majority of the votes cast by whites but not by sufficient margins to overcome the Democratic inclinations of blacks.

In Alabama the perennially vulnerable but persistently victorious Senator Sparkman overwhelmed former Postmaster General Winton Blount. Blount conducted a vigorous and well-financed campaign that contrasted the "Nixon-Blount team" with the "extreme liberal ticket headed in Alabama by Senators McGovern and Sparkman."[18] The seventy-two-

Table 7.6
Percentage of the Vote for Republican Candidates in Atlanta
in 1966, 1970, and 1972,
by Socioeconomic Class and Race

Vote category	1966 (Callaway) Percentage of vote received	(N)[a]	1970 (Suit) Percentage of vote received	(N)[a]	1972 (Thompson) Percentage of vote received	(N)[a]
Lower-class white	32.0	(10,466)	47.3	(7,686)	67.3	(3,976)
Lower-middle-class white	46.0	(14,565)	52.2	(10,989)	62.8	(5,622)
Upper-middle-class white	57.5	(13,523)	58.8	(11,837)	61.5	(5,685)
Upper-class white	81.6	(16,726)	72.7	(14,543)	65.1	(6,542)
Black	51.8	(13,556)	42.0	(11,021)	9.1	(6,026)
Fulton County[b]	58.7	(116,054)	56.2	(163,276)	48.3	(173,349)

[a](N) denotes the number of votes upon which the percentages are based.

[b]County-vote percentages are based on the total number of votes cast in the county.

[18]Austin Scott, in the *Washington Post*, November 7, 1972; and Don F. Wasson, in the *Atlanta Journal and Constitution*, September 24, 1972.

year-old Sparkman, clearly showing his age, faced the Nixon landslide and the third-party candidacy of John LeFlore, a black civil-rights activist from Mobile who ran on the National Democratic Party of Alabama ticket and threatened to drain away a substantial black vote that otherwise would have gone to Sparkman. Early in the campaign, it appeared that Sparkman might be in serious trouble. But Blount's campaign managers increasingly seemed more attuned to Madison Avenue than to the voters who had swept into office Big Jim Folsom and George Wallace. LeFlore's candidacy foundered, ultimately taking only a fraction of the votes that John Cashin had won in the 1970 gubernatorial race. Sparkman received an endorsement from Wallace and successfully disassociated himself from the McGovern ticket, which crashed in Alabama with hardly more than a quarter of the votes. Even the Nixon administration seemed ambivalent toward the election. Sparkman was chairman of the Banking and Currency Committee and a consistent supporter of the Nixon administration, while the second ranking Democrat on the committee was William Proxmire of Wisconsin, a liberal critic of the administration. The White House alternated between supporting a former cabinet member and sending a "Dear John" letter expressing appreciation for Sparkman's support in the Senate. Sparkman swept 62.3 percent of the vote, as compared with Blount's 33.1 percent, with most of the remainder going to LeFlore. Sparkman won everywhere, carrying blacks and whites, rural dwellers and urbanites.

If the Nixon administration hedged its bets in Alabama, it was downright antagonistic toward the Republican senatorial candidate in Mississippi. The Republicans in Mississippi had not shown any noticeable enthusiasm for putting up a candidate to oppose Senator Eastland until James Meredith, who had desegregated the University of Mississippi ten years before, filed in the Republican primary. Apparently at the urging of Republican friends, automobile dealer Gil Carmichael then entered the primary as the white hope to turn back Meredith.[19] Carmichael easily won the nomination and went on to conduct a game campaign against the veteran Eastland. But Eastland, who was chairman of the Senate judiciary committee, was an acknowledged friend of the Nixon administration. When Vice-President Agnew visited Mississippi during the campaign, he would not permit Carmichael on the speaker's platform or mention his name. Although the election was never in doubt, Carmichael made a relatively impressive showing, winning just over 39 percent of the vote, the best showing by a Mississippi Republican in the twentieth century and one no doubt related to the fact that Nixon won almost four out of every five votes cast in the state, which, as in the 1964 presidential election, again made Mississippi the most Republican state in the union.

There were no statewide elections in Florida in 1972, and in Arkansas and Louisiana the Republicans offered only token challenges in state elec-

[19] *Memphis Commercial Appeal*, June 6, 1972.

tions. Both Governor Bumpers and Senator McClellan won reelection easily in Arkansas, while in Louisiana Bennett Johnson's major opposition came from former Governor John McKeithen, who ran as an independent, rather than from the anemic effort of Republican Ben C. Toledano. In Louisiana Republican David Treen captured a seat in the House of Representatives to break the Democratic monopoly of the Louisiana congressional delegation, which, combined with the election of two Republican congressmen from Mississippi, meant that the G.O.P. held at least one congressional seat in every southern state. Additionally as a result of the 1972 elections, the congressional Dixieland Band was no longer all white. Andrew Young of Atlanta and Barbara Jordan of Houston won seats in the House of Representatives to head a list of some six hundred black southerners elected to office in 1972, which meant that well over eleven hundred elected officials in the eleven southern states were blacks.[20] The days when white Democrats monopolized the offices in the county courthouses and city halls across the region and malapportioned state legislatures pondered new methods to endorse segregation had clearly come to an end. And that left the crucial question: What difference had it all made?

[20]Voter Education Project figures, as reported in the *Washington Post*, February 6, 13, 1973.

CHAPTER **8**

CONCLUSION

When V. O. Key published his monumental *Southern Politics* in 1949, he painted a rather gloomy portrait of a poor and politically stagnant region, Democratic in its affiliations and New Dealish in its inclinations, but one wherein the legitimate grievances of its abundant have-nots were largely thwarted by the iron grip of four major institutions which Key portrayed as underpinning the southern polity. These were (1) disfranchisement, (2) the one-party system, (3) malapportionment, and (4) the edifice of Jim Crow. At best these symbiotic arrangements effectively minimized public participation, party discipline, and party responsibility and diffused the focus of issues by deflecting campaigns toward a parochial and too often irrelevant friends-and-neighbors stump politics, and, at their too familiar worst, they encouraged the time-honored racebaiting which historically had proven effective in setting the region's black and white have-nots against each other.

But Key also saw room for hope. In his last chapter, entitled "Is There a Way Out?" he asserted that "southern liberalism is not to be underestimated," that "fundamentally within southern politics there is a powerful strain of agrarian liberalism," and that "an underlying liberal drive permeates southern politics."[1] Since in his view "southern political regionalism derives basically from the influence of the Negro," Key concluded hopefully that "if the Negro is gradually assimilated into political life, the underlying southern liberalism will undoubtedly be mightily strengthened."[2] Key's concluding note of optimism soon received strong reinforcement with the publication of *A Two-Party South?* written by his research associate, Alexander Heard. While sharing Key's consciousness of the irrational and unpredictable elements of political life, Heard called attention to increasing sources of two-party competition and accordingly to the improving prospects for a "liberal Democratic politics in the South."[3]

[1]V. O. Key, Jr., *Southern Politics in State and Nation,* (New York: Alfred A. Knopf, 1949), p. 670.
[2]Ibid., pp. 665, 670.
[3]Alexander Heard, *A Two-Party South?* (Chapel Hill: University of North Carolina Press, 1952), p. 248.

184

During the decade following World War II, the cautious optimism of Key and Heard seemed well-founded. The postwar tendencies toward a neopopulist politics in the South encouraged liberal hopes and sent to southern statehouses and to Congress such relatively loyal New Dealers as Governors James Folsom, Kerr Scott, Sidney McMath, and Earl Long and Senators John Sparkman, Estes Kefauver, and Albert Gore. For the most part, such candidates relied upon rural votes, especially from the predominately white hill country; votes from the lower-status white precincts in the cities; and the votes of the gradually growing number of black voters who until quite recently have been mainly urban dwellers. Neopopulists like James Folsom and Earl Long ran best in rural areas, but the returns suggest the fundamental class orientation of their followings. Despite significant state-to-state variations and exceptions, this coalition of farmers and mill workers of the countryside and working-class whites and the blacks of the cities, united behind populist economic programs and common-man campaign styles rather than racebaiting, generated much of the thrust in southern state politics during the decade following World War II.

These voting patterns were clearly etched in the presidential election of 1952, in which General Dwight D. Eisenhower carried four southern states, all of them in the peripheral South, and made an impressive showing throughout the region. Like other Republicans before him, Eisenhower won the votes of Appalachian and Ozark mountaineers. He was also the choice of a substantial number of citizens who had voted Dixiecrat four years before and who, having made their break with the national Democrats, continued their anti-civil-rights rebellion by supporting the Republican ticket. But even more important to Eisenhower's success in the South were the ballots cast by prospering urban-suburban voters, who found the Republican candidate's personal appeal and economic conservatism too attractive to resist. Eisenhower's campaign established the G.O.P. as the party of affluent voters in the cities and suburbs, and the election returns of 1952 conformed with considerable precision to Alexander Heard's speculations in *A Two-Party South?* The merchants, businessmen, and landowners of the black belt and the business-professional-white-collar residents of the cities and suburbs, all of whom were economically conservative and for the most part reasonably prosperous, were seemingly being driven out of the Democratic party, while the less affluent whites of the cities and the countryside and the newly emerging Negro voters, all economic liberals, in varying degrees remained loyal to the Democrats.

In the 1952 presidential election, the southern electorate divided along relatively rational lines of economic self-interest in an election that marked the beginning of a genuinely competitive two-party presidential politics in the South and also witnessed a significant increase in voter turnout. Voter participation in the South still remained far behind the national average, but by the early 1950s two of the South's distinctive political institutions—disfranchisement, which had been under attack since the *Smith* v. *Allwright* decision of 1944, and the one-party system—showed signs of slippage, and the behavior of southern voting groups suggested a movement toward a more participatory and class-based politics.

It was at this point that another peculiar southern institution came under direct challenge with the *Brown* v. *Board of Education* decision of May 1954. Although in its implementation decision of 1955 the Court permitted a pattern of gradual compliance, which for a decade produced the barest tokenism, the magnitude of a decision declaring the foundation of the southern social system to be illegal was readily apparent. But in the hope that after the initial shock of social change the freeing of blacks from the caste system would also free whites from the requirement of defending it and thus would hasten the emergence of a two-party, New Dealish politics in the South, liberally oriented political analysts underrated the intensity of white opposition to the *Brown* decision and to the civil-rights movement generally. Southern state executive officials and their malapportioned legislatures launched a program of massive resistance to school desegregation during the 1950s, and during the 1960s the white backlash against the pace and extent of civil-rights progress was frequently reflected in seismic political jolts. In the face of white hostility to social change, blacks became increasingly organized and more unified in their balloting.

The racial hysteria on the part of a considerable number of southern politicians and the racial fears on the part of many white voters drove a wedge between blacks and less affluent whites, much as in the 1890s. With prosperity increasing and memories of the Great Depression fading, many rural and lower-income whites saw themselves threatened more by social change than by economic exploitation. In state and local politics, the Folsoms and Earl Longs gave way to the Wallaces and McKeithens. Orval Faubus, George Wallace, Ross Barnett, Jimmie Davis, and John McKeithen were among those who combined racism, a white common-man campaign style, and, often, little in the way of constructive programs to rally support in rural areas and in lower-income white urban districts.

But massive resistance did encourage a political dialectic of its own. The two groups in southern society most disturbed by the excesses of the movement were blacks and the affluent whites of the cities and suburbs. This coalition provided important support for some of the South's better-known moderates of the period, men like LeRoy Collins, Carl Sanders, and deLesseps Morrison. In the racial crisis in Little Rock, the alliance of blacks and affluent whites ultimately provided the political stability that led to the reopening of the public high schools. In Atlanta the same coalition kept progressive Mayor Ivan Allen in office and made Charles Weltner the Democratic nominee for congressman in Atlanta's Fifth District. In

Birmingham, it ultimately retired Eugene "Bull" Connor from city office, although this event was delayed, since the county board of registrars placed every obstacle in the path of prospective black voters and since a large proportion of the more prestigious white residential neighborhoods lay outside the city limits. The extent of the changes in voting patterns generated by the politics of massive resistance could be exaggerated, of course, but the heating up of the race question did fundamentally transform the evolution of the New Dealish patterns that had marked the late 1940s and the early 1950s.

Similarly, the civil-rights question influenced the emerging patterns of two-party politics. The first impact was temporarily to make the G.O.P. the party attracting a coalition of blacks and higher status-whites; Eisenhower carried both the affluent white precincts and the black districts in most southern cities in 1956. But this alignment soon dissolved as Presidents John Kennedy and Lyndon Johnson consolidated the Democratic position among minorities by vigorously championing minority rights. The civil-rights movement and federal legislation accomplished during the 1960s what federal court decisions alone had not been able to do in the 1950s, namely, the destruction of the de jure Jim Crow system, an event that sent political shock tremors throughout the region. The civil-rights movement also spread northward, and what had once been quaintly regarded as a problem unique to the wicked South now threatened to split the New Deal coalition outside the South. In this situation, the national Republicans shifted to their famed Southern Strategy.

The logic and the results of the Southern Strategy are well known. The rural and lower-income whites who fairly consistently supported the national Democratic ticket also tended to vote for the Faubuses and Wallaces. Ironically, the urbane and racially liberal Adlai E. Stevenson and the equally urbane and racially liberal—and also Catholic—John F. Kennedy generally ran best among the same white voter groups who evidenced the strongest concern for white supremacy and, more often than not, the greatest support for those gubernatorial candidates who most uninhibitedly vowed to thwart the liberal policies of the national Democratic party. In the presidential election of 1960 and in several senatorial contests in 1962, Republican candidates made some significant gains in areas that were normally citadels of Democratic solidarity. By abandoning civil rights in the name of states' rights, the Goldwater Republicans presumably sought to broaden these beachheads into a general polarization of southern voters along racial lines. This design was successful in the Deep South, where Goldwater won a large majority of the votes cast by whites. In the cities of the southern heartland he projected an essentially classless appeal, winning equally impressive margins in white working-class districts and affluent neighborhoods. In the peripheral South, however, Goldwater largely failed to break the Democratic voting habits of lower-income whites, while there as elsewhere driving blacks into virtually solid opposition. Nationally, of course, the Goldwater campaign was a disaster. Only in the Deep South were racial fears of sufficient salience to solidify the bulk of the white vote. Goldwater's Southern strategy failed to live up to the expectations of its sponsors, but it further warped the emerging two-party system by attracting lower-income whites, especially in the Deep South, whose partisan identification had normally been Democratic and by repelling normally Republican mountain whites and highly educated suburbanites, particularly in the Rim South.

Both voter registration and voter turnout shot upward during the 1960s, but the long-awaited and largely simultaneous enfranchisement of lower-income whites and blacks was a mixed blessing. During the decade well over six million new names were estimated to have been added to southern registration rolls, of which roughly 30 percent belonged to blacks and 70 percent to whites; there clearly appears to be a causal relationship between the addition of some four and a half million new white voters to the registration rolls and the election successes of Wallace, Lester Maddox, James Johnson, and other common-man, "good ole boy" segregationists.

The 1968 presidential election sharply etched the developing voting tendencies in the region. George Wallace appealed to the traditionally Democratic white voters in rural-small town counties and in the working-class districts in the cities. Richard Nixon was the candidate of the urban bourgeoisie, and he was Wallace's chief competitor among white voters generally. Black voters formed the base of Hubert Humphrey's following. In the broadest sense, both survey research data and voting patterns demonstrate that Wallace's blend of populist economics and social reaction appealed to lower-income whites; Nixon's economic conservatism and defense of social stability paralleled the attitudes of the better educated and more secure urban-suburban affluents; and Humphrey's welfare economics and racial liberalism reflected the views of blacks, liberal whites, and other minorities.

Recent state elections have suggested a shift away from the politics of Goldwater, Wallace, and racial turmoil. Moderate Republicans—Winthrop Rockefeller in Arkansas, A. Linwood Holton in Virginia, Howard Baker and Winfield Dunn in Tennessee, James Holshouser in North Carolina—have enjoyed at least temporary successes in the upper South, while a wave of progressive Democrats—Reubin Askew and Lawton Chiles of Florida, Dale Bumpers of Arkansas, William Waller of Mississippi, Jimmy Carter of Georgia, John West of South Carolina, Edwin Edwards and Bennett Johnston of Louisiana, for example—have been swept into office. The difficulties involved in evaluating this apparent orgy of progressive moderation exemplify the problems of dealing with contemporary history. It would appear, however, that the new southern moderation was more antiestablishment than issue-oriented, a proposition that is at least indirectly supported by voting returns, in that these New South Democrats in their primary-election victories did not appeal with any consistency to specific voter groups, and liberals Ralph Yarborough and Albert Gore succumbed as readily as did more conservative contenders.

George Wallace's victories in the Democratic presidential primaries and the continuing storm over busing during 1972 evidenced the powerful strain of social conservatism that underlay the surge of New South moderation. As the vote in the Florida referenda elections suggested, white southerners had accepted desegregation but not much more than that. Attractive new faces similar to those that had fared so well in 1970 were largely unsuccessful in 1972, as Nick Galifianakis and David Pryor, among others, fell before conservative opponents. In the 1972 presidential election, Nixon combined Republican and Wallace votes to sweep the Solid South with a 70.5 percent majority, leaving McGovern, like Humphrey before him, with little voter base beyond blacks and other minority groups. The New Deal coalition of have-nots, which had collapsed in successive presidential elections, seemed in various stages of disintegration in state politics. A notable exception was Henry Howell, who demonstrated strong appeal to urban lower-status voters regardless of race in his two strong but unsuccessful bids for the Virginia governorship. In Texas Frances "Sissy" Farenthold attracted a similar following in her 1972 effort for the Democratic gubernatorial nomination, although her campaign foundered when she tried again for the same office in 1974. Nevertheless, when an avowed liberal who is both female and Catholic not only wins a runoff spot in a Texas gubernatorial primary but also makes a creditable contest against a well-financed, conservative opponent, surely things are changing in southern politics.

Indeed, during the quarter-century since *Southern Politics* was written, all four institutional supports for the politics of the old Solid South have crumbled under the combined assault of the Bulldozer Revolution and the Second Reconstruction. In virtually all aspects of public life and commerce, de jure Jim Crow has been destroyed. In fact, in the matter of school desegregation, minority children were more likely to attend schools with substantial numbers of nonminority children in the South than elsewhere in the nation.[4] Similarly, the reapportionment revolution that began with *Baker* v. *Carr* and *Reynolds* v. *Sims* has so equalized, at least arithmetically, the apportionment of seats in the U.S. House of Representatives and the state legislatures that Georgia's county-unit system and Florida's pork-choppers seemed as quaintly outmoded as the convict-lease system.[5] As for suffrage, the South's massive disfranchisement has been dramati-

[4]*Race Relations Reporter*, April 23, 1973; *Today's Education*, May 1973.
[5]See Richard C. Cortner, *The Apportionment Cases* (Knoxville: University of Tennessee Press, 1970); and Robert G. Dixon, Jr., *Democratic Representation: Reapportionment in Law and Politics* (New York: Oxford University Press, 1968).

cally reversed, with southern voter turnout in presidential elections soaring by 183.8 percent between 1948 and 1968, compared to a national increase of 34 percent. A regional differential still remained: the mean southern turnout in 1968 was 51.9 percent, as compared with 67.6 percent in the non-South. But this still represented a quantum leap from the old days of the "purified" southern electorate. Whereas in 1948 an estimated 12 percent of black southerners, or 595,000, were registered to vote, 3,324,000, or 66.3 percent, were registered by 1970, and white registration had climbed to 83.3 percent of the white voting-age population. Approximately 16.5 percent of southern registrants in 1970 were blacks.[6]

Finally, there was the dramatic demise of the one-party system, from the once reliably solid Democracy to the solidly Republican South in the presidential election of 1972. As spectacular as that transformation was, a more reliable indicator of sustained Republican growth was the percentage of Republican seats in the U.S. House of Representatives and in the state legislatures, as indicated in figures 8.1 and 8.2. The G.O.P. held 34, or 31.5 percent, of the South's 108 House seats in 1974, which declined to 27, or 25 percent, as a result of that year's elections. In 1972 Republicans occupied 253, or 14 percent, of the region's 1,807 state legislative seats, and by 1974 the Republicans had elected seven U.S. senators and six governors.[7]

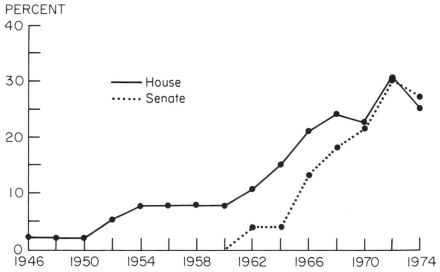

Fig. 8.1. Percentage of southern seats in the U.S. House of Representatives and Senate held by Republicans, 1946–74

[6]Voter Education Project, *V.E.P. News* 4 (January–February 1970); and "Voter Registration in the South: Spring-Summer, 1970" (Voter Education Fact Sheet, August 1970).
[7]The senators were Tower (Texas, 1961), Thurmond (South Carolina, 1966), Baker (Tennessee, 1966), Gurney (Florida, 1968), Brock (Tennessee, 1970), Helms (North Carolina,

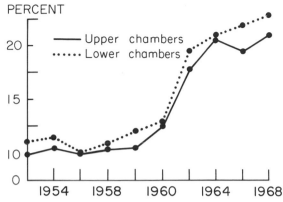

Fig. 8.2. Percentage of seats in southern state legislatures held by Republicans, 1952–68

Elementary logic would suggest that the demise of the institutional pillars of the old politics would unleash new and unpredictable currents. Key argued that "the predominant consideration in the architecture of southern political institutions has been to assure locally a subordination of the Negro population, and, externally, to block threatened interferences from the outside with these local arrangements."[8] Assuming that Key was correct, and in large measure we believe that he was, the collapse of the caste system would of necessity force basic changes in political arrangements. The South had absorbed—sometimes with grace, more often with turmoil—a profound social revolution, and once again race relations were in a state of flux. While in racial matters opinion polls consistently showed growing toleration on the part of southern whites,[9] the racial issue remained deeply embedded in southern and indeed American politics. Voting returns presented in this volume and elsewhere testify to the political vitality of the racial issue, and, despite hopeful trends in opinion polls, that issue is apt to remain politically salient in the foreseeable future. The deeply rooted contradictions entrenched in the social fabric of the South by her tragic history have demonstrated a perverse persistency.

Legislative reapportionment surely was a significant advance, but the rough consensus of political scientists who have studied the effects of *Baker* v. *Carr* on the decision-making process in state legislatures may be

---

1972), and Scott (Virginia, 1972). The governors were Rockefeller (Arkansas, 1966), Kirk (Florida, 1966), Holton (Virginia, 1969), Dunn (Tennessee, 1970), Holshouser (North Carolina, 1972), and Edwards (South Carolina, 1974).

[8]Key, *Southern Politics*, p. 665.

[9]Herbert H. Hyman and Paul B. Sheatsley, "Attitudes Toward Desegregation," *Scientific American* 195 (December 1956): 35–39; idem, "Attitudes Toward Desegregation," *Scientific American* 211 (July 1964): 2–9; and Andrew M. Greeley and Paul B. Sheatsley, "Attitudes Toward Racial Integration," *Scientific American* 225 (December 1971): 13–19.

summarized with the observation that "the policy choices of malapportioned legislatures are not noticeably different from the policy choices of well-apportioned legislatures," and consequently "reapportionment is not likely to bring about any significant policy changes."[10] The one man-one vote formula is in no way inconsistent with the most brutal partisan gerrymandering, and the debate over the relative merits of multi- and single-member legislative districts reflected one of the paradoxes of reapportionment. In many southern states and municipalities the multi-member district was preferred by dominant white Democrats because it minimized the election of blacks and Republicans. On the other hand, it did force the gerrymandered urban delegation to respect the political clout of all constituent groups. But when the federal courts began to frown on such arrangements, and the blacks began to demand single-member districts for blacks to be elected in, the consequent urban delegations, their membership bolstered by reapportionment, also lost much of whatever unity they had possessed, and the rear guard of rural conservatives found new allies in the burgeoning suburban delegations. Both the multi- and the single-member district formulae, it seems, contained pitfalls for urban citizens whose hopes had soared on the heels of *Baker* v. *Carr*. The situation was analogous to the dilemma of the man who took a mouthful of scalding hot coffee: the next thing he did was going to be wrong.

Similarly, higher voter participation and the blossoming of the two-party system, while laudable in terms of democratic theory, have sharpened political conflict and raised basic questions about voter alignments and the ultimate voter base of the southern Democratic and Republican parties. In the 1968 presidential election, Wallace, Humphrey, and Nixon each received approximately one-third of the votes cast in the southern states. In the cities, as has been indicated, each appealed to relatively identifiable voter groups, and, generally, this was also true on the county level of analysis. How these three voting groups will fit into a two-party system is, in a simplified sort of way, the basic question of contemporary southern politics. In state and local politics the Wallace and the Humphrey voters have remained in the Democratic party, though with declining regularity, leaving the Republicans with numerically inadequate bases in the suburbs and the mountains, although exceptions to this pattern are numerous.

Partisan identification has been the best single predictor of the way an individual will cast his vote, of course, but here, again, the evidence is suggestive but by no means conclusive. Certainly the Democrats suffered mas-

[10]Thomas R. Dye, *Politics, Economics, and the Public: Policy Outcomes in the American States* (Chicago: Rand McNally, 1966), p. 280; Bill Kovach, "Some Lessons of Reapportionment," *Reporter*, September 21, 1967, pp. 26–32; Robert S. Friedman, "The Reapportionment Myth," *National Civic Review*, April 1960, pp. 184–88; and Herbert Jacob, "The Consequences of Malapportionment: A Note of Caution," *Social Forces* 43 (December 1964): 256–61.

sive defections during the latter 1960s. According to our survey data, approximately 64 percent of white southerners in 1964 called themselves Democrats; the remaining 36 percent divided about evenly between Republicans and independents. By 1970, the most recent year Institute of Social Research survey data were available to us, the relative number of white Republican partisans continued to hover around 18 percent, but the percentage of white Democrats had dropped from just over 64 percent to approximately 44 percent, and the number of white independents had vaulted from approximately 18 percent to 38 percent. This substantial shift from Democrat to independent was true of both upper- and lower-income whites. In the higher-income half of the southern white population in 1970, roughly 41 percent were Democrats, 38 percent independents, and 21 percent Republicans; in the lower-income half of the white sample, about 46 percent were Democrats, 38 percent independents, and 16 percent Republicans. An overwhelming 80 percent of black southerners identified themselves as Democrats. The shortage of self-confessed Republicans has meant that the G.O.P. could win state elections only when short-term factors were heavily in its favor.

The fact that the bulk of the blacks and a substantial minority of whites were Democratic partisans has helped to account for the general-election victories of attractive, nonvulnerable Democrats like Reubin Askew and Dale Bumpers in the early 1970s. It has also reinforced the degree to which the Republican party at the state and local level in the South has so long confronted, and may continue to face, formidable obstacles, despite the impressive presidential sweep of 1972. Republican growth outside the mountains, where it has lasted, has been built downward from presidential politics, not upward from the grass roots. Lacking the Democrats' broad base of party identifiers (the G.O.P.'s reliable mountain and suburban base in the recent past has provided Republicans with roughly a third of the vote in a typical southern state), Republicans have had to gear for elections one at a time, taking advantage of an attractive candidate, a vulnerable opponent, a favorable issue, a windfall split in the opposing state Democratic party. Hence, attractive Republican candidates have done well where they could find vulnerable Democrats with a divided party behind them who were open on a given issue, such as liberalism in the case of Robert King High and LeRoy Collins in Florida, the Kennedy image and an apparent inability to sell fried chicken on the part of John J. Hooker in Tennessee, and the stubborn courage of conviction plus languished home ties in the case of Albert Gore. Republican challengers have enjoyed the advantages of the underdog, and the upset victories by Jesse Helms and James Holshouser in North Carolina and William Scott in Virginia are particularly significant in that their opponents—Nick Galifianakis, Hargrove Bowles, and William Spong, respectively—were generally attractive and not generally regarded as vulnerable.

But the price of all this was high, and the future is unsure. Such strenuous campaigns to convince non-Republican identifiers are expensive, and they invite the kind of highly personalized, emotional, and frequently mud-slinging campaigns that have long marred Democratic primaries. Further, the resulting accretion of Republican officeholders, being based on no united design, produces no consistent pattern. Generally, G.O.P. candidates in the Deep South have campaigned as states' rights conservatives, attempting to link their opponents to the liberal policies of the national Democratic party. In the Rim South moderate Republican candidates in the Eisenhower tradition have been more frequent.

A good argument can be made that logically the South should be Republican. In the rest of the nation, the Democratic party is broadly the home of religious, ethnic, and racial minorities and of organized labor. The Republican party is the party of white Protestants, especially those residing in affluent suburbs and in rural-small town areas. Yet in the South, most whites are enthusiastically Protestant; rural-small town Protestants are particularly numerous; ethnic enclaves and labor unionists are few; and the position of the nouveau affluent has been strengthened by the out-migration of poor blacks and whites and the in-migration of upper-status whites lured by growing prosperity. Indeed, the major barriers between the South and the Republican party are the Civil War, Reconstruction, and one hundred years of history.

Matthews and Prothro, in their *Negroes and the New Southern Politics*, offered at least guarded support for the speculations of Key and Heard that the substantial entry of blacks into southern political life might lead to a biracial coalition of the poor. In the concluding chapter of their study, Matthews and Prothro observed: "It is the upper-middle-class, economically conservative, racially moderate whites who need to be driven from the Democratic party into the Republican, not the region's segregationists. Then, and only then, will a politics of class prevail over a politics of race in the South as in the rest of the nation."[11] Matthews and Prothro pointed out that blacks had much to gain from what they called "highly volatile, 'populist' coalitions with heavily segregationist white workers."[12] In the backwash of the Great Depression and the New Deal, that is, when Key and Heard wrote, this populist alliance seemed fairly self-evident. By 1972, the balancing of economic issues with what Richard Scammon and Ben Wattenberg have called the Social Issue was a much more perilous matter.

Important strains of the southern historical legacy militated against the development of a politics based on a realistic assessment of economic self-interest, and this tendency was compounded by the lack of an ade-

[11]Donald R. Matthews and James W. Prothro, *Negroes and the New Southern Politics* (New York: Harcourt, Brace and World, 1966), p. 475.
[12]Ibid., p. 479.

quate institutional foundation for a meaningful southern liberalism. The South has little in the way of ethnic-religious minorities with liberal Democratic voting traditions, and the weakness of southern labor unions deprived the region of another foundation upon which the northern New Deal coalition has rested. Political machines have existed in the South, but, with the exception of some Chicano and urban black communities, they have not performed the function of educating lower-status citizens to the relationship between politics and bread-and-butter issues that northern machines have traditionally done. The South's distinctive historical evolution and the absence of basic aspects of the New Deal coalition have contributed to a politics which might be described as less structured and more individual and personal than was customary on the national level. That is, lacking the structure provided by a disciplined party organization, a union, the block club of a political machine, or the social pressure of an ethnic group, southern whites, in comparison with northerners, have been not only less inclined to vote but more inclined to use their ballots in state and local politics to express personal beliefs or prejudices rather than socioeconomic self-interest.

Most Americans, North or South, appear to possess little in the way of a coherent political philosophy, and therefore the group orientation of a voter has been extremely significant to political behavior. But the basically tripartite group orientation of southern voters as it has emerged during the era of the Second Reconstruction so ill comported with the two-party model and has so set the South against itself politically that the wan, populist dream of a biracial coalition of the poor seemed to stand essentially little chance. Both voting and survey research data reinforce the portrait of a southern electorate that, unshackled at last from the most severe institutional constraints of disfranchisement, malapportionment, the one-party system, and Jim Crow, found itself still confounded by its peculiar historical legacy.

One of the most striking trend lines in the survey data was the growing divergence in opinion between blacks and whites in which southern blacks consistently anchored the liberal position, nonsoutherners hovered in the middle, and southern whites grew increasingly conservative. There has been a sharp decline in the number of whites (but not of blacks) who identified themselves as Democrats. Similarly, our own survey data analysis supports the findings of Alfred Hero and others that there has been a substantial decline in support for economic welfare measures on the part of whites, especially the lower-income half of the white population, but relatively little decline in support on the part of blacks. The chasm between blacks and lower-income whites widened on such fundamental matters as partisan identification, economic welfare measures, civil liberties, and governmental intervention in support of black economic advancement. Long-term voting patterns strongly suggested that holding the bulk of blacks and lower-status whites in the same party is going to be extremely difficult.

How all of this translated into long-term partisan voter divisions is by no means clear as yet. The party-systems mode of analysis assumes normally stable voting patterns, anchored by partisan identification, which tend to remain quite consistent until upheavals sufficiently traumatic to effect the masses of voters catalyze a critical period of realignment. The Eisenhower campaign of 1952 marked a significant break with past patterns of presidential voting, but not until the emergence of the civil-rights issue did a matter directly affecting huge numbers of voters become politically salient. The Republican Southern Strategy and the civil-rights laws of the mid-1960s, combined with the third-party effort of George Wallace, seemed to provide the basic ingredients for realignment. V. O. Key presented the classic definition for this phenomenon when he described "a category of elections in which voters are, at least from impressionistic evidence, unusually deeply concerned, in which the extent of electoral involvement is relatively quite high, and in which the decisive results of the voting reveal a sharp alteration of the pre-existing cleavage within the electorate."[13] Southern political competition in the mid and late 1960s met all of these criteria. Voters evidenced great concern with politics, and electoral involvement shot upward, with turnout reaching its peak in the 1968 presidential election and then leveling off, in some states receding, during the early 1970s in both state and presidential elections. The disentegration of the New Deal coalition and of the national Democratic party's position in the South in the presidential elections of 1968 and 1972 clearly indicated sharp alterations in electoral cleavage. All of these facts strongly suggested that the South had just passed through a critical period of realignment and entered the era of the sixth party system, with the G.O.P. enjoying a solidly Republican (white) southern base in presidential politics and perhaps with time in state politics as well.[14] However, Key added to his definition of critical elections the crucial admonition: "Moreover, and perhaps this is the truly differentiating characteristic of this sort of election, the realignment made manifest in the voting in such elections seems to persist for several succeeding elections."[15] Thus, despite persuasive evidence, the central question remained unanswered

[13]V. O. Key, Jr., "A Theory of Critical Elections," *Journal of Politics* 17 (February 1955): 4.

[14]See generally Kevin P. Phillips, *The Emerging Republican Majority* (New Rochelle: Arlington House, 1969); Nelson W. Polsby, "An Emerging Republican Majority?" *The Public Interest* 14 (Fall 1969): 119–26; E. M. Schreiber, "Where the Ducks Are: Southern Strategy versus Fourth Party," *Public Opinion Quarterly* 35 (Summer 1971): 157–67; Gerald M. Pomper, "From Confusion to Clarity: Issues and American Voters, 1956–68," *American Political Science Review* 66 (June 1972): 415–28; and Norval D. Glenn, "Class and Party Support in the United States: Recent and Emerging Trends," *Public Opinion Quarterly* 37 (Spring 1973): 1–20.

[15]Key, "A Theory of Critical Elections," p. 4.

and invited the speculation of political scientists and the judgment of future political historians. Indeed, the off-year elections of 1974 further clouded the question, as economic recession and the shadow of Watergate moved American voters to punish the G.O.P. severely. While this retribution was less extreme in the South than elsewhere, previous Republican gains were seriously eroded, especially in the Rim South, by the loss of the governorship of Tennessee, of the indicted Edward Gurney's Senate seat in Florida, and a net loss of seven House seats.[16] In North Carolina, Republicans were reduced from 15 to 1 in the state senate and from 35 to 10 in the house, and the G.O.P. lost 14 legislative seats in Tennessee and 11 in Florida. Only a bizarre Democratic split in South Carolina produced a gubernatorial victory to bolster the dampened spirits of southern Republicans.[17]

While the prospects for critical realignment in the South were clouded by the election of 1974, they were reinforced in the Congress, where the southern delegation stood to lose power, especially in the Senate. Whereas southern senators had chaired ten of the eighteen committees in 1970, by 1975 they chaired only six, and while these still included the "Big Four" of appropriations (McClellan), armed services (Stennis), finance (Long), and foreign relations (Sparkman), plus agriculture (Talmadge) and judiciary (Eastland), the advanced age of the chairmen promised retirements that would transfer power to more liberal northern Democrats. Russell Long was the youngest southern chairman, and Herman Talmadge was the next-to-youngest. Between Talmadge and the next ranking southern Democrat in line to chair a committee stood twenty-two northern and western Democrats. Hence the likely retirements of Stennis in 1976 and of McClellan, Sparkman, and Eastland in 1978 would turn their chairmanships over to nonsoutherners. In the House, retirement or death has in recent years sig-

[16]In Tennessee Ray Blanton, a conservative former Democratic congressman from West Tennessee who had been badly beaten in his 1972 attempt to oust Senator Howard Baker, defeated Lamar Alexander, the Republican nominee to succeed Governor Winfield Dunn. In Florida, Representative Bill Gunter was upset in the Democratic senatorial primary by former Secretary of State Richard Stone, who then defeated the Republican nominee, drugstore millionaire Jack Eckerd. Nine Republican House seats were lost, including two each in Virginia, North Carolina, and Tennessee, as follows (with the defeated Republican in parentheses): Georgia Fourth to Elliott H. Levitas (Ben B. Blackburn); North Carolina Fifth to Stephen L. Neal (Wilmer Mizell) and Eighth to W. G. Hefner (Earl B. Ruth); South Carolina Sixth to John W. Jenrette (Edward L. Young); Tennessee Third to Marilyn Lloyd (LaMar Baker) and Eighth to Harold E. Ford (Dan Kuykendall); Texas Thirteenth to Jack Hightower (Robert Price); Virginia Eighth to Herbert E. Harris (Stanford E. Parris) and Tenth to Joseph L. Fisher (Joel T. Broyhill). Two Democratic seats were lost (with the defeated Democrat in parentheses): Florida Fifth to Richard Kelly (Jo Ann Saunders), and Louisiana Sixth to W. Henson Moore (Jeff LaCaze). Blackburn was Georgia's only Republican congressman, and Ford became the South's third black congressman.

[17]State Senator James B. Edwards, a conservative Republican, defeated retired General William C. Westmoreland in the primary and then won the general election by capitalizing on a Democratic debacle. His opponent, twenty-eight-year House veteran William Jennings Bryan Dorn, had lost to reform Democrat Charles D. "Pug" Ravenel in the primary, who subsequently was declared ineligible by the state supreme court, because he failed to meet a five-year state residency requirement.

nificantly reduced the ranks of conservative Democratic oligarchs, as have primary victories by younger Democrats, general election victories by Republicans, and, following the elections of 1974, the resignation under fire of Wilbur Mills (Ark.) as chairman of the House Ways and Means Committee and the unhorsing by the Democratic Caucus of three other southern committee chairmen: W. R. Poage (Tex.) of Agriculture; F. Edward Herbert (La.) of Armed Services; and Wright Patman (Tex.) of Banking and Currency. At the same time, the ratio of nonsouthern to southern Democratic congressmen has dramatically changed at the expense of the latter. In 1946 there were only 85 Democrats elected to the House from the nonsouthern states; in 1974 there were 201, and meanwhile the southern Democratic House ranks have been significantly eroded by the election of southern Republicans.

The decline of the congressional Old Guard, which promised to disrupt the Republican-Dixiecrat coalition and to narrow the North-South split in the congressional Democratic party, and the Republican set-backs in the 1974 elections suggested a politics of continuity. But projections based upon such secular, short-term surge forces as Watergate and recession are risky, and the apparently vengeful mood of those who voted in 1974 reflected a deepening disillusionment with political life. Whether the recession would slow the disintegration of the New Deal coalition was unclear, but southern electoral returns and survey evidence during the postwar years pointed overwhelmingly toward the coalition's decay. It is true that electoral fragmentation, popular cynicism toward government, and the disintegration of the New Deal coalition have been national as well as southern phenomena, and we seek here neither to deny the convergence factor nor to speculate on the relative strengths of the northernization of the South or the southernization of the North. The increasing national salience of the Social Issue since the bread-and-butter politics of the New Deal has intensified the disharmonies between the major parties and their traditional supporters. Generally, the white-collar class has been more conservative than the blue-collar class on most economic issues, but the blue-collar class has been more conservative than the white-collar class on a variety of social issues relating to civil liberties and civil rights, international involvement, patriotism, law enforcement, and the like. Hence, as Norval Glenn has observed, "the Democratic Party, in seeking the support of blacks, has alienated many of its white working-class members, and the generalized conservatism of the powerful conservative wing of the Republican Party is inconsistent with many of the characteristic values and attitudes of the affluent and well-educated classes, who tend to be liberal on many non-economic issues."[18] Electoral instability and ambivalence toward party have increased nationally, and George Wallace has been in a position to capitalize upon this

[18]Norval D. Glenn, "Sources of the Shift to Political Independence: Some Evidence from a Cohort Analysis," *Social Science Quarterly* 53 (December 1972): 518.

process of disaggregation by simultaneously appealing to economic and social fears.

But in the South, the historical legacy of cultural distinctiveness, the persistence of which John Shelton Reed has recently demonstrated in *The Enduring South*,[19] must more than any other factor explain the alarmingly wide divergences of opinion reflected in our survey data. Once having shed their inherited Democratic label, upper-status white Republicans in the South are not likely to remain troubled by partisan ambivalence, for as Norval Glenn concluded, "at present, white-collar whites in the South represent a combination of conservative attitudes on both economic and noneconomic issues which is probably unique among the major categories of the population in the United States."[20] Blue-collar whites in the South have never been particularly conservative on economic issues, but they, too, have shared that collective legacy that Wilbur Cash called *The Mind of the South*, a legacy that the despairing Cash, in his intensive love-hate relationship with his native region, saw as an amalgam of pride, bravery, honor, loyalty, courtesy, and generosity at its best, together with its characteristic vices of the past—"violence, intolerance, aversion and suspicion toward new ideas, an incapacity for analysis, an inclination to act from feeling rather than from thought, an exaggerated individualism and a too narrow concept of social responsibility, attachment to fictions and false values, above all too great attachment to racial values and a tendency to justify cruelty and injustice in the name of those values, sentimentality and a lack of realism."[21]

The "new political history" has persistently demonstrated the importance of ethnocultural factors in determining long-term voting behavior and party identification. In a summary of findings of recent research in political history, Joel H. Silbey and Samuel T. McSeveney have observed that "clashing religious and ethnic perspectives more often than anything else shape group attitudes toward politics and lead particular groups to identify with those political institutions that seem either to reflect their specific viewpoints or to serve their specific interests. . . . Economic differences within the society have occasionally influenced voting behavior but usually have been subordinate to these cultural tensions except in periods of intense economic dislocations such as the 1890s and 1930s."[22] The legacy of

[19] *The Enduring South: Subcultural Persistence in Mass Society* (Lexington, Mass.: D. C. Heath, 1972). Reed argues that southern whites constitute an ethnic group wherein family and church are far more powerful agents of socialization than are school and media and that southerners are more likely to be conventionally religious, to accept the private use of force, and to be anchored in their homeplace.

[20] Glenn, "Class and Party Support in the United States," p. 17.

[21] Wilbur J. Cash, *The Mind of the South* (New York: Alfred A. Knopf, 1941), pp. 439–40.

[22] *Voters, Parties and Elections: Quantitative Essays in the History of American Popular Voters Behavior* (Lexington, Mass.: Xerox College Publishing, 1972), p. 3.

slavery, segregation, and white supremacy leaves little doubt about the basic ethnocultural division in southern society.

The South of the 1970s is not the same South that the tortured Wilbur Cash knew. Gone are the Jim Crow signs and ordinances, the yahoo legislatures with their prohibition and monkey laws, and the triumphant "nigger-baiting" demagogues, and many of the social and political dilemmas of the South are symptomatic of a national malaise. But given the region's decidedly un-American experience with defeat, poverty, and guilt,[23] history seems to have placed a peculiar kind of hex upon her, not as an immutable curse but as a pernicious source of devilment that confounds our more rational and optimistic predictions and masks deeply-rooted continuity behind the symptoms of basic change. The Republican sweep of the South in 1972 may well have reflected a quite traditional southern triumph, under a new partisan label, of her more dominant social conservatism over her game but historically outweighed populism.

[23]See C. Vann Woodward, "The Irony of Southern History," and "A Second Look at the Theme of Irony," *The Burden of Southern History*, rev. ed. (Baton Rouge: Louisiana State University Press, 1968).

NOTE ON METHODOLOGY
AND DATA SOURCES

The basic research for this study of southern politics was the collection and analysis of county and precinct election returns. To organize and interpret what ultimately amounted to a massive accumulation of data, we sought a research design which would be applicable to the South as a whole and which would permit state-to-state comparisons of the voting behavior of the South's geographic and cultural subregions over time. In devising such a model, we were influenced by Bernard Cosman, who, in his study of the 1964 presidential election in the South, divided southern counties into 4 "sectors"; Perry H. Howard, who divided Louisiana's 64 parishes into 9 "voter type areas"; and Numan V. Bartley, who divided Georgia's 159 counties into 8 analytical categories.[1] For this study we constructed an ecological model which assigned the 1,109 counties and 25 independent cities[2] in the South to the following eight subregions:

1. *The mountain South.* This category is defined both geographically and politically. Geographically, we included the 118 southern counties listed in Thomas R. Ford's standard study, *The Southern Appalachian Region*,[3] plus 37 Arkansas counties in the Ozarks and Ouichitas. Addi-

[1]Bernard Cosman, *Five States for Goldwater: Continuity and Change in Southern Presidential Voting Patterns* (University: University of Alabama Press, 1966); Perry H. Howard, *Political Tendencies in Louisiana* (Baton Rouge: Louisiana State University Press, 1971); and Numan V. Bartley, *From Thurmond to Wallace: Political Tendencies in Georgia, 1948–1968* (Baltimore: Johns Hopkins Press, 1970).

[2]The figures reflect the total number of counties and independent Virginia cities in 1948. This number varies because Virginia's peculiar annexation and incorporation laws have encouraged the creation of independent cities which report their election returns separately from the county in which they are located; occasionally entire counties are annexed by cities and thereby removed from the county list. In 1948 Virginia contained one hundred counties and twenty-five independent cities; by 1970 the count was ninety-six counties and thirty-eight independent cities. See Chester W. Bain, *Annexation in Virginia* (Charlottesville: University of Virginia Press, 1966); and idem, *"A Body Incorporate": The Evolution of City-County Separation in Virginia* (Charlottesville: University of Virginia Press, 1967). In 1960 the total number of counties and independent cities in the South was 1,142; in 1970 there were 1,143.

[3]Thomas R. Ford, ed., *The Southern Appalachian Region: A Survey* (Lexington: University of Kentucky Press, 1962). We, of course, excluded the 72 counties in Kentucky and West Virginia, bringing the number of counties down from Ford's 190.

tionally, we expanded this definition to include 22 highland "traditionally Republican" counties, which were generally contiguous to the Appalachian mountain counties and which, in our judgment, behaved politically more like mountain counties than like counties of any other category.[4] The result was a 1960 total of 177 mountain counties and 7 independent cities that cast just under 17 percent of the total southern vote for president in 1948 and 10.8 percent in 1972.

2. *The Piedmont South.* Piedmont counties are defined as those counties located between the fall line and the Appalachian Mountains, including the Nashville Basin but excluding any county which according to the 1960 Census was 40 percent or more nonwhite in population. This definition encompassed a 1960 total of 163 counties and independent cities that in 1948 cast just over 16 percent of the southern presidential vote and in 1972 cast 16.8 percent.

3. *The black-belt South.* Any county containing a 1960 nonwhite population of 40 percent or more was placed in this category. In addition, several Deep South metropolitan counties located in the arc stretching through the southern black belt from Montgomery, Alabama, to Columbia, South Carolina, were included in this group even if they did not contain 40 percent nonwhite population.[5] The black belt in 1960 included 244 counties and independent cities that in 1948 cast just over 9 percent of the southern vote for president and 12.4 percent in 1972.

4. *The white-belt South.* A residual term of convenience, this subdivision designates those counties of the tidewater, coastal plains, delta, and gulf slope—the white lowland counties generally—whose populations are over 60 percent white. This category in 1960 contained 320 counties and independent cities and in 1948 tallied approximately 31 percent of the presidential vote and 30.3 percent in 1972.

5. *South Florida.* This area includes the 30 Florida counties lying south of the northern boundaries of Volusia, Lake, Sumter, and Citrus counties and roughly defines a rapidly developing area in which the political culture has differed qualitatively from the more Deep South pattern associated with northern Florida.[6] Although a peripheral region, south Florida cast 7.5 percent of the total southern vote for president in 1948 and 13.4 percent in 1972.

[4]These twenty-two counties are Madison and Green in Virginia; Surry, Stokes, Yadkin, Davie, Catawba, Lincoln, and Polk in North Carolina; Pickett, Carroll, Henderson, Decatur, McNairy, Hardin, Wayne, and Lawrence in Tennessee; and Cherokee, Walker, Winston, Marion, and Franklin in Alabama. Otherwise, occasional isolated "traditionally Republican" counties or small clusters, such as the "German counties" in central and west Texas, were categorized within whichever geographical group they fell, as discussed below.

[5]These counties are Montgomery in Alabama; Muscogee, Bibb, Richmond, and Dougherty in Georgia; and Richland and Charleston in South Carolina, which along with Hinds County, Mississippi, comprise the black-belt metropolitan counties.

[6]See Hugh D. Price, *The Negro and Southern Politics: A Chapter of Florida History* (New York: New York University Press, 1957).

6. *Catholic Louisiana.* The 19 non-black-belt Louisiana parishes estimated to contain a population more than 50 percent Catholic inherited a
French Catholic culture which in many ways has differed significantly from
that of Protestant north Louisiana or the Protestant South generally.[7]
These counties cast something over 4 percent of the southern presidential
vote in 1948 and only 2 percent in 1972.

7. *West Texas.* Another peripheral region, west Texas shares much in
common with the Great Plains states. For this study, west Texas was defined in a negative way as that portion of Texas left over after eastern
Texas, which is historically and culturally "southern," and Mexican-
American Texas, described below, were removed.[8] As defined here, west
Texas contains 146 counties that in 1948 cast just over 13 percent of the
southern presidential vote and in 1972 cast 12.4 percent.

8. *Mexican-American Texas.* The 36 southwestern counties clustering
along the Rio Grande River that in 1950 were estimated to contain a Latin
American population of 40 percent or more were designated Mexican-
American Texas.[9] These counties reported approximately 2 percent of the
total southern vote for president in 1948 and under 2 percent in 1972.

While recognizing the South's constituent parts insofar as cultural
geography is concerned, this eight-dimensional taxonomy was a horizontal
division and did not take into account rural-urban differences within the
region and within subregions. Consequently, we designated all counties
according to the following demographic criteria:

1. *Metropolitan,* which includes counties containing a city of greater
than 50,000 population in 1960, as well as such obviously metropolitan suburban areas as Jefferson Parish in Louisiana and Chesterfield County in
Virginia. In 1960 there were 85 metropolitan counties, which in 1948 cast
almost 37 percent of the southern presidential vote and in 1972 cast 48
percent.

2. *Urban,* which includes counties containing a city of between 20,000
and 50,000 population in 1960. As expected, the counties in this category
(109 in 1960) cast a limited share of the southern vote—approximately 13
percent in the presidential election of 1948 and 13.3 percent in 1972.

---

[7]William C. Havard, Rudolf Heberle, and Perry H. Howard, *The Louisiana Elections of 1960* (Baton Rouge: Louisiana State University Press, 1963), p. 14; and Howard, *Political Tendencies in Louisiana,* pp. 3–17.

[8]The east Texas region encompasses the coastal and blackland prairies and the timber and piney woods region originally settled primarily by migrants from Alabama, Georgia, Louisiana, Mississippi, and Tennessee. It contained the bulk of the plantations and slaves at the time of the Civil War, and it includes all counties that in 1960 were 16 percent or more nonwhite in population, with the single exception of Gonzales County. See William T. Chambers, *The Geography of Texas* (Austin: Steck, 1946), pp. 1–110. We did choose to consider the Dallas-Fort Worth metropolitan complex as an entity and for that reason assigned Dallas County, usually considered an east Texas city, to our west Texas category.

[9]James R. Soukup, Clifton McCleskey, and Harry Holloway, *Party and Factional Division in Texas* (Austin: University of Texas Press, 1964), pp. 126–38.

3. *Rural-small town*, which constituted all remaining counties (948 in 1960) and cast just over 50 percent of the vote for president in 1948 and 38.6 percent in 1972.

Thus, all southern counties were assigned both a geographical-cultural and a demographic code, in addition to their individual and state codes. Naturally, this model fits some states considerably better than others, and, in any case, it properly invites subcategorization into smaller and more variegated dimensions, such as the Tennessee Valley counties of north Alabama, the Florida parishes of Louisiana, the Southside counties of Virginia, and so on. Our purpose in describing the model in some detail is not to defend it but to explain our overall approach to the problem of politically analyzing a vast and complex region and to identify the units of analysis in the ecological correlations that appear in the text. We did compute correlation coefficients utilizing election returns from each county, most massively by comparing county returns in successive presidential elections in the South, which of course involved more than eleven hundred units of analysis in each computation. Most of our correlation analysis, however, was based upon ecological units and was intended to test for continuity and discontinuity in state and regional voting patterns. Not surprisingly, the ecological correlation coefficients, positive or negative, tended to be higher than county coefficients, but, for the most part, the differences were small.[10]

But what concerned us more than our unsophisticated methodology was the crudeness of the data. For all its potential, political ecology based upon county-level data is inherently limited by the aggregate nature of the total county vote. Most counties contain both affluent and poor voters and both black and white voters. Our county topology does not distinguish between wealthy and poor counties, but even if it did, it is uncertain precisely what could be concluded from such a division. The poorest counties in the South, generally speaking, are the black-belt and mountain counties, but during most of the period covered by our study, the voters in the black belt were not for the most part the poor blacks but the whites living among them, who were not always poor by any means. Obviously the electorate has changed in the black belt, as it has to a lesser degree in the mountains, since a higher percentage of mountain whites also have voted in recent years than in the past. Thus, even with sophisticated methodological techniques, it would be difficult to generalize about poverty and voting behavior over time on the basis of county and subregional data alone.

What was needed, then, was a more precise method for determining the behavior of voter groups, a quest which led us into the most difficult and demanding part of the research in this study. We obtained precinct returns for presidential, gubernatorial, and senatorial primary and general elec-

---

[10]The units of analysis for the ecological correlations were: white-belt metropolitan, white-belt urban, white-belt rural, black-belt metropolitan, black-belt urban, black-belt rural, etc.

tions since 1948, and we included other selected state and local elections, constitutional amendment votes, and various referenda which offered (or seemed to offer) voters an opportunity to express fundamental social and political preferences at the polls. Precinct returns were obtained for the following 27 cities:

Alabama: Birmingham, Gadsden, Mobile, and Montgomery
Arkansas: Little Rock
Florida: Jacksonville and Miami
Georgia: Atlanta and Macon
Louisiana: Baton Rouge, New Orleans, and Shreveport
Mississippi: Jackson
North Carolina: Charlotte, Greensboro, High Point, and Raleigh
South Carolina: Charleston and Columbia
Tennessee: Memphis and Nashville
Texas: Fort Worth, Houston, and Waco
Virginia: Norfolk, Richmond, and Roanoke

These cities were chosen somewhat arbitrarily but generally with an eye toward a reasonable sampling of cities from the states and subregions of the South.

Within each city we constructed a five-dimensional taxonomy of precincts: (1) black,[11] (2) lower-class white, (3) lower-middle-class white, (4) upper-middle-class white, (5) upper-class white. These classifications were based on *U.S. Census of Population: 1950 Census Tract Statistics*[12] and *U.S. Census of Population and Housing: 1960 Census Tracts* (PHC series) and then were checked against the 1970 census tracts, which began to appear after this study was in progress, and adjusted when necessary. Census tracts were first divided by racial composition. Predominately black tracts were designated as such, and racially mixed tracts were eliminated. For the predominately white tracts, an index was constructed which gave equal weight to median family income, median house value, and median years of education. These indices were then broken down into quartiles and designated lower-class, lower-middle-class, upper-middle-class, and upper-class. The tracts were transcribed on transparent sheets and laid over precinct maps, and rarely did tract and precinct lines coincide. Fortunately, the tracts were normally larger than the precincts, and what made the entire procedure feasible was the lack of necessity for classifying

[11]For various reasons no attempt was made to divide black precincts by socioeconomic class. In part, this decision was based on practical considerations. During the post-World War II period, the socioeconomic composition of black neighborhoods has tended to change more rapidly than that of white neighborhoods, and the problems associated with accurate categorization of black precincts of socioeconomic class for twenty-seven cities were awesome. Equally important, the politics of the Second Reconstruction only occasionally permitted black voters the luxury of dividing along class lines. See Bartley, *From Thurmond to Wallace*, pp. 35–56.

[12]In a number of smaller cities included in this study, there were no published *Census of Population* tracts for 1950, and information in the *Census of Housing* was substituted.

all precincts. When in doubt about the socioeconomic composition of a precinct, we threw it out. We were particularly careful to maintain a cordon sanitaire around the black precincts, given the rapidity with which neighborhoods have changed their racial composition. Some cities maintain registration records by race, which greatly simplified this problem.[13] In any case, our procedure categorized the precincts of each city relative to that city's particular socioeconomic profile, and, of course, cities differ, not only in size and wealth but also in political and sociological personality.

Our precinct data are not surgically clean, and, even if they were, they would still be relatively crude. It is easy enough, at least since the mid-1960s, to locate all-black precincts and thus to be able to speak with some assurance of black voter behavior. But, even here, generalizations are open to suspicion. That black voters in Charleston and Columbia voted for certain candidates is not proof that blacks residing in rural areas or smaller towns or, for that matter, other South Carolina cities voted in a like fashion. In white neighborhoods the problems are greater. It is true that, by and large, cities tend to be residentially segregated by class as well as race (cities generally have high prestige and low prestige neighborhoods). But residential homogeneity is by no means complete. For example, a precinct properly classified as lower-status white may contain apartment complexes housing people of different socioeconomic characteristics. Even if it is assumed that precinct categories do accurately reflect the socioeconomic status attributed to them, the fallacy inherent in generalizing from some upper- or lower- or middle-class white precincts to others, as in the case of blacks, is still applicable. Nevertheless, taking into account the pitfalls and fallacies to which political analysis is heir, the precinct data, viewed in the aggregate, provide that crucial access to racial and class patterns of voting that county returns generally lack and without which an analysis of southern politics would be necessarily superficial.

The accumulation of this mountain of data involved three basic problems: the location of precinct maps, precinct returns, and county returns. Of these, the precinct maps presented the greatest obstacles. Cities redraw precinct lines, renumber existing precincts, and otherwise bewilder researchers to accommodate population shifts, changes in voter registration, or sometimes, one suspects, the whim of city or county officials. In the larger cities such changes are usually frequent; in the smaller cities precinct boundaries may remain unchanged over a period of several years. In any case, analyzing precinct returns over a period of more than two decades requires any number of precinct maps for each city. Often the search for long outdated precinct maps proved a frustrating experience. Municipal and

---

[13]Best of all was the city of Macon, Georgia, which decreed Jim Crow voting booths and reported election returns as "white" and "colored." Alas, this fine old practice, which appealed to both white supremists and political analysts, fell victim to the 1964 Civil Rights Act, complicating the chores of precinct classification.

county governments are not organized to ease the professional problems of academic researchers, and especially not historians. One learns to glow with appreciation and the joy of belated discovery when one finally locates those marvelous little old ladies of both sexes whose habit it is to hide away in some dusty corner copies of the old precinct maps at the time new ones are being drafted. One learns, also, to regard with a shudder the gleaming edifice of a new government office building, as the movement into it often consigns such out-of-date records to oblivion. As one retreats into the 1950s and the 1940s, the availability of precinct information becomes ever more limited. In at least one city in every state, however, we managed through luck and assiduous scavenging to carry our analysis back at least to the early 1950s and in most cases to the late 1940s.

The collection of precinct returns presented similar though somewhat less severe problems. Local governmental officials are more likely to retain the precinct returns than the maps needed to interpet them, and newspapers in many cities conscientiously print precinct tallies for significant elections.[14] No other southern state remotely matches Louisiana, where the secretary of state performs a yeoman service by compiling and publishing parish precinct statistics for all state primary and general elections.[15] For Texas elections in 1966 and 1968, Lance Tarrance has edited two editions of *Texas Precinct Votes*, which include not only precinct returns but also precinct maps for all 254 Texas counties.[16] During recent years, public record keeping, at least in the larger southern metropolitan counties, has undoubtedly improved. But despite developments that promise to simplify precinct data acquisition in the future, historians still face challenges, as anyone who has scrounged around some of the more unkempt metropolitan courthouses and city halls in search of precinct returns can testify. Occasional gaps in our precinct data resulting from inability to locate election returns in some cities are further testimonial.

County-level returns are considerably easier to acquire, although even here locating returns from primary elections held in the early 1950s can be troublesome. Alexander Heard and Donald S. Strong's *Southern Primaries and Elections, 1920-1949*[17] is invaluable for the early postwar period, and Richard M. Scammon's multivolume *America Votes* is equally helpful for general-election returns during the 1950s and 1960s.[18] Most of the county-

[14]Newspaper returns do present problems. To beat publication deadlines the newspapers sometimes go to press with incomplete returns, and the reprinting of election results offers one more opportunity for errors. Nevertheless, in a number of cases newspapers were the only sources available.

[15]Wade O. Martin, Jr., comp., *Primary Election Returns* and *General Election Returns* (Baton Rouge: Office of the Secretary of State, 1948–).

[16]V. Lance Tarrance, Jr., ed., *Texas Precinct Votes, 1966* (Austin: Politics, Inc., 1967); and idem, *Texas Precinct Votes '68* (Dallas: Southern Methodist University Press, 1969).

[17]University: University of Alabama Press, 1950.

[18]Richard M. Scammon, comp., *America Votes: A Handbook of Contemporary American Election Statistics*, 10 vols. (Washington, D.C.: Governmental Affairs Institute, 1956–73). We

level general-election data used in this study were supplied in machine-
readable form by the Inter-University Consortium for Political Research,
University of Michigan, which has extensive general-election holdings and
was provided by the authors in machine-readable form the county-level
primary-election returns collected for this study.[19] The only published collection of Southwide primary election statistics during the past two decades
is Richard M. Scammon, comp., *Southern Primaries '58.*[20] The following
sources for election statistics by state proved helpful:

Alabama
> *Alabama Official and Statistical Register*, published quadrennially by
> the State Department of Archives and History, Montgomery

Arkansas
> *Arkansas Almanac*, published biennially by Arkansas Almanac Com-
> pany, Little Rock

Florida
> *Report of the Secretary of State of Florida*, published biennially,
> Tallahassee
> Annie M. Hartsfield and Elston E. Roady, comps., *Florida Votes,
> 1920–1962* (Tallahassee: Institute of Governmental Research
> Florida State University, 1963)

Georgia
> *Georgia Official and Statistical Register*, published biennially by the
> Department of Archives and History, Atlanta

Louisiana
> *Report of the Secretary of State*, published biennially, Baton Rouge
> *Louisiana Almanac and Fact Book* (New Orleans: Louisiana Almanac
> and Fact Book, 1949)

Mississippi
> *Mississippi Official and Statistical Register*, published quadrennially
> by the secretary of state, Jackson
> Tip. H. Allen, Jr., *Mississippi Votes: The Presidential and Guberna-
> torial Elections, 1947–64* (State College: Mississippi State Univer-
> sity Press, 1967)
> F. Glenn Abney, *Mississippi Election Statistics, 1900–1967* (University:
> University of Mississippi Press, 1969)

---

are additionally indebted to Professor Scammon for permitting us to xerox extensive county
data in his possession. Scammon, comp., *America at the Polls: A Handbook of American
Presidential Election Statistics, 1920–1964* (Pittsburgh: University of Pittsburgh Press, 1965),
is a convenient source for presidential returns.

[19]For a statement on servicing policies and a summary of data holdings of the Survey Research Archive, see *A Guide to Resources and Services* (Ann Arbor: Inter-University Consortium for Political Research, updated periodically).

[20]Washington, D.C.: Governmental Affairs Institute, 1959.

North Carolina
> *North Carolina Manual*, published biennially by the secretary of state, Raleigh
> Donald R. Matthews et al., comps., *North Carolina Votes: General Election Returns by County . . . 1868-1960* (Chapel Hill: University of North Carolina Press, 1962)

South Carolina
> *Supplemental Report of the Secretary of State*, published biennially, Columbia
> *South Carolina Almanac* (Columbia: Pramac Associates, 1968–)

Tennessee
> *Tennessee Blue Book*, published biennially by the secretary of state, Nashville
> Joe C. Carr and Shirley Hassler, *Fifty Years of Tennessee Elections, 1916-1966* (Nashville: State Government, n.d.)
> _____, *Fifty Years of Tennessee Primary Elections, 1918-1968* (Nashville: State Government, n.d.)

Texas
> *Texas Almanac*, published biennially by A. H. Belo, Dallas
> Texas Election Research Project Committee, *Texas Votes: Selected General and Special Election Statistics, 1944-1963* (Austin: University of Texas Press, 1964)

Virginia
> Ralph Eisenberg, ed., *Virginia Votes, 1924-1968* (Charlotte: University of Virginia Press, 1971)

With the data collected, categorized, and coded in the fashion described, each county and each precinct return was punched on the standard Hollerith card. Given more than 1,100 counties and almost as many precincts,[21] and with presidential elections, senatorial and gubernatorial primaries, runoffs and elections, selected referenda and constitutional amendments, and other local, district, and state contests that for one reason or another tempted our attention, we were working with a data bank well in excess of 70,000 cards. From these data, our arithmetic programs computed total votes and percentages by county and subregion within states (and in the case of presidential elections for the South as a whole) and by precinct category within cities, and these results became the units of analysis for computation of Pearson product-moment, candidate-to-candidate coefficients of correlation.[22]

---

[21] The coding of precincts in a medium-sized city typically would produce around twenty for 1948 and as many as forty by 1972.

[22] The recent proliferation of literature bearing on the problems and advantages of quantitative history is welcome testimony not only to the increasing use of these techniques by historians but also more generally to the healthy degree to which social scientists have recovered

To serve as a check on our analysis of voting returns and to provide information on an individual level, we commissioned the Survey Research Center at the University of Michigan to run a secondary analysis from its survey research data bank. As we had done with our precinct data, we created a five-part taxonomy, with black respondents treated independently and white respondents quartered on the basis of three independent variables: (1) years of education, (2) occupation of head of household, and (3) total family income. As our analysis proceeded, it proved more feasible to collapse these categories into a tripartite division, with the black sample remaining consistent and the white respondents divided by education between those who had completed high school and those who had not; by occupation between those who worked in blue-collar occupational categories (unskilled, service, farm, protective service, unemployed, skilled, semiskilled) and those who labored in white-collar positions (clerical, sales, buyers, agents, brokers, professionals, semiprofessional, self-employed, business managers, officials); and by income according to a sliding scale that varied from, in 1952, those who lived on less than $4,000 family income and those who made $4,000 or more to, in 1970, those families who earned less than $7,500 and those who earned $7,500 or more, which reflected both inflation and the increasing prosperity of the region. This tripartite taxonomy assured that the value of N was greater than one hundred in most categories. For example, the N's for figure 5.1, showing voter turnout in presidential elections by race and education, were: for low-education white, 196 in 1952, 197 in 1956, 226 in 1960, 134 in 1964, and 136 in 1968; for high-education whites, 119 in 1952, 209 in 1956, 275 in 1960, 193 in 1964, and 188 in 1968; and for blacks, 94 in 1952, 69 in 1956, 70 in 1960, 213 in 1964, and 124 in 1968.

As dependent variables we chose the following:

1. A query as to the respondent's vote in that year's presidential election.

---

from W. S. Robinson's shattering blow of 1950. In "Ecological Correlations and the Behavior of Individuals," *American Sociological Review* 15 (June 1950): 351–57, Robinson sought to demonstrate mathematically that ecological correlations, which we have used extensively for this study, could so distort the true underlying relationships revealed by individual correlations that the former mode of social research ought to be abandoned. One finds little fault with Robinson's mathematics. Curiously, however, he seemed quite invalidly to assume that political and social ecologists simply equated correlation with causation, and he demonstrated an apparent blindness to the importance of detecting spurious bivariate correlations and thereby identifying significant third variables. For a more balanced assessment of the strengths and weaknesses of correlation analysis, see Austin Ranney, "The Utility and Limitations of Aggregate Data in the Study of Electoral Behavior," in his *Essays on the Behavioral Study of Politics* (Urbana: University of Illinois Press, 1962), pp. 91–102; and Thomas B. Alexander, "Some Natural Limits of Quantification in History" (Paper delivered at the thirty-seventh annual meeting of the Southern Historical Association, Houston, Texas, November 8, 1971 [mimeographed]). A more technical critique of Robinson's article is Leo A. Goodman, "Some Alternatives to Ecological Correlation," *American Journal of Sociology* 64 (May 1959): 610–25.

2. A party identification question, which read: "Generally speaking, do you usually think of yourself as a Republican, a Democrat, an Independent, or what?"
3. A New Deal question, which in 1956 and 1960 solicited a response to the statement: "The government in Washington ought to see to it that everybody who wants to work can find a job." In 1964 and 1968 the statement read: "In general . . . the government in Washington should see to it that every person has a job and a good standard of living."
4. A fair-employment question that in 1956 and 1960 read: "If Negroes are not getting fair treatment in jobs and housing, the government in Washington should see to it that they do." In 1964 and 1968 it read: "Some people feel that if Negroes are not getting fair treatment in jobs the government in Washington ought to see to it that they do. Others feel that this is not the federal government's business."
5. A school desegregation question, which in 1956 and 1960 sought a response to the statement: "The government in Washington should stay out of the question of whether white and colored children go to the same schools." In 1964, 1968, and 1970 it read: "Some people say that the government in Washington should see to it that white and Negro children are allowed to go to the same schools. Others claim that this is not the government's business."
6. Several other questions concerning political efficacy and social attitudes, the results of which were briefly summarized in chapter 6.

The results of six surveys during the years 1952–70 were incorporated into our analysis. As noted above, the wording for some of the questions used in our analysis was inconsistent over time, thus requiring qualifications on their interpretation. To bolster the size of our sample, we included respondents from the border states—Kentucky, Maryland, Oklahoma, West Virginia, and the District of Columbia—as well as from the eleven southern states. Compared with some in-depth attitudinal studies conducted in recent years,[23] our design was rather modest. What we did achieve, within the reservations stated, was a view of individual respondents by race and social class over a period of almost two decades.

Finally, over a period of several years we interviewed politicians, staff members, journalists, and generally persons whose credentials suggested that they were knowledgeable about southern political affairs. While a broad range of interviews were conducted, they were not systematic, they did not involve scientific samples or questionnaires, and although notes were taken, the interviews were not recorded or transcribed. A list of persons interviewed is located at the end of this appendix.

[23]Notably, Donald R. Matthews and James W. Prothro, *Negroes and the New Southern Politics* (New York: Harcourt, Brace and World, 1966); and Alfred O. Hero, Jr., *The Southerner and World Affairs* (Baton Rouge: Louisiana State University Press, 1965).

For all our interest in and indebtedness to the "new" political history, with its self-conscious concern for a broad theoretical framework, for methodology, and for drawing on a substantial data base, we acknowledge an abiding indebtedness to the "old" political history which emerged from the political mapmaking of Frederick Jackson Turner and Charles A. Beard and was carried on in political science by Wilfred E. Binkley, Samuel Lubell, and V. O. Key, especially in *Southern Politics*. In dealing with so vast a topic, the virtues of simplicity, when coupled with precision, are compelling.

Persons Interviewed

Senator James B. Allen, Alabama
Representative Charles E. Bennett, Florida, Third District
Representative Ben Blackburn, Georgia, Fourth District
Harold Bradley, Tennessee House of Representatives
Representative James T. Broyhill, North Carolina, Tenth District
Representative Patrick T. Caffery, Louisiana, Third District
Representative William L. Dickinson, Alabama, Second District
Edythe Edwards, legislative aide to Representative James Broyhill, North
    Carolina, Tenth District
Representative W. Jack Edwards, Alabama, First District
Guy Friddell, *Norfolk Virginia-Pilot*
Representative Richard H. Fulton, Tennessee, Fifth District
Representative Henry B. Gonzales, Texas, Twentieth District
Senator Albert Gore, Tennessee
Jim Groot, administrative assistant to Senator Edward Gurney, Florida
Representative John Paul Hammerschmidt, Arkansas, Third District
Sam Harris, *Arkansas Gazette*
Charles Holmes, administrative assistant to Representative Bob Eckhart,
    Texas, Eighth District
Thomas Hooker, administrative assistant to Representative William V.
    Chappel, Florida, Fourth District
Representative Walter Jones, North Carolina, First District
Tom W. Lambeth, administrative assistant to Representative L. Richardson
    Preyer, North Carolina, Sixth District
Representative Gillespie V. Montgomery, Mississippi, Fourth District
Ken Morrell, *Nashville Banner*
Robert Mason, *Norfolk Virginian-Pilot*
Edmund Orgill, former Mayor, Memphis, Tennessee

Representative L. Richardson Preyer, North Carolina, Sixth District
Representative James H. Quillen, Tennessee, First District
John Seigenthaler, *Nashville Tennessean*
Luther W. Shaw, administrative assistant to Representative Roy A. Taylor,
    North Carolina, Eleventh District
Representative Floyd D. Spence, South Carolina, Second District
Senator William Spong, Virginia
Representative W. S. Stuckey, Georgia, Eighth District
Senator Herman Talmadge, Georgia
Senator Strom Thurmond, South Carolina
Representative G. William Whitehurst, Virginia, Second District
Representative C. W. Bill Young, Florida, Eighth District
Edwin Yoder, *Greensboro Daily News*

BIBLIOGRAPHICAL ESSAY

Almost a quarter-century ago, V. O. Key wrote: "Of books about the South there is no end," a comment that remains as true today as then. The best bibliographical guides to literature on the modern South are Arthur S. Link and Rembert W. Patrick, eds., *Writing Southern History: Essays in Historiography in Honor of Fletcher M. Green* (Baton Rouge: Louisiana State University Press, 1965); Elizabeth W. Miller and Mary L. Fisher, comps., *The Negro in America: A Bibliography* (Cambridge, Mass.: Harvard University Press, 1970); and James M. McPherson et al., *Blacks in America: Bibliographical Essays* (Garden City, N.Y.: Doubleday, 1971).

The study of recent southern politics begins, of course, with V. O. Key, Jr., with the assistance of Alexander Heard, *Southern Politics in State and Nation* (New York: Alfred A. Knopf, 1949). No one yet has matched Key in grace of style and subtlety of analysis. Other classic works indispensable to an understanding of southern politics are Wilbur J. Cash, *The Mind of the South* (New York: Alfred A. Knopf, 1941); Gunnar Myrdal, *An American Dilemma: The Negro Problem and Modern Democracy*, 2 vols. (New York: Harper and Brothers, 1944); C. Vann Woodward, *The Burden of Southern History*, rev. ed. (Baton Rouge: Louisiana State University Press, 1968); and idem, *The Strange Career of Jim Crow*, 3d ed., rev. (New York: Oxford University Press, 1974). *The Mind of the South* emphasizes southern continuity, a theme that has recently received reinforcement in John Shelton Reed, *The Enduring South: Subcultural Persistence in Mass Society* (Lexington, Mass.: D. C. Heath, 1972). The best general study of the years immediately preceding the period covered in this study is George B. Tindall, *The Emergence of the New South, 1913–1945* (Baton Rouge: Louisiana State University Press, 1967), which is volume 10 of Wendell Holmes Stephenson and E. Merton Coulter, eds., *A History of the South*. Other good general studies of the modern South include Francis Butler Simkins and Charles Pierce Roland, *A History of the South*, 4th ed. (New York: Alfred A. Knopf, 1972); John S. Ezell, *The South Since 1865* (New York: Macmillan, 1963); and Thomas D. Clark and Albert D. Kirwan, *The South Since Appomattox* (New York: Oxford University Press, 1967).

The most thorough analysis of southern politics in the post-World War II period is William C. Havard, ed., *The Changing Politics of the South* (Baton Rouge: Louisiana State University Press, 1972), which includes chapters on each of the eleven southern states written by well-known political scientists. George Brown

Tindall, *The Disruption of the Solid South* (Athens: University of Georgia Press, 1972), is a thoughtful discussion of the emergence of a two-party system in the South. In a popular vein, Neal R. Peirce, *The Deep South States of America: People, Politics, and Power in the Seven Deep South States* (New York: W. W. Norton, 1974), is well-written and revealing. Other important interpretive works on the nature of southern political conflict include Dewey W. Grantham, Jr., *The Democratic South* (Athens: University of Georgia Press, 1963); T. Harry Williams, *Romance and Realism in Southern Politics* (Athens: University of Georgia Press, 1961); Howard Zinn, *The Southern Mystique* (New York: Alfred A. Knopf, 1964); and Jasper Berry Shannon, *Toward a New Politics in the South* (Knoxville: University of Tennessee Press, 1949).

Among the best of a number of collective works containing provocative essays on the South and southern politics are Charles G. Sellers, Jr., ed., *The Southerner as American* (Chapel Hill: University of North Carolina Press, 1960); Frank E. Vandiver, ed., *The Idea of the South: Pursuit of a Central Theme* (Chicago: University of Chicago Press, 1964); Allan P. Sindler, ed., *Change in the Contemporary South* (Durham: Duke University Press, 1963); Robert B. Highsaw, ed., *The Deep South in Transformation* (University: University of Alabama Press, 1964); Willie Morris, ed., *The South Today: 100 Years after Appomattox* (New York: Harper and Row, 1965); and Dewey W. Grantham, Jr., ed., *The South and the Sectional Image: The Sectional Theme Since Reconstruction* (New York: Harper and Row, 1966). Taylor Cole and John H. Hallowell, eds., *The Southern Political Scene, 1938-1948* (Gainesville: University of Florida Press, 1948), and Avery Leiserson, ed., *The American South in the 1960's* (New York: Praeger, 1964), are collections of essays that appeared in special editions of *The Journal of Politics*. Cortez A. M. Ewing, *Primary Elections in the South: A Study in Uniparty Politics* (Norman: University of Oklahoma Press, 1953), is a good introduction to the intricacies of Democratic primary-election politics.

The interrelationship between race and politics has been a continuing theme in recent literature. Numan V. Bartley, *The Rise of Massive Resistance: Race and Politics in the South during the 1950s* (Baton Rouge: Louisiana State University Press, 1969), the most complete examination of the politics of massive resistance, focuses on the conservative reaction to social change, as do James W. Vander Zanden, *Race Relations in Transition: The Segregation Crisis in the South* (New York: Random House, 1965), and Robert Earl Black, "Southern Governors and the Negro: Race as a Campaign Issue since 1954" (Ph.D. diss., Harvard University, 1968). Other works dealing with various aspects of school desegregation, civil rights, and white resistance include Neil R. McMillen, *The Citizens' Council: Organized Resistance to the Second Reconstruction, 1954-64* (Urbana: University of Illinois Press, 1971); Benjamin Muse, *Ten Years of Prelude: The Story of Integration since the Supreme Court's 1954 Decision* (New York: Viking Press, 1964); and idem, *The American Negro Revolution: From Nonviolence to Black Power, 1963-1967* (Bloomington: Indiana University Press, 1968); Reed Sarratt, *The Ordeal of Desegregation: The First Decade* (New York: Harper and Row, 1966); William Peters, *The Southern Temper* (Garden City: Doubleday, 1959); Don Shoemaker, ed., *With All Deliberate Speed: Segregation-Desegregation in Southern Schools* (New York: Harper and Brothers, 1957); Albert P. Blaustein and Clarence C. Ferguson, Jr., *Desegregation and the Law: The Meaning and Effect of the School Segregation Cases*, 2d ed., rev. (New York: Vintage Books, 1962); Daniel M. Berman, *It Is So Ordered: The Supreme Court Rules on School Segregation* (New York: W. W. Norton; 1966); J. W. Peltason, *Fifty-Eight Lonely Men: Southern Federal Judges and School Desegregation*, 2d ed. (Urbana: University of Illinois Press, 1971); Loren Miller, *The Petitioners: The Story of the Supreme Court of the United States and the Negro* (New York: Random House Pantheon Books, 1966); Gary Orfield, *The Reconstruction of Southern Education: The Schools and the 1964 Civil Rights Act* (New York: John Wiley and Sons, 1969); Allan Wolk, *The Presidency and Black Civil Rights* (Rutherford: Fairleigh Dickinson University Press, 1971); Donald S. Strong, *Negroes, Ballots and Judges* (University: University of Alabama Press, 1970); Foster Rhea Dulles, *The Civil Rights Commission: 1957–1965* (East Lansing: Michigan State University Press, 1968); and Chandler Davidson, *Biracial Politics* (Baton Rouge: Louisiana State University Press, 1972). Additionally, the volumes of *Phylon* and *The Journal of Negro Education* are filled with articles on southern race relations and black politics and education.

The monthly reports on the southern states in *Southern School News* (September 1954–June 1965), published by the Southern Education Reporting Service, are excellent for following developments in southern politics as well as in race relations. Also helpful are the "State of the Southern States" quarterly reports in *New South*, published by the Southern Regional Council, during the period Winter 1966–Fall 1969. The Southern Education Reporting Service Library in Nashville, Tennessee (the bulk of its material reproduced on microfilm under the title *Facts on Film*), and the Southern Regional Council Library in Atlanta, Georgia, contain extensive newspaper clipping files on southern politics and race relations. The various reports of the United States Commission on Civil Rights (1959–) are also valuable on a variety of subjects relating to race relations.

A number of recent studies of American politics have contained implications about southern political developments. Among the more important of these are Walter Dean Burnham, *Critical Elections and the Mainspring of American Politics* (New York: W. W. Norton, 1970); Kevin P. Phillips, *The Emerging Republican Majority* (New Rochelle: Arlington House, 1969); Richard M. Scammon and Ben J. Wattenberg, *The Real Majority* (New York: Coward-McAnn, 1970); Frederick G. Dutton, *Changing Sources of Power: American Politics in the 1970's* (New York: McGraw-Hill, 1971); David S. Broder, *The Party's Over: The Failure of Politics in America* (New York: Harper and Row, 1971); James L. Sundquist, *Dynamics of the Party System: Alignment and Realignment of Political Parties in the United States* (Washington, D.C.: The Brookings Institution, 1973); and a series of perceptive works by Samuel Lubell: *The Future of American Politics*, 2d. ed., rev. (Garden City: Doubleday, 1956); *Revolt of the Moderates* (New York: Harper and Brothers, 1956); *White and Black: Test of a Nation* (New York: Harper and Row, 1964); and *The Hidden Crisis in American Politics* (New York: W. W. Norton, 1970). Reg Murphy and Hal Gulliver, *The Southern Strategy* (New York: Charles Scribner's Sons, 1971), is disappointing. Angus Campbell et al., *The American Voter* (New York: John Wiley and Sons, 1960); E. E. Schattschneider, *The Semisovereign People: A Realist's View of Democracy in America* (New York: Holt, Rinehart and Winston, 1960); and V. O. Key, with Milton Cummings, *The Responsible Electorate: Rationality in Presidential Voting 1936–*

1960 (Cambridge, Mass.: Harvard University Press, 1966), continue to influence those who write about politics and voting, whether in the South or elsewhere in the nation.

For the raw voting data prior to 1950, we have the spinoff data book from the V. O. Key project, Alexander Heard and Donald Strong, eds., *Southern Primaries and Elections, 1920–1949* (University: University of Alabama Press, 1950), which contains county returns for primaries, overwhelmingly Democratic, for governor and senator in the eleven former Confederate states (these data are available on card and tape at the Inter-University Consortium for Political Research in Ann Arbor, Michigan). For county returns in general elections in the recent period, see the *America Votes* series, compiled by Richard M. Scammon for the Government Affairs Institute, beginning with volume 1 in 1956 and published biannually. The primary and precinct returns analyzed in this study will be published by the Johns Hopkins University Press and will also be available through the Inter-University Consortium for Political Research. Two extremely valuable guides for research in recent American political history are Lubomyr R. Wynar, comp., *American Political Parties: A Selected Guide to Parties and Movements in the 20th Century* (Littleton, Colo.: Libraries Unlimited, 1969), and Dwight L. Smith and Lloyd W. Garrison, eds., *The American Political Process: Selected Abstracts of Periodical Literature (1954–1971)* (Santa Barbara, Calif.: ABC Clio, 1972). Also useful are the publications of the *Congressional Quarterly* and, since 1969, the *National Journal*, particularly on the behavior of the branches and agencies of the federal government.

Provocative articles dealing with significant aspects of southern politics include Gerald W. Johnson, "Live Demagogues or Dead Gentlemen?" *Virginia Quarterly Review* 12 (January 1936): 1–14; Daniel M. Robinson, "From Tillman to Long: Some Striking Leaders of the Rural South," *Journal of Southern History* 3 (August 1937): 289–310; Rupert B. Vance, "Rebels and Agrarians All: Studies in One-Party Politics," *Southern Review* 4 (Summer 1938): 26–44; George B. Tindall, "Business Progressivism: Southern Politics in the Twenties," *South Atlantic Quarterly* 62 (Winter 1963): 92–106; Marian D. Irish, "Political Thought and Political Behavior in the South," *Western Political Quarterly* 13 (June 1960): 406–20; Leslie W. Dunbar, "The Changing Mind of the South: The Exposed Nerve," *Journal of Politics* 26 (February 1964): 3–21; Dewey W. Grantham, Jr., "The South and the Reconstruction of American Politics," *Journal of American History* 53 (September 1966): 227–46; and Numan V. Bartley and Hugh Davis Graham, "Whatever Happened to the Solid South?" *New South* 27 (Fall 1972): 28–34.

Among a number of biographies of southern political figures active during the 1950s and 1960s, the most objective and scholarly is Joseph Bruce Gorman, *Kefauver: A Political Biography* (New York: Oxford University Press, 1971), although it is exclusively concerned with Kefauver's career in Congress and in presidential politics. Extremely helpful are W. D. Workman, Jr., *The Bishop from Barnwell: The Political Life and Times of Senator Edgar A. Brown* (Columbia, S.C.: R. L. Bryan, 1963); William G. Jones, *The Wallace Story* (Northport, Ala.: American Southern Publishing, 1966); and Marshall Frady, *Wallace* (New York: World, 1968). Less valuable, but still worth examining, are Jerry D. Conn, *Preston Smith: The Making of a Texas Governor* (Austin: Pemberton Press, 1972);

Alberta M. Lachicotte, *Rebel Senator: Strom Thurmond of South Carolina* (New York: Devin-Adair, 1966); M. Carl Andrews, *No Higher Honor: The Story of Mills E. Godwin, Jr.* (Richmond: Dietz Press, 1970); W. Bradley Twitty, *Y'All Come* (Nashville: Hermitage, 1962), on James E. Folsom; and A. G. Irey, *Luther Hodges: Practical Idealist* (Minneapolis: T. S. Dennison, 1968).

Southern political figures who have recorded their own observations include Luther H. Hodges, *Businessman in the Statehouse: Six Years as Governor of North Carolina* (Chapel Hill: University of North Carolina Press, 1962); Frank E. Smith, *Congressman from Mississippi* (New York: Pantheon, 1964); Francis Pickens Miller, *Man from the Valley: Memoirs of a 20th-Century Virginian* (Chapel Hill: University of North Carolina Press, 1971); Ellis G. Arnall, *The Shore Dimly Seen* (New York: J. B. Lippincott, 1946); James F. Byrnes, *All in One Lifetime* (New York: Harper and Brothers, 1958); Terry Sanford, *But What About the People?* (New York: Harper and Row, 1966); Brooks Hays, *A Southern Moderate Speaks* (Chapel Hill: University of North Carolina Press, 1959); Charles L. Weltner, *Southerner* (New York: J. B. Lippincott, 1966); Ivan Allen, Jr., with Paul Hemphill, *Mayor: Notes on the 60's* (New York: Simon and Schuster, 1971); and Albert Gore, *Let the Glory Out* (New York: Viking Press, 1972). Charles Morgan, Jr., relates the tribulations of a liberal lawyer living in Birmingham and writes knowledgeably about Alabama social and political developments in *A Time to Speak* (New York: Harper and Row, 1964). Other works offering valuable insights from southern moderates and liberals include Harry S. Ashmore, *An Epitaph for Dixie* (New York: W. W. Norton, 1958); James McBride Dabbs, *Who Speaks for the South?* (New York: Funk and Wagnalls, 1964); Ralph McGill, *The South and the Southerner* (Boston: Little, Brown, 1963); Henry Savage, Jr., *Seeds of Time: The Background of Southern Thinking* (New York: Henry Holt and Company, 1959); and Pat Watters, *The South and the Nation* (New York: Pantheon, 1969). William D. Workman, Jr., *The Case for the South* (New York: Devin-Adair, 1960), is a good statement of the white conservative position, as is James J. Kilpatrick, *The Southern Case for School Desegregation* (New York: Crowell-Collier, 1962). Other works such as Herman E. Talmadge, *You and Segregation* (Birmingham: Vulcan, 1955), and Tom P. Brady, *Black Monday* (Winona, Miss.: Association of Citizens' Councils, 1955), are positively frightening.

The best starting point for an examination of economic and demographic change in the South is John C. McKinney and Edgar T. Thompson, eds., *The South in Continuity and Change* (Durham: Duke University Press, 1965), an unusually balanced collection of essays covering a variety of subjects. Valuable analyses of the southern economy include Hammer and Company, *Post-War Industrial Development in the South* (Atlanta: Hammer and Company and the Southern Regional Council, 1956); U.S. Congress, Senate, 84th Cong., 2d sess., *Selected Materials on the Economy of the South: Report of the Committee on Banking and Currency* (Washington, D.C.: U.S. Government Printing Office, 1956); James H. Street, *The New Revolution in the Cotton Economy: Mechanization and Its Consequences* (Chapel Hill: University of North Carolina Press, 1957); Melvin L. Greenhut and W. Tate Whitman, eds., *Essays in Southern Economic Development* (Chapel Hill: University of North Carolina Press, 1964); Marshall R. Colberg, *Human Capital in Southern Development, 1939–1963* (Chapel Hill: University of North Carolina Press, 1965); *Raising the Income and*

Productivity of the South: Speeches Delivered at the 1961 Southern Regional Conference of the Council of State Governments (Frankfort, Ky.: Legislative Research Commission, 1961); Edgar S. Dunn, Jr., *Recent Southern Economic Development as Revealed by the Changing Structure of Employment* (Gainesville: University of Florida Press, 1962); H. M. Douty, "Wage Differentials: Forces and Counterforces," *Monthly Labor Review* 91 (March 1968): 74–81; and John C. McKinney and Linda Brookover Bourque, "The Changing South: National Incorporation of a Region," *American Sociological Review* 36 (June 1971): 399–412.

Rupert B. Vance and Nicholas J. Demerath, eds., *The Urban South* (Chapel Hill: University of North Carolina Press, 1954), and John M. Maclachlan and Joe S. Floyd, Jr., *This Changing South* (Gainesville: University of Florida Press, 1956), are good on population movements, but they should be supplemented with the more recent essays in McKinney and Thompson, *The South in Continuity and Change*. Useful articles on southern population movements include Rudolph Heberle, "The Changing Social Stratification of the South," *Social Forces* 38 (October 1959): 42–50; T. Stanton Dietrich, "The Nature and Directions of Suburbanization in the South," *Social Forces* 39 (December 1960): 181–86; James D. Tarver, "Migration Differentials in Southern Cities and Suburbs," *Social Science Quarterly* 50 (September 1969): 298–324; and Tommy W. Rogers, "Migration Attractiveness of Southern Metropolitan Areas," *Social Science Quarterly* 50 (September 1960): 325–36.

On metropolitan government, especially in Nashville, Baton Rouge, and Miami, see Daniel R. Grant, "Urban and Suburban Nashville: A Case Study in Metropolitanism," *Journal of Politics* 17 (February 1955): 82–99; Gladys M. Kammerer, *The Changing Urban County* (Gainesville: University of Florida Public Administration Clearing Service, 1963); Edward Sofen, *The Miami Metropolitan Experiment* (Bloomington: Indiana University Press, 1963); and three studies by Brett W. Hawkins: *Nashville Metro: The Politics of City-County Consolidation* (Nashville: Vanderbilt University Press, 1966); "Public Opinion and Metropolitan Reorganization in Nashville," *Journal of Politics* 28 (May 1966): 408–18; and "Life Style, Demographic Distance and Voter Support of City-County Consolidation," *Southwestern Social Science Quarterly* 48 (December 1967): 325–38. For Virginia's curious evolution of independent cities, see Chester W. Bain, *Annexation in Virginia* (Charlottesville: University of Virginia Press, 1966), and idem, *"A Body Incorporate": The Evolution of City-County Separation in Virginia* (Charlottesville: University of Virginia Press, 1967).

James W. Martin and Glenn D. Morrow, *Taxation of Manufacturing in the South* (University: University of Alabama Press, 1948); Eva Galambos, *The Tax Structure of the Southern States* (Atlanta: Southern Regional Council, 1969); and idem, *State and Local Taxes in the South, 1973.* (Atlanta: Southern Regional Council, 1973), are studies of the consumer-oriented tax structure common to the region. An important comprehensive, quantitative analysis of the relationship between political variables and state governmental policy outcomes in education, welfare, highways, taxation, and the regulation of public morality is Thomas R. Dye, *Politics, Economics, and the Public: Policy Outcomes in the American States* (Chicago: Rand McNally, 1966). William H. Nicholls, *Southern Tradition and Regional Progress* (Chapel Hill: University of North Carolina Press, 1960), and

Thomas D. Clark, *The Emerging South*, 2d ed. (New York: Oxford University Press, 1968), examine the relationship between economic, social, and political change. Harry S. Ashmore, *The Negro and the Schools* (Chapel Hill: University of North Carolina Press, 1954); Truman M. Pierce et al., *White and Negro Schools in the South: An Analysis of Biracial Education* (Englewood Cliffs: Prentice-Hall, 1955); and Patrick McCauley and Edward D. Ball, eds., *Southern Schools: Progress and Problems* (Nashville: Southern Education Reporting Service, 1959), contain useful statistics concerning who gets what from the southern governmental process. Concentrating on the economic problems of black southerners are Leonard Broom and Norval D. Glenn, *Transformation of the Negro American* (New York: Harper and Row, 1965); Gary S. Becker, *The Economics of Discrimination* (Chicago: University of Chicago Press, 1957); Vivian W. Henderson, *The Economic Status of Negroes in the Nation and in the South* (Atlanta: Southern Regional Council, 1963); and James D. Cowhig and Calvin L. Beale, "Relative Socioeconomic Status of Southern Whites and Nonwhites, 1950 and 1960," *Southwestern Social Science Quarterly* 45 (September 1964): 113–24.

John Dollard, *Caste and Class in a Southern Town*, 3d ed. (Garden City: Doubleday Anchor Books, 1957); Charles S. Johnson, *Shadow of the Plantation* (Chicago: University of Chicago Press, 1934); Allison Davis, Burleigh B. Gardner, and Mary R. Gardner, *Deep South: A Social Anthropological Study of Caste and Class* (Chicago: University of Chicago Press, 1941); and Hortense Powdermaker, *After Freedom: A Cultural Study in the Deep South* (New York: Russell and Russell, 1939), are among older studies of cultural behavior in the southern lowlands that remain valuable. Also somewhat dated but still worth attention is Karl A. Bosworth, *Black Belt County: Rural Government in the Cotton Country of Alabama* (University: University of Alabama Press, 1941). Morton Rubin, *Plantation County* (Chapel Hill: University of North Carolina Press, 1951), is an excellent study of an Alabama black-belt county reexamined fifteen years later in National Education Association Commission on Professional Rights and Responsibilities, *Report of an Investigation: Wilcox County, Alabama, A Study of Social, Economic, and Educational Bankruptcy* (Washington, D.C.: National Education Association, 1967). Bob Smith, *They Closed Their Schools: Prince Edward County, Virginia 1951–1964* (Chapel Hill: North Carolina, 1965), demonstrates to what extent black-belt whites were sometimes willing to go to avoid social equality, and Frederick M. Wirt, *Politics of Southern Equality* (Chicago: Aldine, 1970), delves into the impact of federal civil-rights legislation upon social behavior in a Mississippi lowlands county.

On the southern mountain area Thomas R. Ford, ed., *The Southern Appalachian Region: A Survey* (Lexington: University of Kentucky Press, 1962); Jack E. Weller, *Yesterday's People: Life in Contemporary Appalachia* (Lexington: University of Kentucky Press, 1966); Elmora M. Matthews, *Neighbor and Kin: Life in a Tennessee Ridge Community* (Nashville: Vanderbilt University Press, 1965); and Harry M. Caudill, *Night Comes to the Cumberlands: A Biography of a Depressed Area* (Boston: Little, Brown, 1963) are good. Karl A. Bosworth, *Tennessee Valley County: Rural Government in the Hill Country of Alabama* (University: University of Alabama Press, 1941), is a helpful older study. Solon T. Kimball and Marian Pearsall, *The Talladega Story: A Study in Community Process* (University: University of Alabama Press, 1954), and Peter Schuck and Harrison Wellford, "Democracy and the Good Life in a Company Town: The Case of St. Mary's, Georgia," *Harper's* 244 (May 1972): 56–66, discuss two southern communities heavily dependent on textile mills, and John K. Moreland, *Millways of Kent* (Chapel Hill: University of North Carolina Press, 1958), studies one group of southern mill workers. The standard study of southern labor is F. Ray Marshall, *Labor in the South* (Cambridge, Mass.: Harvard University Press, 1967).

Robert L. Crain and Morton Inger, *School Desegregation in New Orleans: A Comparative Study of the Failure of Social Control* (Chicago: University of Chicago Press, 1966), examines the leadership in a number of southern cities, and Robert L. Crain, *The Politics of School Desegregation: Comparative Case Studies of Community Structure and Policy-Making* (Chicago: Aldine, 1968), extends the study to nonsouthern cities. Alfred O. Hero, Jr., *The Southerner and World Affairs* (Baton Rouge: Louisiana State University, 1965), a superior work ranging over a far wider scope than the title implies, includes perceptive observations about leadership and attitudes in the urban South. M. Kent Jennings, *Community Influentials: The Elites of Atlanta* (Glencoe: Free Press, 1964), is a solid study, and Ernest Q. Campbell and Thomas F. Pettigrew, *Christians in Racial Crisis: A Study of Little Rock's Ministry* (Washington, D.C.: Public Affairs Press, 1959), offers perceptive insights into social behavior in Little Rock. Also helpful on urban political behavior in the South are Corinne Silverman, *The Little Rock Story*, rev. ed. (University: University of Alabama Press, 1959); M. Kent Jennings and Harmon Zeigler, "Class, Party, and Race in Four Types of Elections: The Case of Atlanta," *Journal of Politics* 28 (May 1966): 391–407; idem, "A Moderate's Victory in a Southern Congressional District," *Public Opinion Quarterly* 28 (Winter 1964): 595–603; Alvin Boskoff and Harmon Zeigler, *Voting Patterns in a Local Election* (New York: J. B. Lippincott, 1964); Alvin Boskoff, "Social and Cultural Patterns in a Suburban Area: Their Significance for Urban Change in the South," *Journal of Social Issues* 12 (January 1966): 85–100; James Chubbuck, Edwin Renwick, and Joe E. Walker, "The Emergence of Coalition Politics in New Orleans," *New South* 26 (Winter 1971): 16–25; E. Larry Dickens, "Microcosm in Texas: An Achilles Heel for a Liberal Coalition," *New South* 26 (Summer 1971): 10–18; Chandler Davidson and Douglas Longshore, "Houston Elects a Mayor," *New South* 27 (Spring 1972): 47–61; Norman I. Lustig, "The Relationships Between Demographic Characteristics and Pro-Integration Vote of White Precincts in a Metropolitan Southern County," *Social Forces* 40 (March 1962): 205–8; and M. Richard Cramer, "School Desegregation and New Industry: The Southern Community Leaders' Viewpoint," *Social Forces* 41 (May 1963): 384–89. William H. Barnwell, *In Richard's World: The Battle of Charleston, 1966* (Boston: Houghton Mifflin, 1968), is a moving examination of the enormous distance separating the upper-class whites in Charleston from the blacks living a few blocks away.

The Mexican-American counties in southern Texas are examined in William Madsen, *Mexican-Americans of South Texas* (New York: Holt, Rinehart and Winston, 1964); Harley L. Browning and S. Dale McLemore, *A Statistical Profile of the Spanish Surname Population of Texas* (Austin: University of Texas Press, 1964); and Cliften McCleskey and Bruce Merrill, "Mexican American Political Behavior in Texas," *Social Science Quarterly* 43 (March 1973): 785–98. The politics of southern Louisiana Catholics are examined in the appropriate chapter in John H. Fenton, *The Catholic Vote* (New Orleans: Hauser, 1960).

On state politics in the South, the relevant chapters in Key, *Southern Politics*, and Havard, *The Changing Politics of the South*, are the essential beginning points, and the most comprehensive state-by-state bibliography is in Bartley, *The Rise of*

Massive Resistance, pp. 358–66. Some of the most useful guides to state politics are as follows. Boyce A. Drummond, Jr., "Arkansas Politics: A Study of a One-Party System" (Ph.D. diss., University of Chicago, 1957), and Thomas F. Pettigrew and Ernest Q. Campbell, "Faubus and Segregation: An Analysis of Arkansas Voting," *Public Opinion Quarterly* 24 (Fall 1960): 436–47, are helpful on Arkansas political developments. Hugh D. Price, *The Negro and Southern Politics: A Chapter of Florida History* (New York: New York University Press, 1957), and William C. Havard and Loren P. Beth, *The Politics of Mis-Representation: Rural-Urban Conflict in the Florida Legislature* (Baton Rouge: Louisiana State University Press, 1962), delve into aspects of Florida politics. Charlton W. Tebeau, *A History of Florida* (Coral Gables: University of Miami Press, 1971), is an excellent state history that devotes adequate attention to the modern period of Florida history. *Florida State University Governmental Research Bulletin*, published by the Institute of Governmental Research (1964–), contains valuable reports on Florida politics.

Joseph L. Bernd, *Grass Roots Politics in Georgia: The County Unit System and the Importance of the Individual Voting Community in Bifactional Elections, 1942–1954* (Atlanta: Emory University Research Committee, 1960); Charles B. Pyles, "Race and Ruralism in Georgia Elections, 1948–1966" (Ph.D. diss., University of Georgia, 1967); and Numan V. Bartley, *From Thurmond to Wallace: Political Tendencies in Georgia, 1948–1968* (Baltimore: Johns Hopkins Press, 1970), examine trends in Georgia politics. The functioning of Georgia's peculiar county-unit system is covered in Louis T. Rigdon II, *Georgia's County Unit System* (Decatur, Ga.: Selective Books, 1961); William G. Cornelius, "The County Unit System of Georgia: Facts and Prospects," *Western Political Quarterly* 14 (December 1961): 942–60; and Albert B. Saye, "Revolution by Judicial Action in Georgia," *Western Political Quarterly* 17 (March 1964): 10–14.

Perry H. Howard, *Political Tendencies in Louisiana*, rev. ed. (Baton Rouge: Louisiana State University Press, 1971), is an excellent ecological analysis, stressing continuity in Louisiana politics. Also valuable are Allan P. Sindler, *Huey Long's Louisiana: State Politics, 1920–1952* (Baltimore: Johns Hopkins Press, 1956); William C. Havard, Rudolf Heberle, and Perry H. Howard, *The Louisiana Elections of 1960* (Baton Rouge: Louisiana State University Press, 1963); and William C. Havard and Robert F. Steamer, "Louisiana Secedes: Collapse of a Compromise," *Massachusetts Review* 1 (October 1959): 134–46. Journalistic accounts dealing with the Long faction in the state Democratic party include Stan Opotowsky, *The Longs of Louisiana* (New York: E. P. Dutton, 1960), a readable account with a pro-Long bias; Thomas Martin, *Dynasty: The Longs of Louisiana* (New York: G. T. Putnam's Sons, 1960), which is anti-Long; and A. J. Liebling, *The Earl of Louisiana* (New York: Simon and Schuster, 1961), a journalistic classic overtly friendly toward Earl K. Long. Among numerous books dealing with aspects of the civil-rights movement and white resistance in Mississippi, Hodding Carter III, *The South Strikes Back* (Garden City: Doubleday, 1959), and James W. Silver, *Mississippi: The Closed Society*, 2d ed. (New York: Harcourt, Brace and World, 1966), are good.

Extremely useful on North Carolina Democratic party factionalism is James R. Spence, *The Making of a Governor: The Moore-Preyer-Lake Primaries of 1964* (Winston-Salem, N.C.: John F. Blair, 1968). Also helpful are Hugh T. Lefler and Albert R. Newsome, *North Carolina: The History of a Southern State*, rev. ed. (Chapel Hill: University of North Carolina Press, 1963), and Jack D. Fleer, *North*

Carolina Politics: An Introduction (Chapel Hill: University of North Carolina Press, 1968). For insight into the evolution of county government in the South in historical depth, see Joseph S. Ferrell, ed., *County Government in North Carolina* (Chapel Hill: University of North Carolina Institute of Government, 1968).

On South Carolina, Ernest M. Lander, Jr., *A History of South Carolina, 1865–1960*, 2d ed. (Columbia: University of South Carolina Press, 1970), and Howard H. Quint, *Profile in Black and White: A Frank Portrait of South Carolina* (Washington, D.C.: Public Affairs Press, 1958), are helpful. An excellent series of articles by Donald L. Fowler in the *University of South Carolina Governmental Review* includes "Negro Voting—1966 S.C. Democratic Primary," vol. 7 (August 1966); "Two-Party Politics: 1966," vol. 9 (May 1967); and "The 1968 General Election in S.C.," vol. 11 (May 1969). See also Ralph Eisenberg's illuminating case study, "The Logroll South Carolina Style," in *Cases in State and Local Government*, ed. Richard T. Frost (Englewood Cliffs: Prentice-Hall, 1961), pp. 155–63.

Hugh Davis Graham, *Crisis in Print: Desegregation and the Press in Tennessee* (Nashville: Vanderbilt University Press, 1967), and Norman L. Parks, "Tennessee Politics since Kefauver and Reece: A 'Generalist' View," *Journal of Politics* 28 (February 1966): 144–68, are good on Tennessee. For the earlier period, see William Goodman, *Inherited Domain: Political Parties in Tennessee* (Knoxville: University of Tennessee Bureau of Public Administration, 1954), and William R. Majors, "Gordon Browning and Tennessee Politics: 1949–1953," *Tennessee Historical Quarterly* 27 (Summer 1969): 166–81. The growth of the black franchise is treated in M. Jerome Diamond, "The Impact of the Negro Vote in Contemporary Tennessee Politics," *Tennessee Law Review* 54 (1967): 435–81.

Texas political conflicts are analyzed in James R. Soukup, Clifton McCleskey, and Harry Holloway, *Party and Factional Division in Texas* (Austin: University of Texas Press, 1964); Clifton McCleskey, *The Government and Politics of Texas*, 3d ed. (Boston: Little, Brown, 1969); Dan Nimmo and William Oden, *The Texas Political System* (Englewood Cliffs: Prentice-Hall, 1971); and a series of case studies by O. Douglas Weeks: *Texas Presidential Politics in 1952* (Austin: University of Texas Press, 1953), *Texas One-Party Politics in 1956* (Austin: University of Texas Press, 1957), *Texas in the 1960 Presidential Election* (Austin: University of Texas Press, 1961), and *Texas in 1964: A One-Party State Again?* (Austin: University of Texas Press, 1965). The best study of Virginia politics is J. Harvie Wilkinson III, *Harry Byrd and the Changing Face of Virginia Politics, 1945–1966* (Charlottesville: University of Virginia Press, 1968), which stresses the political impact of growing urbanism in the state and which was written as a senior thesis at Yale! A number of articles by Ralph Eisenberg in the *University of Virginia News Letter* examine specific elections in Virginia during the 1960's. Also helpful are Benjamin Muse, *Virginia's Massive Resistance* (Bloomington: Indiana University Press, 1961); Robbins L. Gates, *The Making of Massive Resistance: Virginia's Politics of Public School Desegregation, 1954–1956* (Chapel Hill: University of North Carolina Press, 1962); William F. Ogburn and Charles M. Grigg, "Factors Related to the Virginia Vote on Segregation," *Social Forces* 34 (May 1956): 301–8; and Virginius Dabney, *Virginia: The New Dominion* (Garden City: Doubleday, 1971).

The reentry of black voters into southern politics is examined in Donald R. Matthews and James W. Prothro, *Negroes and the New Southern Politics* (New York: Harcourt, Brace and World, 1966), and Pat Watters and Reese Cleghorn,

Climbing Jacob's Ladder: The Arrival of Negroes in Southern Politics (New York: Harcourt, Brace and World, 1967). Important statistics on both black and white voter registration are available in Margaret Price, *The Negro Voter in the South* (Atlanta: Southern Regional Council, 1957); idem, *The Negro and the Ballot in the South* (Atlanta: Southern Regional Council, 1959); *Voter Registration in the South: Summer, 1966* (Atlanta: Voter Education Project, Southern Regional Council, 1966); *Voter Registration in the South: Summer, 1968* (Atlanta: Voter Education Project, Southern Regional Council, 1968); United States Commission on Civil Rights, *Political Participation* (Washington, D.C.: U.S. Government Printing Office, 1968); and Voter Education Project, *V.E.P. News* (monthly, January 1967–). Other noteworthy studies of Negro political participation in the South are Harry Holloway, *The Politics of the Southern Negro: From Exclusion to Big City Organization* (New York: Random House, 1969); Andrew Buni, *The Negro in Virginia Politics, 1902-1965* (Charlottesville: University of Virginia Press, 1967); William R. Keech, *The Impact of Negro Voting: The Role of the Quest for Equality* (Chicago: Rand McNally, 1968); Everett C. Ladd, Jr., *Negro Political Leadership in the South* (Ithaca: Cornell University Press, 1966); Davidson, *Biracial Politics* (previously cited); Alfred Clubok, John DeGrove, and Charles Farris, "The Manipulated Negro Vote: Preconditions and Consequences," *Journal of Politics* 26 (February 1964): 112–29; and Jack Walker, "Negro Voting in Atlanta: 1953–1961," *Phylon* 24 (Winter 1963): 379–87. Frederic D. Ogden, *The Poll Tax in the South* (University: University of Alabama Press, 1958), is a good study of one barrier to an expanded franchise, and a perceptive case study is Dick Smith, "Texas and the Poll Tax," *Southwestern Social Science Quarterly* 45 (September 1964): 167–73. In *Negroes, Ballots, and Judges*, previously cited, Donald Strong examines the federal voting rights legislation of 1957, 1960, and 1965 and the white resistance to these laws in three Deep South states. Also significant are Donald S. Strong, *Registration of Voters in Alabama* (University: University of Alabama Press, 1956); Olive H. Shadgett, *Voter Registration in Georgia: A Study of Its Administration* (Athens: University of Georgia Press, 1955); and United States Commission on Civil Rights, *Voting in Mississippi* (Washington, D.C.: U.S. Government Printing Office, 1965).

The most thorough analyses of survey research data pertaining to the South are Matthews and Prothro, *Negroes and the New Southern Politics*, and Hero, *The Southerner and World Affairs*, both mentioned previously. Melvin M. Tumin et al., *Desegregation: Resistance and Readiness* (Princeton: Princeton University Press, 1958), is an in-depth attitudinal study conducted in Guilford County, North Carolina, and Thomas F. Pettigrew, "Regional Differences in Anti-Negro Prejudice," *Journal of Abnormal and Social Psychology* 59 (July 1959): 28–36, is revealing. National attitudinal studies containing significant information about the South and southerners include William Brink and Louis Harris, *The Negro Revolution in America* (New York: Simon and Schuster, 1964); idem, *Black and White: A Study of U.S. Racial Attitudes Today* (New York: Simon and Schuster, 1967); Samuel A. Stouffer, *Communism, Conformity and Civil Liberties: A Cross-Section of the Nation Speaks Its Mind* (Garden City: Doubleday, 1955); Lloyd A. Free and Hadley Cantril, *The Political Beliefs of Americans: A Study of Public Opinion* (New Brunswick: Rutgers University, 1967); and Seymour M. Lipset, *Political Man: The Social Bases of Politics* (Garden City: Doubleday, 1960). Mildred A. Schwartz, *Trends in White Attitudes Toward Negroes* (Chicago: University of Chicago, NORC #119,

1967), is very helpful, as are Herbert H. Hyman and Paul B. Sheatsley, "Attitudes Toward Desegregation," *Scientific American* 195 (December 1956): 35–39; idem, "Attitudes Toward Desegregation," *Scientific American* 211 (July 1964): 2–9; and Andrew M. Greeley and Paul B. Sheatsley, "Attitudes Toward Racial Integration," *Scientific American* 225 (December 1971): 13–19. Throughout the 1960s Hazel Erskine periodically reported in the *Public Opinion Quarterly* on survey research in race relations, as follows: on civil rights, Spring 1962, pp. 137–48; on black housing, Fall 1967, pp. 482–98; on demonstrations and race riots, Winter 1967–68, pp. 655–77; on Negro employment, Spring 1968, pp. 132–53; and on the speed of racial integration, Fall 1968, pp. 513–24.

The voting behavior of southern congressmen is examined in H. Wayne Shannon, *Party, Constituency and Congressional Voting: A Study of Legislative Behavior in the United States House of Representatives* (Baton Rouge: Louisiana State University Press, 1968), and Hubert R. Fowler, *The Unsolid South: Voting Behavior of Southern Senators, 1947–1960* (University: University of Alabama Press, 1968). Michael Barone, Grant Ujifusa, and Douglas Matthews, *The Almanac of American Politics: The Senators, the Representatives—Their Records, States Districts, 1972* (Boston: Gambit, 1972), is a superior reference work. Malcolm E. Jewell, *Legislative Representation in the Contemporary South* (Durham: Duke University Press, 1967), is an excellent examination of state legislative politics. During the 1950s and early 1960s southern legislatures, like those elsewhere in the nation, were often grossly malapportioned. See Paul T. David and Ralph Eisenberg, *Devaluation of the Urban and Surburban Vote: A Statistical Investigation of Long-Term Trends in State Legislative Representation* (Charlottesville: University of Virginia Press, 1961); Gordon Baker, *Rural Versus Urban Political Power: The Nature and Consequence of Unbalanced Representation* (Garden City: Doubleday, 1955); idem, *The Reapportionment Revolution* (New York: Random House, 1967); Robert G. Dixon, Jr., *Democratic Representation: Reapportionment in Law and Politics* (New York: Oxford University Press, 1968); and Preston W. Edsall, "State Legislatures and Legislative Representation," *Journal of Politics* 30 (May 1968): 277–90.

On the emergence of a two-party system in the South, the place to begin is Alexander Heard, *A Two-Party South?* (Chapel Hill: University of North Carolina Press, 1952), which continues to reward reexamination. Presidential politics in the South during the 1950s is examined in a series of works by Donald S. Strong, *The 1952 Presidential Election in the South* (University: Bureau of Public Information, University of Alabama, 1956), and in idem, *Urban Republicanism in the South* (University: Bureau of Public Information, University of Alabama, 1960). See also Strong's "Further Reflections on Southern Politics," *Journal of Politics* 33 (May 1971): 239–56. Bernard Cosman discusses southern Republicanism during the early 1960s in "Presidential Republicanism in the South, 1960" *Journal of Politics* 24 (May 1962): 303–322; *Five States for Goldwater: Continuity and Change in Southern Presidential Voting Patterns* (University: University of Alabama Press, 1966); *The Case of the Goldwater Delegates: Deep South Republican Leadership* (University: University of Alabama Press, 1966); and "Republicanism in the South: Goldwater's Impact Upon Voting Alignments in Congressional, Gubernatorial, and Senatorial Races," *Southwestern Social Science Quarterly* 48 (June 1967): 13–23. Walter Dean Burnham, "The Alabama Senatorial Election of 1962: Return of Inter-

Party Competition," *Journal of Politics* 26 (November 1964): 798–829, is an excellent case study, as is Kenneth N. Vines, *Two Parties for Shreveport* (New York: Henry Holt and Co., 1959). Two-party competition in state legislative elections is covered in Jewell, *Legislative Representation in the Contemporary South.* Also suggestive is Gerald Pomper, "Future Southern Congressional Politics," *Southwestern Social Science Quarterly* 44 (June 1963): 14–24. Of varying degrees of usefulness are Donald L. Fowler, *Presidential Voting in South Carolina, 1948–1964* (Columbia: University of South Carolina Press, 1966); Paul Casdorph, *A History of the Republican Party in Texas, 1865–1965* (Austin: Pemberton Press, 1965); William J. Crotty, "The Role of the County Chairman in the Contemporary Party System in North Carolina" (Ph.D. diss., University of North Carolina, 1964); James W. Prothro, Ernest Q. Campbell, and Charles M. Grigg, "Two-Party Voting in the South: Class vs. Party Identification," *American Political Science Review* 52 (March 1958): 131–39; Anthony M. Orum and Edward W. McCranie, "Class, Tradition, and Partisan Alignments in a Southern Urban Electorate," *Journal of Politics* 32 (February 1970): 156–76; and the following works in volumes 1 and 2 of *Tulane Studies in Political Science*: L. Vaughan Howard and David R. Deener, "Presidential Politics in Louisiana, 1952" (1954); Leonard Reissman, K. H. Silvert, Cliff W. Wing, Jr., "The New Orleans Voter" (1955); and Kenneth N. Vines, "Republicanism in New Orleans" (1955).

The Ripon Society has sponsored valuable studies, including *Election '64: A Ripon Society Report* (Cambridge, Mass.: Ripon Society, 1965); John C. Topping, Jr., John R. Lazarek, and William H. Linder, *Southern Republicanism and the New South* (Cambridge, Mass.: Republicans for Progress and the Ripon Society, 1966); and Michael S. Lottman, "The G.O.P. and the South: An 84-page State-by-State Report," *Ripon Forum* 6 (July–August 1970): 9–86. The Republican National Committee, unlike its Democratic counterpart, periodically publishes statistical information, among the best of which is Research Division, Republican National Committee, *The 1968 Elections: A Summary Report with Supporting Tables* (Washington, D.C., 1969).

INDEX

Abernethy, Tom, 82
Acuff, Roy, 15
Agnew, Spiro, 158, 164, 182
Agrarianism, 5, 6, 8
Alabama: black voter registration, 40; change in voting behavior, 108–9; factionalism, 37–40, 47; Folsom administration, 37–38; gubernatorial elections, 67–68; gubernatorial primary turnout, 17; racial issue, 67–68; Republican party, 82–83, 98–100; school desegregation, 117; senatorial elections, 39–40, 98–99, 181–82; socioeconomic class vote, 40, 68, 118; Wallace administration, 117–19
Alexander, Hugh Q., 101
Alford, Dale, 56, 121
Alger, Bruce, 108
Allen, Clifford, 44
Allen, Ivan, Jr., 71, 113, 186
Allen, Melba Till, 172
Almond, J. Lindsay, 75
Andrews, George, 108
Andrews, T. Coleman, 90
Anti-Masons, 5
Arkansas: county organization, 30; factionalism, 37; Faubus administration, 53–57; gubernatorial elections, 53–57, 147–48, 182–83; gubernatorial primary turnout, 16n, 17; presidential election of 1928, 12; primary election of 1972, 170; school-desegregation crisis, 53, 55, 56, 57, 121; senatorial elections, 39, 40, 50, 82–83, 100, 119, 181–82; socioeconomic class vote, 56, 121–22, 148; supremacy of one-party politics, 25, 50
Arnall, Ellis G., 114, 115, 116
Askew, Reubin, 145, 146, 147, 162, 167, 188, 193
Aycock, C. C., 155

Baker, Howard, Jr., 105, 109n, 123, 178, 188
Baker v. *Carr*, 111, 189, 191, 192
Barnes, Ben, 168
Barnett, Ross R., 71, 73, 74, 119, 120, 186
Bass, Ross, 78, 105, 109
Battle, John S., 83, 84
Battle, Laurie C., 39
Battle, William C., 142, 144
Beckworth, Lindley, 42
Bennett, Bruce, 55
Bentsen, Lloyd, 109n, 159, 160, 161
Bethea, A. W., 152
Bilbo, Theodore G., 119, 120
Black belt: Dixiecrat revolt, 85; McGovern vote, 174–75; in Mississippi, 72, 73; Nixon vote, 95; organization of Citizens' Council movement, 52; Republican vote, 87–88; support for conservative candidates, 26; Wallace appeal to voters, 68
Blacks: attitude of on federal civil-rights guarantees, 138–39; effect of civil-rights law on voter participation by, 111; fair treatment in employment of, 138; Kennedy's appeal to, 92; politicians' concessions to, 29–30; position of on social and economic policy, 140–41; reaction of to white supremacy, 53; Republican vote by, 87–88; shifting voting alignments by, 80, 125; support of for liberal candidates, 126; turnout of in 1966 election, 125; vote of in 1968 election, 128, 131, 188, 193; voter registration of, 25–26, 40
Blakeley, William A., 78, 96, 97
Blanton, Ray, 172
Blease, Coleman L., 12
Blount, Winton, 164, 181, 182
Blue laws, 4, 8
Boggs, Hale, 58
Boswell, Ted, 170

Rogers, Joseph O., Jr., 123
Roosevelt, Franklin D., 13, 29
Rusk, Jerold G., 7n
Russell, Donald, 123, 124
Russell, Richard B., 171, 172
Rutherford, J. T., 101

Sanders, Barefoot, 170, 179
Sanders, Carl, 69, 71, 148, 149, 150, 186
Sanford, Terry, 76, 94, 167, 168
Scammon, Richard M., 51n
Schattschneider, E. E., 8
School desegregation: acceptance of, 189; Arkansas crisis over, 55, 56, 57, 121; attitudes on federal involvement in, 138; *Brown* v. *Board of Education* decision on, 25, 51, 52, 53, 87, 186; Byrd strategy against, 75; efforts to delay, 53; Florida and, 167; Georgia efforts to avoid, 68–69; Mississippi opposition to, 75; South Carolina vote on, 26; Tennessee political polarization over, 77
School prayers, 167
Scott, Robert, 130, 131, 167
Scott, William L., 142, 177, 178
Scott, W. Kerr, 25, 30, 33, 46, 52, 76, 185
Second Reconstruction of the South, 1, 19, 22, 23, 189
Secret ballot, 7
Sectionalism, 3; characteristics of southern, 18–22
Senatorial elections, 25. *See also names of individual states*
Shallcross, John S., 126
Shannon, Jasper B., 29
Sharkansky, Ira, 20
Shelton, A. C., 166
Shipp, Bill, 149n
Shivers, Allan, 40, 83
Simpson, James A., 39
Slavery, 4
Smathers, George A., 52, 62, 132
Smith, Alfred E., 12
Smith, "Cotton Ed," 97
Smith, Howard, 142, 177
Smith, Preston, 133, 134, 162, 168, 169
Smith, Willis, 30, 52
Smith v. *Allwright*, 97
Socioeconomic class, vote by, 194–95, 199; in presidential election of 1948, 85–86; in presidential election of 1952, 87; in presidential election of 1968, 128–31. *See also names of individual states*
Somers, Robert V., 130, 131, 132
South Carolina: conversion of public schools into private schools, 26, 31; Democratic primary of 1972, 171; election of 1968, 132; factionalism, 31; gubernatorial elections, 52, 125, 150–51, 197; gubernatorial pri-

mary turnout, 17; presidential election of 1924, 12; Republican party, 97, 100, 123; senatorial elections, 26, 29, 31, 97–98, 123–24; socioeconomic class vote, 31, 33, 124–25, 152–53; vote for Eisenhower, 90
Southern Regional Council's Voter Education Project, 109
Spaht, Carlos, 34, 37
Sparkman, John J., 25, 33, 37, 39, 40, 82, 83, 119, 175, 181–82, 185, 197
Spong, William B., 142, 177, 178, 193
Stanley, Thomas B., 84
States' Rights party, 85, 88
Stennis, John, 162, 197
Stephens, A. E. S., 75, 76
Stevenson, Adlai, 86, 87, 90
Stevenson, Coke R., 31, 40
Stewart, Thomas, 44
Strong, Donald, 16n, 18n, 21n
Suit, Hal, 150, 181
Sullivan, Charles L., 154
Sutton, John A., 101
Sutton, Pat, 45
Swan, Jimmie, 119–21

Talmadge, Eugene, 47
Talmadge, Herman, 47, 51, 52, 68, 69, 71, 180, 197
Taylor, Alf, 93
Taylor, Andrew T., 77
Taylor, Pat, 168
Tennessee: black registration, 26; decline of Republican strength, 15; factionalism, 44–46; gubernatorial elections, 78, 153; gubernatorial primary turnout, 16n, 17; presidential election of 1928, 12; presidential primary of 1972, 167–68; racial issue, 76–77; Republican party, 82, 104–5, 123; senatorial elections, 44–46, 77, 104–5, 123, 157–59; socioeconomic class vote, 76–77, 105–6
Texas: conflict between right and left wings of Democratic party, 97; county organization, 30; election of 1968, 133–34; factionalism, 40, 42–44; gubernatorial elections, 78–80, 179–80; gubernatorial primary turnout, 16n, 17; liberalism, 78–80; New Deal alignments, 78, 80, 134; presidential election of 1928, 12; primary elections of 1972, 168–70; Republican party in state contests, 83, 95–97, 104; senatorial elections, 41–44, 78–79, 95–97, 104, 159–62; socioeconomic class vote, 40, 42, 78–79, 133–34, 161–62, 169–70
Third-party system, 85, 88, 90, 196
Thompson, Fletcher M., 180
Thompson, Melvin E., 47
Thrasher, Wilkes T., 101

Thurmond, J. Strom, 26, 29, 85, 86, 97, 178, 179; defection from Democratic party, 123
Tonnies, Ferdinand, 8
Tower, John G., 95, 96, 97, 100, 126, 179
Traylor, Lawrence, 142n
Treen, David C., 156, 183
Treleaven, Harry, 157
Truman, Harry S., 52, 84, 85
Two-party system: effect of civil rights on, 187; effect of ethnocultural groups on, 3–4; fitting southern voters into, 126
Tydings, Millard E., 51
Tyson, John, 109

Urbanization, effect of on southern politics, 19, 21

Vandiver, S. Ernest, 69, 171, 172
Vietnam, southern blacks' position on, 140
Virginia: Byrd machine, 83–84; county organization, 30; emergence of Republican party, 84; end of one-party politics, 142–45; gubernatorial elections, 75–76, 83, 142–45; gubernatorial primary turnout, 16n, 17–18; presidential election of 1928, 12; Progressive movement, 10; racial issue, 75–76; Republican gains in 1972 election, 177–78; senatorial elections, 142, 162; socioeconomic class vote, 143–44
Vote, "normal," 1, 2, 25
Voter behavior: changes in, in 1964 election, 108–9; demographic factors influencing, 22–23; factors influencing, in 1966 election, 125; presidential election of 1952, 185–86; two-party system and, 126, 186. *See also* Socioeconomic class, vote by
Voter registration. *See* Registration
Voter turnout: during 1950s, 25, 185–86; during 1960s, 188; effect of civil-rights law on, 111–12; effect of Progressivism on, 8; in gubernatorial elections, 14–15; in gubernatorial primaries, 16–18; in presidential elections, 5, 13–14, 190, 196
Voting alignments: by blacks, 80, 125; in election of 1974, 197; New Deal, 51, 71, 78, 80, 136, 139, 143, 169; over racial issues, 51, 71; presidential election of 1968, 127–29, 130, 134, 135, 136, 138, 192, 196

Walker, Prentiss, 109, 123
Wallace, George C., 67, 68, 117, 132, 186, 188; in gubernatorial primary of 1970, 164–65; in presidential primary of 1972, 166–70, 189; third party and, 196; vote in 1968 election, 127–30, 173, 192
Wallace, Lurleen Burns, 118, 164
Waller, William L., 154, 188
Warren, Earl, 87
Watson, Albert, 151, 152, 153
Wattenberg, Ben J., 51n
Weaver, Robert C., 96
Weltner, Charles L., 71, 186
West, John Carl, 150, 153, 171, 188
Whig party, 3, 4
White, Cooper, 151
White, Richard, 108n
White backlash, 117, 186
White supremacy, 11; Citizens' Council movement defense of, 52; Democratic party factionalism over, 53; Dixiecrats and, 51; in Louisiana, 58; Maddox support for, 112–13; in Mississippi, 74, 119
Williams, John Bell, 120, 151, 154
Winstead, W. Arthur, 109
Winter, William, 120
Wisdom, John Minor, 102, 103
Woodlief, Wayne, 177
Woods, Charles, 164
Woodward, C. Vann, 5, 19, 20–21
Workman, William D., Jr., 97

Yarborough, Don, 79, 80, 133
Yarborough, Ralph W., 42–44, 78, 80, 104, 109, 157, 169, 170, 189; defeat of, 157, 159–60, 164
Young, Andrew, 183

Zeigler, Eugene N., 171, 175, 178

Library of Congress Cataloging in Publication Data

Bartley, Numan V.
    Southern politics and the second reconstruction.

    Bibliography: p. 214.
    Includes index.
    1. Elections—Southern States.   2. Political par-
ties—Southern States.   3. Southern States—Politics
and government.   I. Graham, Hugh Davis, joint author.
II. Title.
JK1936.A2B37   324'.2'0975   74-24377
ISBN 0-8018-1667-X